The Media Handbook

The eighth edition of *The Media Handbook* continues to provide a practical introduction to the media planning and buying processes.

Starting with the broader context in which media planning occurs, including a basic understanding of competitive spending and target audiences, the book takes readers through the fundamentals of each media channel, leading to the creation of a media plan. Throughout, concepts and calculations are clearly explained. This new edition reflects the changes in how people consume media today with:

- a new chapter on how audiences are defined and created
- reorganization of the media channel chapters to cover planning and buying together
- expanded coverage of digital formats in all channels
- added discussion of measurement
- completely updated data and examples

The Media Handbook, Eighth Edition is the ideal text for courses in media planning and buying in advertising/communication departments.

Supplemental online resources for both students and instructors are also available. For students, there is a list of key media associations and chapter overviews. To assist in their course preparation, instructors will find lecture slides, sample test questions, and new sample media planning exercise scenarios with accompanying practice spreadsheets. These resources are available at www.routledge.com/9780367775568, under Support Material.

Helen Katz is Executive Vice President, Research, at Publicis Media. She has an extensive professional background in media research and has taught advertising and media planning at Michigan State University, DePaul University, and the University of Illinois.

Routledge Communication Series

Jennings Bryant/Dolf Zillmann, Series Editors

For a full list of titles please visit: https://www.routledge.com/Routledge-Communication-Series/book-series/RCS.

The Media Handbook

A Complete Guide to Advertising Media Selection, Planning, Research, and Buying

8th Edition

Helen Katz

Routledge
Taylor & Francis Group

NEW YORK AND LONDON

Cover image: James Teoh Art, iStock/Getty Images

Eighth edition published 2022
by Routledge
605 Third Avenue, New York, NY 10158

and by Routledge
4 Park Square, Milton Park, Abingdon, Oxon, OX14 4RN

Routledge is an imprint of the Taylor & Francis Group, an informa business

First edition published by NTC Business Book 1995
Seventh edition published by Routledge 2019

Library of Congress Cataloging-in-Publication Data
Names: Katz, Helen E. author.
Title: The media handbook : a complete guide to advertising media
    selection, planning, research, and buying / Helen Katz.
Description: 8th Edition. | New York, NY : Routledge, 2022. |
    Series: Routledge communication series | Revised edition of the
    author's The media handbook, 2019. | Includes bibliographical
    references and index. |
Identifiers: LCCN 2021052073 | ISBN 9781032007878 (hardback) |
    ISBN 9780367775568 (paperback) | ISBN 9781003175704 (ebook)
Subjects: LCSH: Advertising media planning. | Mass media and business. |
    Marketing channels.
Classification: LCC HF5826.5 .K38 2022 | DDC 659—dc23/eng/20211220
LC record available at https://lccn.loc.gov/2021052073

ISBN: 9781032007878 (hbk)
ISBN: 9780367775568 (pbk)
ISBN: 9781003175704 (ebk)

DOI: 10.4324/9781003175704

Typeset in Times New Roman
by Apex CoVantage, LLC

Access the Support Material: www.routledge.com/9780367775568

CV 12.16.2022 2249

Contents

9   Putting the Plan Together   179

Exhibits

Foreword

Writing a handbook on media would seem to be a fool's errand since few things change as quickly and profoundly as do media. One might expect any such handbook to be out of date before the proverbial ink dries. What used to be a relatively orderly process of analyzing, planning, and buying media is increasingly a devilishly complex matter. As media options have proliferated and as nearly all media have become digital, our definitions and understanding of "media" and "audience" have radically changed. The lines have blurred between buyers and sellers, between publishers and audiences. Advertisers mostly used to buy media but now they often create it. Audiences used to consume media, but now they also amplify it through social media—sometimes with their own audiences of "followers".

The lines have also blurred between marketing and advertising. Advertisers who once relied on media to reach audiences (and on retail distributors to sell) now often try to build direct relationships with their customers—independent of both media and retail distributors. Advertising happens in the upper funnel, but also at multiple touchpoints, including the point of sale and beyond. Advertising has blurred with customer relationship management.

Digital targeting techniques have enabled advertising to be untethered from media, to be bought and sold instantly through programmatic algorithm-driven auctions. Aversion to advertising has fueled the growth of subscription-based media giants like Netflix and Spotify, moving large chunks of the media audience into advertising-free zones. And then a once-in-a-century global pandemic further accelerated the changes in consumer behavior and media marketplace response.

So how can one possibly hope to describe and explain this complex and constantly morphing world into something as basic and fundamental as a handbook? Yet that is exactly what Helen Katz has done so brilliantly in *The Media Handbook*, now incredibly in its 8th edition. Most of the books in this valuable Routledge imprint only see one edition. A few get up to two or three. But *The Media Handbook* is seeing its 8th edition. How? It is not just by adding in bits about each new media manifestation and trend, though you will find that coverage here. However, this edition, following the 7th by only three years, gives readers more of the essential back story.

While most accounts of media and media planning start with the idea of a campaign, this edition steps back to consider some of the strategic inputs and decisions that can make or break any marketing campaign. How well do we understand the consumer and the marketplace in which the marketer is operating? How do we make sure that we are identifying the right target and approaching in the right voice with the right offer? If we don't have these right, we won't succeed.

Helen's contribution here is to provide an accessible point of entry to this vast and fascinating field. Using the inherent economy of the handbook format, she does not dwell on any single topic. Readers will want to double-click on many of them through further study. Though they won't get all of that detail here, The Media Handbook provides one of the best overviews, one of the most comprehensive road maps to the field. It will be valuable both to novices and to old hands trying to navigate that complicated road.

Scott McDonald, Ph.D.
President and CEO
Advertising Research Foundation

Preface

Welcome to the eighth edition of *The Media Handbook*. As always seems to happen in a three-year period, the world of media has not sat still since the prior edition. While consumers still, at a high level, are "using" media for their entertainment, information, and communication, the channels they choose and how they access content has morphed, yet again. Brands seek deeper and more direct relationships with their audiences, whether in the way they deliver messages or in how they are made available for purchase. The roles of paid, owned, and earned media have adapted to capture the attention of an ever-more distracted consumer, whether through podcast sponsorships, online gaming integrations, or connected TV ads.

This latest edition reflects the latest changes in consumer use of media, and in the media themselves. A new chapter has been added on defining audiences, and planning and buying are now brought together when each media channel is explored, reflecting the increasing closeness of those functions in today's agencies. There is a continued acknowledgment of the importance of data to drive decision-making, whether for programmatic buys or measuring outcomes. Yet, as always, this book recognizes and emphasizes the complexity of media, requiring creativity and data savviness to succeed.

This edition starts out with a brief high-level view of the "big picture" of advertising and media, before jumping straight in to understanding the consumer journey and the importance of overall marketing and advertising objectives. From there, a new chapter focuses on how to translate the "consumer" to the media "audience". This is followed by an introduction to key media terms and calculations, to provide a solid foundation for the reader before embarking on the four chapters that deep-dive into paid, owned, and earned media opportunities. Each covers the landscape for a media channel, consumer usage and trends, and how those channels are planned and bought. This leads into how a plan is put together, and, lastly, how plans and buys are measured and evaluated. All chapters now begin with a set of objectives, to help guide the reader upfront with what they will learn.

Once again, the book includes numerous examples, both real and fictitious, giving a clear sense of how media planning and buying work in the real
world for large and small companies. Examples of research studies, from both
the industry and the academic world, are included to give readers additional
resources to go to for more in-depth information. At the end of the book, a
selection of key resources is offered in the appendices for those who wish to
find out more about a particular service or system.

The Media Handbook provides a basic introduction to the media planning
and buying process to help today's college students or industry professionals
understand how today's advertising media operate, and how media fit into the
larger picture of total brand communications. Whether media is in your job
title or career path, or whether you are just curious to better understand why
you received another ad for the shampoo you purchased online a week ago, the
book illuminates the fundamentals of media planning and buying so that you
can effectively navigate both the art and science of the practice.

Acknowledgments

Many thanks are owed to all the people who helped me with this edition of *The Media Handbook*. These include my long-time mentors and colleagues, Kevin Killion, Wendy Marquardt, Jana O'Brien, Kate Sirkin, and Tracey Scheppach. Thanks are also due to my many industry colleagues who keep me grounded in the ever-changing media business and have helped ensure this latest edition is current and accurate, including Darcy Bowe, Eric Cavanaugh, Tracy Chavez, Julie Erbe, Kathy Heatley, Dijana Jovicic, Lisa Stearn, and David Turman.

My academic roots gave me the foundations for my career, from early mentors such as Kim Rotzoll, Steve Helle, Kent Lancaster, and Bruce Vanden Bergh, and long-time friends and colleagues Wei-Na Lee and T. Bettina Cornwell, who have always supported me both personally and professionally. My Routledge editor, Felisa Salvago-Keyes, continues to provide me with guidance, while trusting me to get the job done. With this edition, I am happy to welcome Marilena Olguta Vilceanu to the team; she has taken charge of some of the ancillaries, including an outstanding new workbook and vastly improved teaching materials. Trevor Zaucha continued his stellar job at keeping the other ancillaries updated and useful.

Once more, I am grateful for the unwavering support of my family. My husband, Eric, and three daughters, Stephanie, Caroline, and Vanessa, always encourage me to try new activities. In writing this during the global Coronavirus pandemic, I was reminded of the values of resilience and endurance, both of which I learned from my parents, Joan and Peter Katz, whose lives required much of each. They instilled in me a passion for learning, a love of writing, and a curiosity for what's new. I hope that all of these are reflected well in the eighth edition. My father is no longer with us, so it is to my mother, Joan Katz, that I dedicate this book.

Introduction

Despite the never-ending changes in advertising that take place every year, there is still a need for a media handbook to provide an overview of how ad messages get in front of audiences. While you as a consumer may feel like you are constantly bombarded by brands trying to get you to buy them (or consider them, or know they exist), the fact is that behind those TV commercials, digital video ads, or sponsored podcasts, much thought and effort went into deciding who should receive that message, where and when, and how often. Teams of people thought about which media channels would be most effective at delivering the ad to a particular target group, while other teams helped to place the media buys or analyzed their impact.

The goal of this book is to provide a complete picture of how media planning, buying, and research work. You will see what each function entails and how they fit together with each other and within the framework of the marketing mix. You will know enough by the end of this book to be able to create your own media plan or undertake a media buy. Even if you are not directly responsible for either of those tasks, a greater understanding of how media fit into the marketing picture will help you communicate with those who do such work. Each chapter builds on and works off the preceding ones, although once you have been through them all, it is designed to be very easy for you to refer to specific tasks or concepts at a later date. At the start of each chapter is a set of learning objectives, to keep you on track. On our companion website, you will find a list of additional resources you can turn to for help in media planning, buying, and research.

Chapter 1

Media in the Big Picture

Learning Outcomes: In this chapter you will learn how to:

- Understand how media fit within marketing
- Explain the relationship between media, consumers, and brands
- Analyze the competitive landscape for an individual brand

It's 7:30 a.m. You wake up and check your mobile phone to see what is happening on Facebook, Twitter, and Instagram. You look at the latest news and weather on your phone apps. At breakfast (while possibly still engaged in those activities), you might watch some of the morning news on TV or ESPN sports highlights on your phone, which are "brought to you" by Budweiser. On the way to work or class, you watch clips from last night's talk shows on your mobile phone, with branded video ads preceding each one.

In that brief time span, you have been immersed in today's world of media. That world includes various media platforms for which advertisers *pay*: radio, digital, television, mobile, newspapers, magazines, and outdoor billboards. Then there are segments of those media in which advertisers insert their brands less overtly to *own* the content. Last, there are social media forms such as Facebook and Twitter, where advertisers try to *earn* the trust and attention of the consumer. In all of these instances, when you listen to music on the radio, go online to post your Instagram story, stream a TV show, or read your favorite magazine, you also receive information through a means of communication or a *medium*. Given this broad definition, you can see that there are, in fact, hundreds of different media available, such as direct mail offers sent to your home, TV screens at the gym, digital coupons, stadium signs, shared bike programs with sponsor names on the wheels, tray liners in airport security bins, and samples handed out at the supermarket. All of these, and many other media, offer us ways of communicating information to an audience. As advertising media professionals, we are interested in looking at media as means of conveying

DOI: 10.4324/9781003175704-1

a specific kind of information—an *advertising message*—about a product or service to consumers.

Media play very important roles in our lives. Media help fulfill two basic needs: They *inform*, and they *entertain*. We turn to media when we want to hear the latest world news or what happened in financial markets, for instance. We also look to media to fill our evenings and weekends with escapist fare to get us out of our everyday, humdrum routines. Television entertains us with movies, dramas, comedies, reality shows, and sports. Radio offers us a wide variety of music, talk, and entertainment. We turn to print or digital magazines to find out more about our favorite hobbies and interests. Newspapers, also in print or digital, help us keep up with the world around us. And digital media, in all its varied forms, provides limitless information and a means of shared entertainment and communication.

The informational role of the media is perhaps best illustrated by considering what happens during an international crisis, such as disputes between countries or national disasters such as hurricanes or major snowstorms. When these occur, millions of people turn to their laptops or mobile devices to get breaking news updates, go to social media to hear that friends or relatives are all safe, or turn to TVs and radios for ongoing news coverage. Then, over the next several days, they seek out newspapers and magazines for more in-depth coverage and follow-up stories.

Media also affect our lives through their entertainment function. Television programs such as *Black-ish* and *Transparent* have not only reflected what has been happening in U.S. society but also helped influence attitudes and behaviors concerning the issues of race and equality. Stories appearing in print or online magazines such as *People* or *Vanity Fair* let us know what is happening in other people's lives, both famous and ordinary. And we take our mobile devices with us everywhere so that we can receive the latest sports scores or watch videos while we relax.

A third primary function of media is to socialize. While the informational and entertainment aspects offer "one-to-many" disseminations of content, the various forms of social media bring people together in a "one-to-one" way, whether that is you sharing pictures or videos through Snapchat and TikTok or putting a favorite recipe on a Pinterest board.

What Media Are Out There?

One way that advertisers differentiate between media channels is to consider whether their brands' messages are *paid for*, *owned* by the advertiser, or *earned* by consumers taking action. This organization is shown in Exhibit 1.1. It is worth noting that the lines between the classifications are not absolute. While brands "own" their name or slogan that is placed or integrated or named at an event as part of a sponsorship deal, they may still have to pay for those rights.

Exhibit 1.1 Today's Media Classification: Paid, Owned, and Earned

Paid	Owned	Earned
TV	Product placement	Word of mouth
Radio	Brand integration	Earned social
Newspapers	Brand website	Organic search
Magazines	Sponsorship	Public relations
Outdoor	Influencers	
Digital display	Custom events	
Digital video		
Digital search		
Paid social		

Whether a brand truly *owns* an influencer is also subject to debate. Moreover, what a brand can earn through social media may well happen as a result of that brand's paid messaging. And importantly, from the consumers' perspective, these are artificial or irrelevant classifications. We will return to this dilemma in later chapters.

The Role of Media in Business

It is important to emphasize here that the focus of this book is commercial media. The communications media we will be talking about are not there simply to beautify the landscape or fill up airtime; they are designed to sell products to customers. Of course, there are also media that convey information but are not commercial in intent. *Consumer Reports* is a magazine that does not carry any advertising. Neither do public television and radio (except for sponsorships). Google Maps and airline safety instructions are informative, but they are not advertisements in and of themselves (even if they can carry advertisements within or near them). And books certainly communicate information to their readers. Here, however, we will concentrate on those media that currently accept advertising messages. It is worth emphasizing the word *currently*. Twenty-five years ago, you did not find commercial messages at supermarkets, schools, doctors' offices, or ski slopes. Today, advertisers can reach people in all of these places. People are willing to cover their vehicles, or sometimes even parts of their bodies, in sponsored ads. Companies are routinely paying people they consider influential to mention their products online, sometimes without the authors publicly acknowledging the payment. While some of these ventures have been criticized, that does not mean similar attempts will not be made again in the future. What is true today may very well change by tomorrow. The generic term *media* (or *medium* in the singular) means different things to different people. To people sitting at home on a Friday evening, *media* means whatever TV shows they stream or games they play on their mobile apps. For the local Honda car dealer, *media* provide ways to advertise this week's deals on CRVs and Civics. And the Local Electric Utility Company uses *media* to remind its customers with their monthly bills that they can get free energy-savings audits.

Strictly speaking, a *medium* may be defined as a means by which something is accomplished, conveyed, or transferred. This deliberately broad definition means that consumer media would cover everything from handbills passed out in parking lots to "for sale" signs taped to lampposts. It could also include the four-page BMW supplement wrapped around the printed edition of the *New York Times*, or digital billboards flashing in Times Square, or the BMW vehicles that contestants drive in Bravo's *Top Chef*.

How the Media Business Evolves

The media business is never static. Like many other industries, companies often start small, grow bigger (through acquisition or mergers), and then face new competition from smaller players. Those changes have effects on both advertisers and consumers. For example, the purchase of NBC Universal by Comcast back in 2013, or the 2021 merger of WarnerMedia and Discovery, can alter the TV networks or movies available or promoted. Viewers might wonder why USA Network airs seemingly endless reruns of *Law & Order: SVU*. That is because both USA Network and Universal Studios (the TV syndication company) are part of Comcast NBCU. One media agency, GroupM, estimated that in 2020 two-thirds of all ad spending went to the top 25 media suppliers, compared to their control of 42 percent of adspend just four years earlier.[1]

The impact this has on advertisers occurs primarily in negotiations where media buyers find themselves with fewer companies to buy from. If they want to place commercials during *Grey's Anatomy* or *The Bachelor* (both on ABC) they may have to accept a package that includes ads on National Geographic Channel or FX or Freeform, all of which are also part of Walt Disney Television. This consolidation occurs in the digital sphere too (such as Facebook's purchase of Giphy or Amazon buying Twitch). So while consumers are being offered more and more media choices (more digital audio offerings, more magazine apps, more ad-supported streaming services), the advertisers trying to reach them find that they must negotiate with fewer and fewer companies selling advertising space or time. This paradox is something we shall revisit later.

Media Versus Communications

In the business world, we think of a medium as a way to transfer and convey information about goods or services from the producer to the consumer, who is a potential buyer of that item. There are various ways to accomplish that in business besides using radio, television, or social media. Product or company publicity, sales brochures, or exhibits can all be useful ways of conveying information to potential buyers. You should note that throughout this book, we will refer to all potential buyers as *consumers*, but we should really think of them as *us*. One of the biggest dangers in media planning or buying is, as we shall learn in Chapter 3, categorizing viewers or listeners or digital users into broad consumer groups (such as "adults 18–49") that make it all too easy to forget that, in the infamous words of one of the founders of the advertising industry, David Ogilvy, "the consumer isn't a moron. She is your wife".[2] And, as we shall also learn in subsequent chapters, technology has enabled advertisers to use mass media in an individualized way to reach their more precise target audiences (e.g., sending dog food company advertising only to homes with dogs) in ways that bring television full circle to a more personalized, one-to-one form of media. Today it is common, although sometimes considered controversial, to deliver digital ads based on the products purchased or programs watched.

Although this book is titled *The Media Handbook*, it is important to think of media in the broadest terms—as communications that may be paid for directly by the advertiser, owned by integrating the brand into the content, or earned by giving people the opportunity to make a direct connection with the brand. Today, most agencies look for integrated ways to contact consumers across all these media, whether that is paying to display their brand of soft drink on *The Voice*, sponsoring a blimp flying over a popular baseball field in the summer, or encouraging consumers to "like" Starbucks on Facebook. The goal of these disparate efforts is to surround the target audience with a holistic campaign that presents them with the same message about the brand in creative ways.

The Role of Media in Consumers' Lives

Today, media play an increasingly prominent role in many of our lives. As the example at the opening of this chapter suggested, we are constantly connected to some form of media from the minute we wake up in the morning, whether that is paid media (radio, TV, digital), owned media (brand influencers), or earned media (social). The number of interactions with media during the day becomes staggering when you stop to think about it. Most likely, within the past 24 hours, you have used several of the following types of media: audio, print, video, digital, out of home, or social.

When you watch a TV program and see a commercial for Budweiser beer that then appears in your Twitter feed, and is mentioned in the local Chicago evening newscast because the brand is a major sponsor of the Chicago Cubs baseball team, you generally don't think about the effort that went into coordinating all of those elements. In fact, if the seams between them are too obvious, then something probably isn't working right! While you, as a member of the reading or listening or viewing audience, are interested primarily in a particular

Exhibit 1.2 Top Global Advertisers in 2019

	Billions of Dollars
Procter & Gamble	$10.1
Samsung Electronics Co.	$10.1
L'Oréal	$9.6
Unilever	$8.5
Amazon	$8.2
Comcast	$7.5
Nestle	$7.3
LMVH Moet Hennessy	$6.5
Alphabet (Google)	$6.4
AT&T	$6.2
Total Top Ten	**$80.4**

Source: Advertising Age World's Largest Advertisers 2019, Adage.com, December 2020.

program or app or site, the medium is interested in you as a potential buyer, offering you up to advertisers who wish to talk to you.

The role of media in conveying information through advertising messages is not something consumers generally consider. Indeed, when they do think about it, they are likely to complain about being inundated by commercial messages! Despite the fact that no one has yet proven definitively and conclusively how advertising works, businesses continue to believe in its power, as evidenced by the estimated $145 billion spent in the United States on advertising in 2020.[3] Exhibit 1.2 shows the top ten global advertisers, each of whom spent at least $6 billion in 2019.

How Media Work with Advertising

Advertising in the media performs the roles of informing, connecting, and entertaining. It informs us of the goods and services that are available for us to purchase and use. Along the way, it often entertains us with some humorous, witty, or clever use of words and pictures. It can connect us with friends and strangers. For example, let's say you have created a new carbonated fruit juice that you want to introduce to the marketplace. Friends and neighbors have tasted it, and they think it's original and tasty. You have talked to several distributors and manufacturers, and they have some interest in producing it. Now, however, the question arises of what to do next. How do you inform people you don't know personally about this wonderful new product?

This is where the media can help. You could create a Facebook page, Instagram page, and Twitter hashtag to promote this brand-new drink online and generate social awareness of it. Perhaps you'd place ads on cooking and nutrition websites that show the product and explain its health benefits over soda. You might create a piece of branded content that appears on Pinterest in the food and drink topic area or place an advertisement on TV announcing this brand-new drink, which you've named Fruitola. Your website could encourage consumers to send in their own ideas for different drinks or recipes that include the brand, as well as having links to the retailers that sell it. Through all of these media channels, you would disseminate your brand message, that "Fruitola refreshes with fruit," to an audience of hundreds, or thousands. You can generate additional publicity by selecting influencers to promote the brand on their social media. Whatever form of communication you use, all involve sending a message through a medium of one kind or another.

Again, it is important to keep in mind that we are talking about media in the broadest sense. So, in trying to promote your Fruitola drink, its TV and digital presence can show people what the product looks like and give more details on its health benefits. Then, you might sponsor a local food festival as a public relations effort to heighten awareness of the product and let people sample it. You could send out press releases in advance to notify the media of the event and thereby generate additional publicity both for the event and for your drink. You could offer retailers a special deal, such as contributing funds to the ads that they run (an advertising allowance), if they will promote the product in their weekly online or radio ads. You might also arrange for samples to be handed out on college campuses or in gyms so that people can learn more about Fruitola. Each medium fulfills a slightly different role, but by advertising the product in a wide variety of media, your overall message—that "Fruitola refreshes with fruit"—is conveyed clearly and consistently.

Media advertising also performs another vital function. It helps offset the cost of the media communication itself to consumers. If we did not have commercials on television or radio or in digital media, the cost of the informational, educational, or social content would have to come through sponsorships, taxes, or government monies. Public broadcasting in the United States derives most of its income through semi-annual pledge drives, during which viewers and listeners are asked to give money to pay for the services. Government funding provides additional revenues. But even here, more and more public broadcasting radio and television stations are accepting restricted forms of paid commercials as long as they are image-oriented and not hard sell.

Tasks in Media

The broad field of advertising media can be broken down into four primary tasks:

1   Planning how best to use media to convey the advertising message to the target consumer (the *media planner*)

2 Buying media space and time for the message (the *media buyer*)
3 Selling that space or time to the advertiser (the *media seller*)
4 Analyzing the relationship between consumers, media, and the brands that
  advertise to them in those media (the *media analyst*)

Beyond these basic roles, however, there is a broad array of other specialty functions, such as content development, e-commerce, software development, and data science.

Most large companies handle the media planning and buying functions through an advertising agency. Smaller firms will usually handle this task themselves through their marketing director or public relations coordinator. The fundamental role of the planner is to decide where and when the message should be placed, how often, and at what cost. The plan is then implemented by the media buyer, who negotiates with the media providers themselves to agree on the space and time needed and to determine or confirm where the ad will appear. In digital, increasing automation has moved most buys to a programmatic marketplace. Nonetheless, the buyer will still deal with the salesperson at the media company, whose job it is to sell as much advertising space or time as possible (or, in the case of branded entertainment, co-develop the content that the brand can own). Throughout this process, the analyst offers insights into how to make media have the greatest impact on the consumers' brand decisions and measures how well it worked.

Media Within Marketing

It is critical to remember that media is part of advertising, which itself is part of marketing. The primary goal of marketing is to attract and retain customers by offering products that meet their needs, and thereby generate sales (and profits). To return to our earlier example where we were wondering how to market our fruit-based carbonated drink, Fruitola, we considered many elements beyond which media to use. To market any product effectively involves not simply advertising it but also figuring out how much to charge for it, where to distribute it, and how to manufacture it. In marketing terms, these critical elements are known as the four P's: product, price, place (distribution), and promotion. Although your job as a media specialist does not necessarily involve making the decisions on all of these criteria, you need a clear understanding of how they work and, more importantly, how they can impact your media decisions and strategy.

In order to sell anything, you must first have a product or service. You have to decide how much you need to charge for it (the price) so that you can make a profit. You must also figure out how and where the product will be made available to people (place, or distribution). Last but not least, you must consider how you will let potential buyers know what you are offering (promotion). Within that last category, there are several key channels of communication: advertising, personal selling, sales promotion, direct marketing, event marketing, and publicity. All can be thought of as media, or ways of conveying information to potential buyers. You see how these elements work in Exhibit 1.3.

One of the most important things to remember here is that the arrows move in many directions. Almost any decision you make concerning media will have an impact on something else in the marketing mix. For example, if you decided to advertise on national television, you would have to ensure that your product was, in fact, available throughout the country. Or if you chose to concentrate your advertising efforts during holiday periods (Memorial Day, Independence Day, and so on), you might consider lowering your price at that time to boost sales even further.

The task of the media planner is to consider all of the marketing information available on the product and to use that information to determine how best to reach the target audience with the brand message through advertising media. In this way, the media plan can be thought of as the pivot point, or hub, of the overall marketing plan (Exhibit 1.4).

Exhibit 1.3 The Marketing Mix

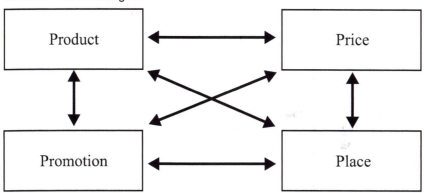

Exhibit 1.4 Putting the Media Plan in Context

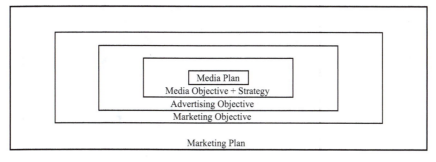

Getting to Know the Consumer

There are two critical pieces of information that a media specialist needs to know in order to successfully market a product. The first is an understanding of how your consumers view and use your product or service. The second is how they view and use different media types. The rest of this chapter will delve into the consumer–brand–media relationship.

Consumers and Brands

First, you must know more about the brand and the product category. A *brand* is the individual product or service that you are trying to sell. It can be thought of as the name on the label. Kellogg's Frosted Flakes cereal is a brand, as is their Froot Loops cereal or their Frosted Mini Wheats variety. The *product category* could either be defined as all brands of sugared cereal or all kinds of cereal. In the case of a service, such as insurance, the product category could be one type of insurance, such as life or home or auto, or all types. The brand would be one particular company such as Allstate, State Farm, or Geico.

One way to think about brands is to consider your own behavior. When you go to the grocery store, you are usually not thinking in terms of product categories or brands. More likely, you are thinking about buying a pack of Ramen noodles, a six-pack of Sprite, or a bag of Doritos. Similarly, when you have to decide which restaurant to go to, you will not categorize them the way marketers do—into quick service, family style, or steakhouses—but will instead think in terms of the types of food—Thai, Mexican, Indian, and so forth. And within those groups, you will probably categorize them by geography, thinking of the specific restaurants by area.

What we need to know as marketers and media specialists, however, is how the consumer decides *which* brands and products to buy, as well as the process he or she goes through when purchasing an item. This is often referred to as the *consumer journey*. It will vary depending on the type of product. While consumers might pick up any brand of floor cleaner, the journey they go through to select the car they drive will take far longer because there are more elements to consider and a higher price involved. Understanding these decision processes will help you determine which media might best be used both to reach your target and to convey the desired message at the right time. For selling your carbonated fruit drink, you could probably use digital display, to increase awareness of your product along with paid search when people are looking for nutritional or diet and fitness information. A company trying to sell a more complex product, however, such as a car or insurance plan, will use a different mix of communication forms to sell its product. A comprehensive understanding of the relationship between the consumer and the brand helps ensure that an ad campaign engages the consumer effectively, which, in turn, will generate more sales of the brand.[4]

Here, we will take a general look at how consumers view and use brands. From there, we can establish some foundations for the media plan. We will start this by going back into the past and looking at what has happened in the marketplace both to the brand and to the product category in which we are interested.

In looking at how consumers use brands, we must answer several key questions. How much do consumers already know about the brand (brand and advertising awareness)? When, where, and how often do they buy it (purchase dynamics)?

What Do People Know About the Brand?

People are potentially exposed to a minimum of 5,000 ads every week, so it isn't surprising that they don't remember many of them. Studies routinely show that the percentage of people who can accurately remember the name of the brand they last saw advertised on television is astoundingly low (typically less than 10 percent). Indeed, you likely know from your own TV or digital video behavior that you try to skip through as many ads as possible. And although we talk about "great" ads that we saw on television last night or saw online, we are probably unlikely to remember the brand that was being advertised. Is Simone Biles the spokesperson for Uber Eats or Grubhub? Does George Clooney promote Nespresso or Keurig? In today's increasingly competitive marketing climate, consumers are also likely to be exposed to more than one brand name in an ad. This *comparison advertising* is extremely common in categories such as pain relievers, automobiles, and detergents. But while your brand, Brand A, emphasizes how much better it is than Brand B, will your target audience remember A or B?

How to Get to Know Consumers and Brands

Finding out how aware your consumers are of your brand and its advertising is quite straightforward, although it is not without pitfalls. The easiest way to do this is through a survey (typically conducted online) in which you simply ask people what they remember about certain ads. You can do this in one of two ways: either *unaided*, where no prompts or assistance are provided, or *aided*, where you offer some kind of memory aid, such as mentioning something from the advertisement or giving an actual list of brand names and asking for further information on the advertising. The unaided method demands more from consumers, asking them to tap deeper into their memories to recall the information you are seeking. With the aided method, you are basically asking people to recognize a brand and/or advertisement when it is placed before them and then prompting them for additional information about it.[5]

There are other issues to keep in mind with brand-awareness research. The most important is that you cannot expect complete accuracy. That is, there is always the danger with any kind of memory check that you will not get full information from the people you survey. Obviously, the longer the time between when people see an ad and when they are questioned about it, the less they will remember about it. Human memory is highly fallible. They may attribute pieces of one ad to another ad or recite a list of brand attributes from Brand A that really belong to Brand B. If you do test consumer awareness of your ads, be sure that you keep in mind the possibility of inaccuracies in the responses.

In addition, you must remember that all of these responses are what consumers *claim* to recognize or recall. Even if you give people a questionnaire to fill out on their own, they may not respond with their real feelings or thoughts. They might not want to offend the interviewer or admit how they really feel, or—for whatever reason—they may not want to tell the truth. For instance, they may have only a vague recollection of your brand's name, but they write down that they are very familiar with it.

Having said that, awareness checks do play a vital role in letting you know more about how your consumers interact with the brand and its advertising. If no one can recall your brand name after it has been advertised on television every day for the past year, then you have a problem. It could be the message isn't convincing at all, or it could be you are advertising it in the wrong medium. Perhaps people can recall the brand name very easily, but nothing about the advertising has stuck in their minds. Many companies conduct *brand tracking research* where they conduct consumer surveys on a regular (weekly, monthly, or quarterly) basis to see to what degree people are aware of their brand and its advertising. This kind of data becomes very useful for monitoring not only the health of the brand over time but also for building statistical models that show the relationship between the media dollars spent and the results obtained. We will cover this in more detail in Chapter 10.

The goal of increasing brand awareness should not be understated. While social media has made it far easier to generate sales of new brands that people were not previously aware of, it is still the case that brands cannot continue to grow without expanding consumer awareness of their offering. People are far more likely to purchase a brand whose name they have heard before than one about which they have no information. There are many companies that conduct this kind of research. Some of the larger ones are listed in Appendix B.

If you want to probe further into people's responses, you can find out more through focus groups, which are groups of five to ten people who are interviewed together by a moderator. They are probed for their beliefs, attitudes, or feelings toward a given brand or product category and its advertising to help in the development of the creative message as well as the marketing and media strategies.

A more in-depth technique for understanding consumers is the use of ethnography. Developed in sociology and anthropology, the technique involves close observation of what consumers are doing. This may include visiting their homes to watch them prepare a meal (for a brand such as Kraft salad dressing) or spending a few hours with them in the gym (for a brand such as Adidas sports shoes). The idea is to see up close how the brand or product category really fits into people's lives.[6]

The Consumer Journey

Many research studies have been conducted over the years to demonstrate the decision process that a consumer typically goes through when buying a routine product. It is often referred to as the consumer journey, since we are envisioning the way that people go along a journey from thinking about a product to buying and using it. Some think of it as a purchase funnel, which looks like a funnel in that it starts with a large group of people thinking about a need they have, and gets progressively narrower since there are fewer people who end up at the end of the funnel, making a purchase.

In its simplest form, this process has three steps:

1 Think
2 Feel
3 Do

The belief here is that people must first *think* about the item (i.e., be aware of it and know it exists). Then they must then develop some kind of attitude or *feeling* toward it (i.e., like it and prefer it to others). Finally, they must take some action with regard to it (decide on it and actually buy it—the *do* part of the model).

The process is, in fact, far more involved than this. We can break these three stages down further, coming up with eight stages of the journey that the consumer typically goes through in buying a product or service. The media selected to influence consumers at each stage will vary, depending on whether the goal is to expand awareness of a new Coke flavor, or encourage greater use of Campbell's Cream of Mushroom soup.

The stages of the process, or journey, are:

1 Need
2 Awareness
3 Preference
4 Search

5   Selection
6   Purchase
7   Use
8   Satisfaction

To begin with, the consumer must first have a *need* to fulfill. He or she then becomes *aware* of the brands available to satisfy that need. After that, several brands are considered acceptable, and a *preference* is developed for one or more of them. The consumer will then *search* for the brand(s) desired and make a *selection* of one over the others. A specific brand is *purchased* and *used*. Finally, the level of *satisfaction* with that purchase helps determine whether or not that brand is bought on a future occasion. This is discussed in detail in the next chapter.

Of course, in reality, life isn't always as simple. As noted, there are occasions (and products) where people hear about or see a product, buy it, and only at that point do they develop attitudes toward it. This is especially true for new product launches, where consumers have not had a chance to develop emotional bearings for the brand or category. Another point to keep in mind is that the decision process can sometimes get stalled at a point before purchase. In our Fruitola example, your target may be made aware of the brand, decide that he'd like to buy it but be unable to find it in the grocery store, and give up. Or he could try it and decide he actually prefers to stick with Coca-Cola's Sprite product.

A more popular theory of decision-making, called *behavioral economics*, posits that consumers do not behave as rationally as we would like to think they do. Moreover, they cannot fully explain why they take certain actions or hold particular beliefs related to brands or services. Therefore, marketers should pay more attention to the actions taken (the *behavior* part) and ask questions in ways that then can be accurately answered.[7]

How the Consumer Buys Products

One of the main drawbacks to using surveys or holding discussions with consumers about how they buy is that they are telling you what they *think* they do, which may be very different from what they actually do in real life. Moreover, measuring brand awareness and advertising recall often ends up being a poor predictor of sales. So, in addition to looking at awareness, or the top of the decision tree, you should also pay attention to what is happening at the bottom of the tree with the purchase cycle. When are people buying your product? How much is bought? Is there some kind of seasonality to their purchases? All of this information will prove to be critical in planning and buying your media and will have a major impact on how and when you schedule your ads.

When Do People Buy?

The answer to this question is more complex than it seems at first. You might say "Well, they buy my product all the time". But if you look more closely at purchase behavior, you will probably detect some kind of pattern. While people are buying houses "all the time," they are more likely to do so when interest rates are low and prices are depressed. People buy cars "all the time," but sales typically increase when the new models come into the showrooms in the fall, and more sales occur in the second half of the month than in the first. There is even a timing component to the purchase of everyday items. Sales of cheese are higher on the weekends and around paydays because that is when people have more money to go shopping. Moving companies are busiest between May and October because that is when most people change their residence. Greeting card sales go up before every holiday (whether traditional holidays, such as Christmas, or "Hallmark holidays," such as Grandparents Day and Father's Day).

If you know when consumers are most likely to buy your product, you can time your media advertising to take advantage of that purchase cycle. For major purchases in particular, you might also want to consider when people are *thinking about* buying. This might occur several weeks or even months before they make the actual purchase. Mr. and Mrs. Anderson might buy a new Toro lawnmower in May, but they will probably start to think about which one to get several months prior to that. This provides you with a valuable opportunity to get your brand's message to the Andersons early in their decision-making process.

How Much Do They Buy?

Another important element of the purchase cycle for the media specialist to know is the differing behavior of a heavy user of a brand versus a past six-month user (total) of the same brand. Coca-Cola Classic offers a variety of packaging options, and the company needs to know who buys cans, plastic bottles, and glass bottles. It turns out, according to MRI-Simmons, that heavy users of Coca-Cola Classic (defined as those who consume six or more servings in the past seven days) are more likely to consume cola in cans. Total users are 10 percent more likely to use cans than all cola drinkers; heavy users are 22 percent more likely to use cans. Heavy users account for just over 20 percent of the Coca-Cola Classic users but consume 68 percent of the volume of the brand, so they are a very important segment to the media specialist. This kind of information is not only important for production and distribution purposes; it can also play a key role in media planning—the users of each size are likely to be different kinds of people with different media habits. Looking at regular cola drinkers, the casual drinker who picks up the individual can is more likely than all cola drinkers to be young, with two children, and live in

Exhibit 1.5 Profile of Regular Cola Glass Bottle Buyers

Ethnic minority
Age 18–34
Census region: West
Live in one of top five markets
Household income $100,000+
Bachelor's degree
Watched *Chicago Fire* and *Chicago Med*
Watched *Family Guy* and *The Simpsons*
Listen to Amazon Music, Audible, and streamed AM/FM stations
Read *Bon Appetit*
Read *Elle* magazine
Read *Men's Health* magazine

Source: 2020 Doublebase MRI-Simmons.

the Southwest or West, while those who purchase the plastic bottles are fairly similar demographically but are more likely to be earning less money and living in the North East. A profile of the regular cola glass bottle buyer is shown in Exhibit 1.5. This group prefers to watch programs such as *Family Guy* and *The Simpsons*, listen to Amazon Music or streamed AM/FM stations, and read *Bon Appetit* or *Men's Health* magazine. Based on these media preferences, your plan for the glass buyer may well differ from that for the can or plastic bottle purchaser.

Understanding the Marketplace

Once you know how consumers view and use your brand, the next step for the media specialist is to examine what has been happening to that brand in the marketplace in recent times. Given this information on past efforts to sell your product, you can decide whether to continue along the same path or try something different in terms of your media planning and buying. Examining the marketplace involves doing an analysis of historical data on both the brand and the product category.

Some of the basic questions the media specialist might ask include the following:

- How long has this brand been available?
- How successful has it been throughout its history?
- How has it been positioned in the past?
- What do you know about the company that makes this brand?

You can think of this as genealogical work—trying to dig up as much background on the brand as possible. You may find that the company has been in business for 150 years, suggesting possible leverage to be gained by emphasizing in the message the long heritage the brand possesses and even placing it in media vehicles that have also been around for a long time. Or perhaps the company has been around forever but is now moving in a different direction and is starting to explore new opportunities, suggesting the use of new or different media. DeWalt is known as a leading power tools company, selling items like power drills and hedge trimmers. But today, it also offers storage containers (for those tools) and heated jackets (to wear while working with its tools). This 100-year old company positions itself as "guaranteed tough," offering "professional workhorse solutions" rather than simply selling tools. The media choices will vary accordingly, depending on the products and services being presented.

What Are the Competitors Up To?

In doing an historical analysis of the brand, you must also deal with competitive issues. That is, you should not only explore and uncover as much marketing and media information as possible about your *own* brand, but you should also do the same for *all* the brands against which you compete or plan to compete. The marketing part of these issues may be divided into three main areas:

1   Product category trends
2   Brand trends and share of market
3   Brand's share of requirements

Product Category Trends

Whether your brand has been available for half a century, two years, or is about to be launched, one of the most important preplanning considerations for the media specialist is what is happening in your product category. If you are creating a media plan for the manufacturer of a Trek mountain bike, you would want to know whether sales of bicycles are increasing, decreasing, or flat. That will immediately influence your media budget and whom you choose to target and how you will go about trying to reach them. In some instances, to determine how the category has fared, you will have to decide what your "category" really is. If you are selling a granola bar, then it might seem obvious that it belongs in the cookie category. But perhaps this is a protein-filled bar designed for endurance athletes that belongs more appropriately in the diet and health food classification. Does a yogurt drink fit better into yogurt products or milk drinks? And what about flash drives—do they belong with software or in the office supplies section, along with pens and paper?

How you define your product category will determine not only your assessment of the strengths or weaknesses of that category but also the direction and potential marketing and media strategies you employ for your particular brand. To take the yogurt drink example, if you decide it is part of the health foods category, you might want to advertise on health-related websites and find a health-oriented influencer to help promote the product. As a milk drink, however, you may prefer to create a promotion with child-oriented companies like My Little Gym or Sesame Workshop. You could create a product integration in a parent-oriented program on TLC (The Learning Channel), or you might choose to advertise the product to both target groups using a combination of those media.

There are numerous stories in advertising lore of how the redefinition of a product category gave new life to a moribund product or service. Perhaps the most renowned case of redefinition is that of Arm & Hammer baking soda. By finding a new use for an established product (keeping refrigerators smelling fresh), the brand positioned itself in two completely distinct categories: baking products and home fresheners. Today, it has a huge market share in the latter category, and it has expanded into numerous other cleaning-related areas, such as carpet freshener and deodorant.

Once you have determined in which product category your brand rightfully belongs (or the category in which you want it to belong), you are then in a position to examine trends in that category. You can do this in one of several ways. You may have access to product category sales from a trade association or manufacturers' group of some kind (such as the Juvenile Products Manufacturers Association, if you are marketing children's toys, or the Cellular Telecommunications and Internet Association [CTIA], if you are marketing mobile phone devices or apps). You can often find such data in trade journals or websites in your particular field (such as *Supermarket News* for supermarket food sales or *Chemical Week* for sales of liquid nitrogen). Overall category sales are gathered and reported by companies such as Euromonitor or Mintel. *Advertising Age* also reports an advertising-to-sales ratio in all major product categories periodically that shows spending on advertising relative to sales. In many larger companies, these data are routinely collected, usually within the marketing department.

In looking at category trends, be careful to look back beyond the past year. In fact, if you can find five to ten years of data, you'll be in a much stronger position to see what the real trends are. Another important point to remember is that there will be many factors to explain the rise or fall of product sales. These trends do not occur in a vacuum. Sales for construction products fell from 2008 to 2014, but this is not because people stopped building houses; rather, due to the recession, the rate of new home construction was lower than it was before 2008 because home loans were much harder to get. It is worth noting, however, that sometimes marketers can *benefit* from changes in consumer habits driven by external factors that work to their advantage. For example, the global COVID-19 pandemic forced many people to work from home rather than go to offices, which was beneficial for companies making casual clothing. For example, Lululemon saw a 40 percent increase in its share value during this time.

Interpreting Sales Trends

Four factors that help explain sales trends are political, economic, sociocultural, and technological. This is referred to as a PEST analysis (the acronym using the first letter of each trend type). Each factor may influence your media choices. For instance, politics can play an important role in the marketing of goods and services, affecting public policies that impact marketers. For companies selling marijuana-related products, what happens at federal, state, and local levels will affect all elements of the marketing process, including distribution, promotion, and even the types of products.[8]

The overall health of the economy will impact companies trying to sell their newest smartphone. In a downturn, for instance, will people wonder whether they can afford to spend the money to purchase a new version of a device they already own. If you decide that, despite the economic downturn, you want to emphasize a sophisticated image for your product, aiming it at innovators who always want to buy the latest equipment, then you might use social media ads targeted to electronics aficionados. If, on the other hand, you choose to emphasize how the new phone has enhanced ways to keep you connected to friends and family, you might look to a broader audience and use programmatic display ads that appear on an array of websites.

Social and cultural changes, while slower to occur, can also explain movements in product sales that have implications for media planning and buying. Generational shifts can have a huge effect on society at large, as well as how marketers act. As people became more environmentally aware and conscious, companies such as Target and Starbucks responded, reducing the use of plastic bags for the former and removing plastic straws for the latter. When brands want to promote their response to issues of sustainability and climate change, they may alter the media channels used to convey those messages, moving from traditional TV or radio ads, for example, to making this the focus of their owned media channels (such as the brand website) or getting more actively involved in community events or sponsorships.[9]

Cultural changes, such as the increasing diversity of the U.S. population, lead to changing tastes and preferences. People of Asian ethnicity are 33 percent more likely than the total population to consume soy sauce and 9 percent less likely to eat ketchup.[10] The marketers of these foods will introduce new flavors or adjust the ingredients in existing brands to accommodate the changing tastes of consumers. Marketers may also try different ways of reaching their target audiences, such as through product sampling in stores or sponsorship of community events or location-based digital campaigns. The heightened awareness of the Black Lives Matter movement following the death of George Floyd in Minnesota in June 2020 led more than 90 brands to pause all their social media advertising the following month to increase pressure on social platforms to remove racist content.

Finally, how people use technology has significant effects on media decisions. The growth in digital forms of media, whether streamed television and audio or digital outdoor billboards, has made many brands adopt a "digital-first" approach to advertising. And with the growth of voice-assisted devices such as Google Home and Amazon Echo, marketers have tried to figure out how to take advantage of voice to deliver brand messages and facilitate sales.

While you as a media specialist may not have to pinpoint all the reasons behind category trends, it is important for you to gain a broad understanding of what is really happening in the category and not simply limit yourself to whether sales are up or down. Having this additional background information will help you decide which media you can or should be using in your plan.

What Should You Measure?

Another important issue when looking at category trends is deciding which you should be measuring. Sales? Units? Volume? The answer to this may ultimately depend on the types of data you are able to obtain, but you need to keep in mind that what seems to be a trend when examining one number may disappear or be reversed if you turn to another. For example, while sales of your Fitbit devices could be going up in dollar terms, you may actually be selling fewer units if sales are rising primarily due to price increases (i.e., you make more money on each unit sold but sell fewer units as a result). When looking at category trends in dollar terms, always remember to factor in the effects of inflation. What may seem to be a 7 percent annual growth rate could turn out to be a 2 to 3 percent rate once you account for inflation. Perhaps the category trend line shows that the number of units of shampoo sold is declining, but volume is holding steady. This might occur if the unit size has been enlarged, so the same total volume is being sold but in larger bottles. Again, ideally, you want to look at several trend lines using diverse measurements so that you can get an overall picture of what is going on in the category.

Brand Trends

When you turn your attention to individual brands, you perform similar analyses to those done at the category level. This time, however, you focus your attention on specific brand names. The use of the plural here is critical: You are not just looking at how *your* brand has been doing over the past several years, but, even more importantly, you need to track how your brand's *competitors* have been faring during that same period. This requires finding the answers to the following questions:

- How many competitors are there?
- How many of these are major, and how many are minor?

In some categories, where there are just a few players, such as the airline industry, you should probably consider all of them; in larger categories, such as fast-food restaurants, where many companies have offerings, you will do better to pay attention to the ones you believe are your most serious threats. In certain instances, it is a good idea to look at all of the competitors regardless of their size; you may find that the fourth-tier player of three years ago has gradually been gaining market share and is now a far bigger concern. In the casual dining restaurant category, the top spenders in the category in 2016 were Applebee's and Olive Garden. By 2020, their biggest competitors were no longer other dine-in restaurants, but rather Doordash and Uber. Together, the two food delivery players spent 57 percent more than the top-spending legacy players.[11]

- How is the category characterized? Is it an oligopoly, where three or four brands define the category, or are there 20 or 30 brands each shouting to be heard?
- How aggressively do the brands in this category compete against one another? For example, is the category advertising driven or promotion driven? Does everyone rely heavily on digital display ads or TV? Do they all have a large presence on social media? You can answer these questions either from your own experience in the category or by looking at any available syndicated data on competitive media expenditures.

For each competitor (or at least for the major ones), you should also find out the following:

- What is the company's financial position? For publicly owned companies, this can be found by looking at stock market information or Standard & Poor's reports, where available, or by obtaining a recent issue of the company's annual report.
- How does the competitor position its brand? To determine this, you will have to use your own judgment. Examine the advertising for the brand and see what is being emphasized. Is it similar to your own current efforts or not? If it is dissimilar, is that because there is an actual difference between the two brands, or do consumers just perceive a distinction between them? And who has the more favorable position?

- How does the competitor promote its brand? Which media are used? How much does the competitor spend to promote its brand? Where and when does it spend its money? The answers to these questions may come from several sources. In the U.S., many large companies and/or their agencies subscribe to syndicated competitive spending data from either Kantar Media or Nielsen. Both show—on weekly, monthly, quarterly, and annual bases—how much money was spent by a brand in each major media category (see Exhibit 1.6). Smaller businesses may simply try to keep track of where their competitors' ads are appearing.

This is not too difficult if you are dealing with a local product, but it gets more complicated the wider the area that you or your competitors try to cover. You can also subscribe to a service that will do the tracking for you.

Share of Market

Once you have looked at the trends for your brand and its competitors, you must then put that information together and see how your brand is faring in the marketplace. The percentage of total category sales that your brand enjoys is known as the *share of market*. You should try to examine how this figure has changed over time. There are published sources for this kind of information, such as NPD Group. Have you been gaining or losing market share in the past few years? Again, it is important to avoid oversimplifying the picture. It could be that you have been losing market share, but so have your major competitors, because of the entry of several new brands into the category. We can see this in the media arena in television. Whereas ten years ago the broadcast networks commanded about half of the prime time viewing audience, today the broadcast affiliates (such as ABC, CBS, FOX, or NBC) account for less than one-third of the tuned-in audience at that time while the remainder are watching something else.

Share of Requirements

One of the most useful pieces of information you can examine is the source of your brand's sales. This is known as the *share of requirements*. It is calculated by taking the percentage of total category volume accounted for by a particular brand's users. Quite simply, it tells you whether your brand is being bought primarily by your customers or by your competitors' customers—and, conversely, how much of your competitors' sales are coming from your brand users. Looking at this figure, you will be able to determine what percentage of the volume you sell is accounted for by your users as opposed to people who usually buy another brand.

Exhibit 1.6 Example of Competitive Reporting Data

| | | | | | Dollars in thousands | | | | | | | | | | | | |

Year	Brand	Industry	Major Category PCC	Sub-Group Category PCC	Network TV	Cable TV	Spanish Language TV	Local TV	National Spot Radio	Local Radio	Magazines	Outdoor	Display	Online Video	Mobile Web	Paid Social	Grand Total
2019	Coca-Cola General Promotion	Confectionary, Snacks & Soft Drinks	F220	F221	$383.7	$21.0	$0.0	$0.0	$5,132.0	$20.0	$0.0	$30,208.0	$1,219.0	$74.3	$1,362.4	$0.0	$38,420.4
2019	Coca-Cola Zero	Confectionary, Snacks & Soft Drinks	F220	F222	$11,357.2	$8,504.8	$5,705.4	$240.0	$0.0	$85.0	$482.1	$0.0	$1,387.3	$230.2	$0.0	$0.0	$27,992.0
2019	Diet Coke	Confectionary, Snacks & Soft Drinks	F220	F222	$84.9	$775.9	$0.0	$0.1	$0.0	$0.3	$0.0	$7.4	$18.3	$0.0	$0.0	$1,208.0	$2,094.9

Source: Kantar Media, 2020

Exhibit 1.7 Example of Share of Requirements

	Total Category Volume	Brand Share of Volume	Brand Share of Requirements
National pretzels	38%	25%	65%
Regional pretzels	42%	29%	69%
Pioneer Pretzels	27%	15%	55%
Other brands	9%	5%	65%

Let's say you are a manufacturer of a local brand of pretzels (Pioneer Pretzels) and you are competing with other regional brands as well as a major national brand. As you can see in Exhibit 1.7, Pioneer Pretzels buyers account for 27 percent of all the pretzels sold in the last 30 days. Of all the pretzels purchased, 15 percent are Pioneer Pretzels, and 12 percent are other brands. This means that 55 percent (15 percent/27 percent) of the total category volume is given to your brand, which gives Pioneer a 55 percent share of requirements. This is the lowest figure among all pretzel types, suggesting that Pioneer's users are not especially brand loyal, which could harm sales and future market share.

There is an extensive body of research on brand loyalty. Byron Sharp, for example, strongly believes in the "duplication of purchase law," which posits that a brand's customer base overlaps with the customer base of other brands, in line with their market share so that a brand shares the most customers with large brands. He notes that the majority of a brand's sales in fact come from light buyers, which means brands must continue to fight for attention, and if marketers focus primarily on their loyal current buyers, they will experience the "law of double jeopardy," which posits that it is not possible to grow sales without expanding market share.[12]

Where Is Your Brand Sold?

Once you have found out as much as possible about how your brand stacks up against the competition, you need to think about geographic and distribution considerations. While online sales have certainly become a significant factor in terms of revenues, particularly in categories such as consumer electronics and clothing, most consumers are still buying brands in the store. In 2020, online sales in the United States accounted for about 14 percent of all retail transactions.[13] This varies by category, of course, and the COVID-19 pandemic rapidly increased online commerce as people could not go inside brick-and-mortar stores. It is important for media specialists to look at where your brand is selling well and where it is doing poorly in terms of markets, regions, or states and in terms of the type of retail outlet. This holds true whether your brand is available nationally, regionally, or locally. Unless your product is sold in just one store or location, there are likely to be some differences in sales according to geography and distribution outlets. What you discover by looking at the sales for your brand in these ways may lead you to develop a media plan with regional or local differences.

Indeed, more and more marketers have adopted a regional approach to selling, realizing that people in Boise have different tastes, customs, and buying habits than people in Boston or Baton Rouge. Marketers are customizing their marketing and media plans (and, in some cases, their products) to meet the needs of specific areas of the country. While some regional differences are obvious, such as higher snowblower sales in Maine than in Arizona, others might seem surprising (such as the fact that insecticides sell most heavily in the South). These types of differences occur not just at the product category level but also for individual brands. Dannon yogurt generally sells better on the East Coast than does Yoplait, which has traditionally been stronger out West.

To understand geographic skews, the media specialist can turn to two pieces of information: development indices and market share.

Development Indices

You could, in theory, obtain sales data from every region or store in the country and look through them to discover your brand's sales picture. But a more efficient method for analyzing geographic strengths and weaknesses is to look at how the product category is doing across the United States and then to look at how the brand is developing over time. Both of these are calculated by using *development indices*.

Category Development Index

The category development index, or CDI, looks at product category sales in each potential region or market. A norm, or average, is calculated at 100, and then each area is assigned a value relative to that, expressed as a percentage. Numbers below 100 indicate the category has lower than average sales in a given region, whereas those above 100 suggest sales of the category are greater than the national average in a certain part of the country. If, on average, 32,500 tractors are sold per month per region across the United States, that might mean 25,000 units are sold in the East, 45,000 in the West, 28,000 in the North, and 32,000 in the South. Eastern sales would index at 77 (25,000/32,500), meaning that sales in that area are 23 percent below the national norm, while sales in the West would have a CDI of 138 (45,000/32,500), indicating that that region's sales are 38 percent higher than average. Those in the South have a CDI of

98 (32,000/32,500), which shows that southern sales are 2 percent lower than the norm, whereas in the North, the CDI would be 86 (28,000/32,500), or 14 percent lower than the average. Based on such information, a company might decide to concentrate its marketing and media efforts in the region with the higher CDI, as that is where there is greater potential for all tractor sales.

Brand Development Index

You should not rely solely on the CDI in making geographic media decisions, however. You also need to look at how your brand stacks up against other brands in the category. One tool for this job is the brand development index, or BDI. The calculation is very similar to that of the CDI. You calculate a norm, or average, for all brands (or chief competitors) in the category, which is again set at 100, and then you see how your own brand is doing in comparison. The John Deere tractor company might find its BDI for tractor sales is 10 percent above average in the eastern region and 5 percent below the norm in the West, suggesting that it is doing better than other brands in the category in the East but slightly less well in comparison in the West.

When you look at the BDI, you need to keep the CDI in mind, too. Once you have these two sets of data, you should compare your BDI to your CDI. In that way, you will be able to find those markets where your brand is doing better than the category overall as well as where your brand appears to be under-performing in the category (see Exhibit 1.8). For John Deere, its eastern BDI is greater than the CDI, so the brand is doing better than the category in that region. In the West, however, its BDI is below the CDI, so there is room for improvement here.

Exhibit 1.8 BDI Versus CDI

Category Index

	High	Low
High	Both brand and category growing	Brand growing and category declining
Low	Brand declining and category growing	Both brand and category declining

Brand Index

Armed with this information, you may choose to adopt one of three possible marketing and media strategies. You can focus your attention on those areas of the country where your brand is doing better than the category, playing to your strengths. Or you might choose to give more attention (and money) to the weaker markets where the category is doing well, but your brand isn't to try to bolster your sales there. Alternately, you might decide to play it safe and concentrate on markets where both category and brand are successful. The one strategy you should avoid is pouring money into areas where both brand and category are doing poorly, as that suggests there is something about all the brands that is not liked or does not meet the needs of those consumers. To try to rectify that situation single-handedly is probably going to be more trouble (and cost) than it is worth.

Market Share by Geography

When looking at the development indices, you can also find out how your competition is doing in each territory and calculate their BDIs. It is common to see that where your brand is doing well, your competitors are having a harder time, and vice versa. The exception here would be for a new or relaunched category where all brands are selling well, such as fruit-flavored hard seltzers.

One way of investigating sales further in geographic terms is to look at your share of the market by region or locality. Is your brand number one in sales in the central region but in third place in the South? Are you neck and neck in New York but a distant second in Florida? Faced with these different scenarios, you should explore some of the possible reasons behind the distinctions. And here you should go back to the other Ps of the marketing process. Perhaps you have place (i.e., distribution) problems in Florida that are harming sales. Maybe your brand is being undercut in price in the South by a local manufacturer. Or it could be that your chief competitor is flooding the local airwaves with promotional messages in New York and drowning out yours. By putting together the information you gather from the development indices with your market share figures, you will start to create a picture of how your brand is doing across the country. That will help you decide what marketing and media tactics might be needed in each situation.

One last scenario to consider is a deliberate geographic restriction on product sales. This may be taken for several reasons. You might choose to test launch a new product in only one market or one region of the country to see how it fares there first. This is what companies such as Uber and Tesla did with their self-driving cars in Phoenix, Arizona. Or you might "create" demand by making your product restricted, as movie studios effectively do when they open a new film only in New York and Los Angeles before the rest of the country to assess consumer response there first, which can then help guide their marketing strategies. In either scenario, the advertising required to support these tactics is going to be far smaller than for products available more broadly.

The media plan will not be the miracle solution to all of the problems you might encounter, and you should not expect it to turn a floundering brand into a superstar. But, as we shall see in subsequent chapters, the better your understanding of the marketing situation your brand is in, the more likely you are to come up with creative solutions to the problems. For example, if your problem is distribution, you might want to include extra trade promotions or incentives in your plan to encourage retailers or distributors to push your brand further. Pricing discrepancies might be alleviated by offering a digital coupon or on-pack premium to offset the lower-priced competitors. And if your consumers are being faced with a barrage of competitive messages in one medium, it might be wise to consider placing your own advertising in completely different media or perhaps move to more owned and earned media to raise your own voice elsewhere. There is also an array of possibilities with geographically targeted ads, such as digital display or mobile ads that are customized to your specific geographic area. More will be said on this in later chapters.

Finally, if possible, you should try to look at your brand's geographic strengths and weaknesses over time to see where the trends are going. Have you always been weaker in the Southwest, or does this seem to have started only in the past year? Is the overall CDI flattening out across the country or moving to different areas? This is likely to occur in new product categories when they are first introduced, as was seen when flavored carbonated water was first introduced. As always, looking at several years of data will help you to avoid acting on "blips" in the numbers that might have disappeared without cause within a few months.

Consumers and Media

Although a successful marketing plan requires a thorough understanding of consumers' relationships with the brand, similarly thorough knowledge is needed to learn the relationships between consumers and media. In subsequent chapters, we will explore in greater detail the characteristics of each major media form, but here we will introduce the notion of the value of media *context*, or environment.

As you start to learn more about the way consumers use and think about your brand, you can also begin to investigate how they use and think about media. Do your tractor owners, for example, rely on the early morning farming report on the radio? How much do they rely on digital media to check on crop prices? With the Fruitola brand, are the people you want to reach with your message about its fresh taste interested in health and fitness? If so, are they following certain influencers, and what do they think about them? In both cases, how do they respond to ad messages or sponsorships appearing in those contexts compared to seeing the same message placed elsewhere?

The impact of context has long been explored by the academic community, primarily by looking at the effects of consumer involvement with the media in which ads appear.[14]

A different approach that has grown popular in the advertising industry is known as *audience first*. Here, rather than analyzing the context in which an ad appears, the focus shifts to a deeper understanding of the people receiving the ad message to ensure that they are seeing or hearing ads that are most relevant for them at that time and place. We will explore this further in Chapter 3.

A Word About Budgets

One of the most important preplanning issues to look at is how much money you have to spend for media for the coming year. You may be given a specific amount upfront, or you may have a range within which to work. In many situations, the media specialist is likely to come up with two or three alternative media plans at different spending levels, showing what could be achieved with $500,000 versus $1,000,000 versus $2,000,000, for example. If possible, you should try to be flexible on the budget at this point, keeping in mind that if you lock yourself into a set figure from the beginning, you may limit your creativity later when you put the plan together. There has been some research on how much is an ideal amount to spend to be both efficient with the funds and effective with the message impact.[15]

Timing and Other Issues

The last major area to explore in the preplanning phase is that of timing. This may include the month of the year, the week of the month, the day of the week, or the hour of the day. While some timing considerations can be rationalized and justified, others may be out of your control. Some companies skew their messages toward pay periods, such as the 15th and 30th of the month, knowing that people are more likely to spend money when they have just been paid. Movie studios traditionally advertised more heavily near the end of the week before people decided what movie to see at the weekend. Other considerations may be out of your control. The CEO of the company that makes your brand of sports drink may demand that you purchase television time during the U.S. Open Golf tournament. He not only likes golf, but he also wants to get tickets to the event. The marketing manager may refuse to have the brand advertised in any magazine that accepts liquor advertisements. Perhaps your candy company has been a sponsor of a local parade for the past 50 years, and you cannot break with that tradition.

There might also be key timing opportunities that you should consider. If you are going into a Summer or Winter Olympics year, you might want to look for some way to tie your brand into that. While this sounds out of the league of any but the largest national advertisers, there may be an Olympic swim team member in your own town whom your brand of swim goggles could support in some way. Or, if your city is celebrating its 200th anniversary and your tool factory has been around for just as long, you could get involved in the preparations for related events. Or maybe next year has been designated the Year of the Child, so you can look for opportunities to promote your diaper brand. Be alert and open to new ideas and opportunities such as these that might come along infrequently and sporadically but could greatly enhance your brand's profile and help sales locally, regionally, or even nationally. We will delve further into timing considerations in Chapter 9.

Summary

The focus of *The Media Handbook* is the role of media in communicating and conveying information about products and services to potential consumers. It starts by looking at how media fit within the broader worlds of advertising and marketing. Understanding the relationship of consumers to both media and brands provides useful background for any media plan. Before creating a new plan, it is important to know as much as possible about the consumer journey, as well as how your brand has performed within its product category. As you examine your brand, consider who its real competitors are and learn about their past and present marketing plans.

As you learn more about consumers' relationships with your brand and its competitors, also consider how they respond to the media that are important to their lives. Think about the context, or environment, of your brand's messages, while you also start to think about your consumers as the potential audience for your plans. Finally, keep in mind any budgeting or timing constraints that will affect your media plan.

Notes

1. "GroupM: Top 25 Media Suppliers Now Control Two-Thirds Of All Ad Spending," Joe Mandese, MediaPost Agency Daily, June 22, 2021.
2. David Ogilvy, *Confessions of an Advertising Man*, London: South Bank Books, 2004.
3. Kantar Media, 2021.
4. Qimei Chen, Yi He, Miao Hu, and Jaisang (Jay) Kim (2020) "Navigating Relationship Norms: An Exploration of How Content Strategies Improve Brand Valuation over Time," *Journal of Advertising*, 49:4, 459–476.
5. Jan Stapel, "Recall and Recognition: A Very Close Relationship," *Journal of Advertising Research*, vol. 38, no. 4, July/August 1998, 41–46. Robert Angell, Matthew

Gorton, Johannes Sauer, Paul Bottomley, and John White, "Don't Distract Me When I'm Media Multitasking: Toward a Theory for Raising Advertising Recall and Recognition," *Journal of Advertising*, vol. 45, no. 2, April–June 2016, 198–210.

6. Russell W. Belk, "Qualitative Research in Advertising," *Journal of Advertising*, vol. 46, no. 1, January–March 2017, 36–47.

7. Gina Sverdlov, "Behavioral Economics for Market Insights Professionals," *Forrester Research*, September 6, 2012.

8. Jeremy Kees and J. Craig Andrews, "Research Issues and Needs at the Intersection of Advertising and Public Policy," *Journal of Advertising*, vol. 48, no. 1, 2019, 126–135.

9. Wei-Na Lee, "Exploring the Role of Culture in Advertising: Resolving Persistent Issues and Responding to Changes," *Journal of Advertising*, vol. 48, no. 1, 2019, 115–125.

10. 2020 Doublebase MRI-Simmons.

11. Kantar Media, 2020.

12. Byron Sharp, *How Brands Grow: What Marketers Don't Know*, Oxford: Oxford University Press, 2010.

13. U.S. Department of Commerce, 2020.

14. Valentine Appel, "Editorial Environment and Advertising Effectiveness," *Journal of Advertising Research*, vol. 27, no. 4, August/September 1987, 11–16. Elizabeth Gigi Taylor and Wei-Na Lee, "A Cross-Media Study of Audience Choice: The Influence of Media Attitudes on Individual Selection of 'Media Repertoires,'" *Proceedings of the 2004 Conference of the American Academy of Advertising*, 39–48. Britta C. Ware, "Magazine Reader Involvement Improves ROI," *ESOMAR, Print Audience Measurement*, June 2003. Maria Christina Moya Schilling, Karin Wood, and Alan Branthwaite, "The Medium Is Part of the Message," *ESOMAR, Reinventing Advertising*, November 2000, 207–229.

15. Yunjae Cheong, Federico de Gregorio, and Kihan Kim, "Advertising Spending Efficiency Among Top U.S. Advertisers from 1985 to 2012: Overspending or Smart Managing?" *Journal of Advertising*, vol. 43, no. 4, November–December 2014, 344–358.

Chapter 2

Media Objectives and Strategies

Learning Outcomes: In this chapter you will learn how to:

*   Differentiate marketing, advertising, and media objectives
*   Explore the stages of the consumer journey
*   Understand how to create media objectives

Setting objectives is something we are all familiar with in our day-to-day lives: "I will make the Dean's List this semester," "I'll get 1,000 Instagram followers," or "My goal is to become the CEO of the company by the time I reach 35." Whatever the objective may be, if you didn't have one, it would be difficult to know what you've achieved!

First, however, it is important to differentiate objectives from strategies. The strategy is the plan that is put in place to reach an overarching goal. Objectives are the steps proposed to deliver on the strategy. Beneath all of these are the tactics needed to achieve the objectives. In the context of a class, your goal of making the Dean's List might have a strategy of focusing solely on your classes during the term. Then your objectives could be to aim for top grades in three of your four classes, while the tactics to achieve that could be extra study sessions in the university library each week.

In the media planning context, you need to establish firm objectives for your plan to demonstrate how it will help your brand achieve its marketing goals. Although you may feel that to execute a media plan you must keep returning to your starting point, moving one step back for every two you go forward, it cannot be overemphasized that *everything* you do on the media planning side must be coordinated with the overall marketing strategy. Therefore, to establish your media objectives—what you intend the media plan to achieve—you must first reaffirm and clarify the goals of your complete advertising program to ensure that your media objectives fit in with the goals set in your brand's marketing objectives.

Once you have determined what your objectives are, you must develop the means to achieve those objectives. Again, to put this in a more personal

DOI: 10.4324/9781003175704-2

context, if your goal is to ace a test, your strategies might include setting aside time every day to study, talking to the professor or person administering the test to get guidance, or taking practice tests beforehand. In the media world, your objectives should guide you on how you are going to achieve your strategy—not in a tactical way (I'm going to use TV ads for 12 weeks at 50 ratings per week) but at the higher level. With our Fruitola example, if the broad strategy is to make consumers see this new carbonated fruit juice as a healthy alternative to regular soda, then your objective could focus on finding health-oriented paid, owned, and earned opportunities to communicate that idea.

With all objectives, it is important to consider how they will be measured. In marketing, these are sometimes referred to as the *key performance indicators*, or *KPIs*. A study undertaken by the Association of National Advertisers in 2021 found that three of the KPIs marketers considered most important for advertising and media were return on investment (ROI), lifetime value of the customer, and conversion to a sale. Yet, when asked which were the most commonly used KPIs, the top two items listed were cost per 1,000 impressions and cost per click, both of which demonstrate the efficiency of the investment, rather than an indicator of the effectiveness of the campaign or meeting broader objectives.[1]

How the Marketing Objective Leads to the Media Objective

It is worth noting that the media specialist is likely to be presented with the marketing objective rather than having to develop it on his or her own. It usually comes in the form of a Client Brief, which puts the media objectives within the broader context of the overall goals for the brand. The marketing objectives should be stated in some quantifiable form, such as "sell *x* thousand more widgets in 2022 than in 2021" or "increase awareness of Brand X to 75 percent within calendar year 2023." It may relate to any of the major marketing functions, such as increasing shelf space in the store or increasing the number of distribution channels for your product. Frequently, it is expressed in terms of specific volume and share goals, such as "within calendar year 2023, bring Brand Z's total volume sold to 25 percent of the total category, raising its market share from 35 percent to 38 percent."

If the marketing objective is vague or ill-defined, simply "increasing awareness" or "improving distribution," then at the end of the year (or whatever time period has been set to meet the goal), there is likely to be considerable debate over whether the plan was successful. It is going to be more difficult for the media specialist to devise the strategies to achieve those objectives. Even if awareness does improve, how much higher must it go for the media plan to be considered a success?

Along with understanding the marketing objective, the media specialist should also look at *how* that objective will be achieved, or what strategy to take, because that will affect what the media plan is supposed to do. Examples might be to increase product penetration among potential users by taking sales away from competitors or bringing new users into the marketplace. Alternately, the strategy might be to encourage people to use your brand more frequently, perhaps offering new uses for it. To increase the sales of Kraft Singles cheese, the marketing objective might be to get current users to buy additional packs of the product for use in new and different ways besides just for sandwiches. For the media plan, this could lead to an objective of increasing the frequency with which target users are exposed to the message to remind them of the various ways they can use the product by demonstrating the uses in recipes. Your strategy would then focus on looking at media (paid for or created specifically for the brand) that could provide recipes that include the cheese slices.

For a hospital with the marketing objective of introducing a new children's critical care unit and encouraging more people in the community to choose that facility for their pediatric medical needs, the media objective could be to reach 75 percent of people who live within a 10-mile radius to inform them of the expertise available at the new unit. The strategy would focus on how best to achieve that objective (geo-targeted media or social platforms, for example). Clearly, the marketing objective has a major impact on how the media plan develops, affecting the target audience, communications used, and media selected.

Media and the Advertising Objective

As we noted earlier, the marketing objective may relate to any of the four major areas of the marketing mix (product, promotion, distribution, or price). Therefore, before establishing specific media objectives, it is also essential to focus on how media affect your advertising goals. While your ultimate *marketing* goal for most goods is to sell more products (or services or enhanced image), unless your audience finds out about the product through the media that you use, that goal is unlikely to be reached. You need to be aware, at the same time, of the other marketing mix elements. If the product is weak, your media advertising will have little impact. Similarly, if you advertise your product heavily, but it is out of stock online or in stores, sales will likely not improve.

Frequently, the objective of your advertising is tied to the stage at which the target audience is in the consumer journey, or their decision-making process. As we noted in Chapter 1, this process breaks down into three very broad areas: think, feel, and do (or, in psychology, the *cognitive*, *affective*, and *conative* stages). Once you have decided that you need a new smartphone, you will *think* about what brands are available. Then, you will consider how you *feel* about each one of them. Finally, you will select a particular brand and take action (*do*) and buy it.

Stages of the Consumer Journey

This process can be better understood by revisiting the eight main stages of the consumer journey introduced in Chapter 1:

1 Need
2 Awareness
3 Preference
4 Search
5 Selection
6 Purchase
7 Use
8 Satisfaction

Need

Before you can hope to sell any more widgets, people have to have a reason to buy them. Contrary to what many advertising critics maintain, advertising does not persuade people to buy something they do not need. Indeed, it is often easier to think of this first stage in the journey as reflecting people's *wants*; in today's industrial society, most people are able to satisfy their basic needs, such as food and shelter.

Even when people buy products that seem pointless, such as Starbucks' unicorn Frappuccino or a fidget spinner, they may feel they have a *need* to indulge in it just for fun. And while you might argue that no one really has a *need* for a $150,000 Tesla vehicle, the person who chooses to purchase one clearly feels that he or she deserves this luxury automobile. Defining what the need might be for the product helps the marketer understand the motivations behind why people might buy it, which in turn may provide some clues as to ways of reaching those people through media. Although everyone buys shampoo, if you can segment the target into different groups according to their motivation for use, you could reach each one through a variety of media forms. People who are most concerned with how their hair looks may be reached via fashion and beauty influencers. Those who want a shampoo with built-in conditioner to help in their busy lives may respond to digital ads appearing on working parent websites that offer advice on juggling multiple roles. For the ones who are looking for the most natural ingredients in their shampoo, social media ads in eco-friendly content or conversations might be most appropriate. Research conducted directly with target consumers may reveal that different segments actually have different relationships with their shampoo, leading you, as a planner, to determine what ways media can help your shampoo brands best fit in consumers' lives, such as a Pinterest board on time-saving tips, content integration in a fashion-oriented reality show, a YouTube channel focused on fashion, or an app featuring natural products. These and other media options are covered in greater details in subsequent chapters, but you should understand how different consumer needs can often lead to different media choices.

Awareness

Once the consumer has determined that he or she needs a particular product, it is the job of marketing to make the consumer aware of the choices that are available. For the media specialist, this means reaching that consumer in the right place and often enough so that your brand's message is the most relevant and convincing. And it is not enough to simply make people aware of your *brand*; the real goal here is to make them aware of your brand's *message*. You might well be able to reach 95 percent of all cat owners to make them aware of the new cat food that you sell, but unless they also learn that your product provides 100 percent of a cat's daily nutritional requirement, which is more than any other competitor, your advertising is unlikely to increase sales. Of course, keep in mind that your message could get lost in the clutter of other cat food ads unless you ensure that the message is delivered in a meaningful way that fits in with your target's life, instead of being unwanted advertising bombardment.

Preference

Based on the various choices the consumer sees and hears, he or she will then develop specific brand preferences. Ideally, the marketer would like that consumer to develop *brand loyalty* so that every time Isabella needs to buy a new pair of running shoes, for example, she always chooses Saucony. A media plan to enhance preference might include a co-promotional program with Avon to provide that brand's running shoes to breast cancer survivors participating in Avon's annual walkathons or a sponsorship of local races where Saucony representatives let you try on their shoes.

Search

Once the target audience decides it might prefer your brand over others, the audience's next task is to find out where to purchase the item. Here, media advertising can be a big help by notifying people of the places that sell your product. The fastest way most consumers search today is on Google, simply typing in the brand name or checking on a store's website. Advertisers can buy keyword searches so that whenever consumers are searching for the brand (or category), it is yours that comes up first. But other media offer search-assisting opportunities, too, such as listing local area stores or dealers that stock the brand in a TV or radio ad or on a billboard. If your audience cannot find the product when it's time to buy it, then not even the best advertising placed in the most appropriate media will help increase sales.

Selection

Brand selection may seem like an easy stage in the consumer journey. If Rachel has decided already that she prefers Cover Girl nail polish over others, and she has learned that it is sold in Walmart stores, then isn't it obvious that she will buy it? Not necessarily. Today's consumer is faced with so many different brands that, once in the store and standing in front of the shelf, she may decide to go with Revlon instead because it is on sale, or it is packaged more attractively, or it comes in larger bottles. The selection process is a crucial stage for the marketer and the media specialist to consider. From a media perspective, the nail polish user may be encouraged by in-store vehicles such as in-pack premiums or point-of-purchase radio or a digital coupon that comes up on her phone. Personal experience can also be very important at this stage. Someone who has come into the store to buy a mid-range laptop may be encouraged to select your more expensive model by being offered one year of free parts and service by the dealer.

Purchase and Use

Clearly, the ultimate goal of marketing and media plans is to persuade consumers to purchase the product. But if they buy it and never use it, then there is no reason for them to ever buy another one. No marketer can remain successful by continually targeting new product users; the cost of securing new users is much higher than retaining current ones. Often, one marketing and media objective is that of encouraging consumers to *use* the brand. In media planning terms, this might involve increasing the message frequency so that users are reminded of the different ways in which the brand can be used. A good example of this, in past years, has been Campbell's Soup, which often places recipes in its ads to encourage people to use more of the product and, hence, purchase it more frequently. Academic research has looked at the relationship between ad frequency and purchase intentions.[2]

Sometimes a simple conversation with current users can provide important information on how best to market to them. Whether through focus groups, online communities, or social media, marketers can learn a lot just by listening. That, in turn, can suggest ways that the media message could help solve a problem or offer information. If you are marketing a chocolate bar to kids, then hearing the nutritional concerns of mothers might steer you toward putting some of your media dollars where those parents are consuming media, with messages of reassurance about the nutritional quality of that product.

Satisfaction

The final stage in the consumer journey is really a feedback loop into the earlier ones. If people come to your restaurant but are dissatisfied with the quality of the food or friendliness of the staff, then their dissatisfaction will likely mean they won't return to your venue again. What is worse, they may tell their friends about their bad experience and decrease your potential sales even further. In a world of Instagram, Facebook, Twitter, and other social media, it is easier than ever to spread the (bad) word. Customer satisfaction is extremely important for future success. *Satisfaction* is generally not listed as the primary marketing or media objective of a plan, but it should nonetheless be kept in mind when deciding where and when to place your advertising message. Social media can be used by the marketer to offer reassurance or an outlet to respond when issues arise with a brand or its communications. And social conversations, whether online or offline, can be readily monitored to keep abreast of consumer satisfaction. When Dove placed a video ad for its body lotion on Facebook showing a black woman turning into a white one, it faced an immediate outcry. The company quickly pulled the ad and apologized on Twitter to reassure consumers that it did not intend to make any racist comment.

Advertising Objectives and the Consumer Journey

To see how advertising objectives might fit in with each stage of the consumer journey, let's look at an example. If your client is the city's professional soccer team, the Stars, and they are trying to increase the number of people who attend home games, you may not have to create a "need" for your offering since anyone who likes sports feels the "need" to attend live games. It is likely, however, that you would want to increase awareness of your team. So, your advertising objective might be to boost awareness of the Stars from a baseline measure of 40 percent to 70 percent among young people under the age of 25 within a 50-mile radius of the city.

It could be that many people have heard about the team, but they are still choosing to attend baseball games instead. Here, your advertising objective would be to improve *preference*, so that instead of two out of ten people under 25 choosing to go to a soccer game over baseball, three out of ten do so. Setting advertising objectives for the subsequent stages in the consumer journey is somewhat less common because it is believed that advertising has a less direct role to play here. But you still want to encourage your target to *use* your team by attending games, setting your advertising objective to boost visits to your games from an average of one time per year to four, perhaps by offering promotional tickets on social media or hosting special events at the stadium.

Media and the Consumer Journey

The advertising media will also affect each of these stages in the consumer journey. To continue with the soccer team example, you might boost *awareness* of the team through widespread local TV and radio ads, outdoor billboards, or digital ads in the communities where you believe there are high concentrations of young adults. Consumer *preference* could be encouraged by sending emails to potential visitors offering them two tickets for the price of one. They could be helped in the *search* process by putting ads that provide maps to your stadium in local print or digital newspapers or by buying search keywords on local or regional tourist websites. *Selection* might be helped by bringing some of the bigger soccer stars in from out of town and offering the opportunity for fans to meet them, which you promote via social media. These special events could then earn you publicity in local media. Finally, to get current team supporters to *use* the team and attend more games, you could have some of the soccer players send tweets to those supporters to encourage them to come to future games.

Let's take another example. Say you are in the market for a new automobile. That puts you in the initial stages of *needing* a new car. You see some TV ads for various makes and models, which increases your awareness of what is available. Three of the cars that interest you are the Toyota Corolla, the Honda Civic, and the Hyundai Elantra. You go to several automotive websites, check out the cars' resale values on kellybluebook.com, pick up the *Consumer Reports* issue on new cars, and decide that these models fit your needs. Now you have developed a *preference* for these particular models out of the hundreds that are available. Your next step would be to visit some car dealerships to *search* out the cars themselves. Here, your interaction with the salespeople is likely to play a major role in influencing your decision. You will also probably talk to friends and colleagues, check out what people say on social media about the different vehicles, and look more closely online at each car's specifications. Faced with all of the information you have gathered, you *select* the Civic. You negotiate a deal and drive the car home; now you can *use* it, and, based on your experiences, you will develop a degree of *satisfaction* with your new purchase. If you are happy with the car, you may well buy another Honda the next time you are in the market for a vehicle.

The media's role is important at several points in the process. Television advertising is frequently used to create or enhance *awareness*, informing people of the qualities of the brand and what it has to offer. Both TV and magazines can help develop consumer *preference*. Here, you might see ads that compare the Honda Civic to other cars in the same class or that cite the awards and rankings the car has received in automotive competitions. As we noted previously, personal contacts and social media may be critical, too. Local ads on spot radio and television and outdoor billboards, along with keyword searches online and in mobile, help reach consumers who are *searching* for your brand.

To encourage people to *select* your offering, the media may emphasize special discounts or added features, such as a 60,000-mile warranty or $1,000 cashback. Getting people to *use* the product is also important. While this is not an issue in the case of an automobile, it can be for other consumer products. Nestlé, for instance, uses ads that feature recipes for foods made with its Toll House chocolate chips in order to encourage people to take the product off the shelf. Having people talk positively about their post-purchase experiences on social media has become increasingly important for brands and for other potential customers.

As with the marketing objective, the more measurable the advertising objective is, the easier it will be to determine whether it has been achieved. This can be done either through specific testing after the ads have run for a while or by setting up a market test and determining the effect of advertising on sales.

Media Objectives and ROI

An important consideration before you develop any media objectives is that of *ROI*, which stands for return on investment. This financially oriented term is used to help those at the top of the company (chief executive officer, chief financial officer, etc.) understand how the money being spent on media is helping generate profits. That is, for every dollar spent in media, how much is *returned* to the company in terms of sales or awareness or customer goodwill? As the media specialty has grown increasingly sophisticated and more measurable (with more digital distribution), marketers have put greater pressure on those working in media to prove that their dollars are well spent.

One of the ways this is done is through statistical modeling (described further in Chapter 4). This combines an analysis of economics with the use of statistical metrics or models. The idea here is that statistical models can be created to explain, mathematically, the value of each dollar spent in media by comparing the amounts invested in each media form to the results achieved. These results may be in terms of product sales or consumer awareness or brand preferences.

This is not an easy process, in part because not everything is easily quantifiable. How can JC Penney "prove" that its product integration into the popular TV program *Project Runway* is what causes sales of its fashion clothing to go up? Perhaps it was the concurrent TV or digital advertising that caused it. Or possibly it was the absence of its competitor, Kohl's, on the air during the same time period. Or maybe it was heavy promotional activity that helped sales. These econometric models attempt to parse out all the causes of changes in sales. When sales are increasing, everyone wants to take credit for it. The harder challenge is explaining what is *not* working—what causes sales to decline? Often it may be far broader economic trends, from the recession of 2020 to drastic weather patterns. An unusually warm (or wet or cold) period is often cited as the reason for sales of products to go down. A colder-than-normal summer can cause havoc on sales of suntan lotion, while a sudden freeze will cause a rapid halt to Starbucks' chilled coffee drinks. While the media specialist cannot be held responsible for all these external events, he or she may be required to help demonstrate the accountability of the media included in the plan.

Establishing Media Objectives

Armed with clear and concise marketing and advertising objectives that are in sync with how your brand's consumers think about and respond to the brand and to media, you are now ready for the most important part of the media planning process: setting media objectives. As with the other goals, once you have a clearly defined course set for you, it becomes much easier to figure out how to get there. There are three main elements involved in the media objectives:

1   Defining the target audience
2   Setting broad communication objectives
3   Considering creative requirements

Defining the Target Audience

Although you haven't yet started to put a plan together, you are probably beginning to realize that much of the most important work needs to be done beforehand to establish the media objectives. Defining the target audience is one key step you must take in the objective-setting process, for only by knowing whom you wish to reach through the media will you be able to put together a schedule that will convey your brand's message to the right people. Here, we will cover this within the context of creating media objectives. Chapter 3 will go into greater detail on how to develop the target.

Ideally, the target audience for your media plan should be identical to the audience for the overall marketing plan. Since most of a brand's sales are typically generated by its current users, the target audience definition is likely to include some product usage qualification. A marketing plan that is intended to increase sales of Pantene shampoo–conditioner combinations might have as its target audience women aged between 25 to 54 years old who currently use shampoo–conditioners, with an annual household income of more than $50,000. Life stage can be a crucial factor, too. A plan geared toward increasing awareness of your Motorola wireless video baby monitor might define its target as adults between 25 to 49 years old who have had a child in the past year.

Often, however, you will find that the media target may be both more and less precise than the marketing target. This is largely because the media themselves have traditionally been bought and sold on the basis of fairly basic demographics, such as age, sex, income, education, or race. For example, while your brand of Terra sweet potato chips may be aiming to sell 20,000 more packets this year by expanding its user base and capturing more sales from young adult gourmet lovers who enjoy entertaining and eating out, when it comes to creating your media objectives your target may be adults 18 to 34 who are college-educated and have an annual household income of more than $30,000. This is a more precise definition in that it specifies a particular age category as well as particular income and education levels, but it does not take into account (at least, in terms of definition) lifestyle variables (like eating out, entertaining, and fine foods).

As media has become more data-driven, however, we are seeing the growth of more precise and lifestyle/product-usage-based targeting, especially in digital channels. While traditional media such as television focused solely on age/sex targets, digital media flourished by using household-level information from data companies such as Experian or Epsilon to deliver ads to those homes that are known to have certain characteristics or product habits. For example, Purina could send its dog food ads only to homes known to have a dog. As television advertising has evolved, it has moved more to this type of approach, using household-level information linked to smart TV registrations or cable/satellite subscriptions. The approach is similar to digital, with operators or networks delivering ads solely to the households of interest. It has been found to deliver significantly more in terms of the message impact (by linking addressable ad exposure to actual sales) and media efficiency (money saved by only paying to reach homes the advertiser wants, thereby reducing waste). We will explore this further in Chapter 5.

One element that will be as true tomorrow as it is today is that the media target should be identical to the creative target. While this may seem blatantly obvious, occasionally the research and account teams will develop a complex and precise target audience, but the creative team will march forward with their own ideas of whom the message should speak to. That leaves the media department in confusion. Just as the media specialists should have seen and understood the marketing objectives, they should also be familiar with the creative brief, a document that lays out for the copywriter and art director the fundamental information about who or what the brand is, what the communication goals are for the campaign, and who the message targets. Ideally, all of the target definitions will match!

Communication Objectives

When it comes to writing down what you expect the advertising message to do for your brand, you will find that all of a sudden you are dealing with the art, rather than the science, of media planning. These objectives are measurable to some degree through communications tests with the target audience that find out what information the audience is taking away from the message. In addition, media calculations can be made to estimate what the plan should achieve in terms of how many of the targets will be reached and how often (with what frequency). But many of the criteria you need to use to establish what the goals should be are more evaluative and rely on your judgment and subjective responses to everything that you know about the brand, its advertising, and the marketplace. These objectives must also be in line with the overall marketing strategy of the brand. If you are trying to increase your market share in the athletic shoe category by 2 percentage points by increasing distribution into mass merchandise outlets, then your communication objective might involve increasing awareness of your brand among your target audience by 15 percent within the first three months of the campaign.

Communication objectives will vary depending upon the kind of product you are promoting. For launching a new brand of cat litter, you probably want your advertising to generate awareness of the product. If you are advertising Charmin toilet paper, however, which has been around for decades, your message will more likely serve as a reminder to consumers of the qualities of the product, such as its softness or strength. These differing objectives will also affect your reach and frequency goals. For a new product, you would want to establish some broad reach to drive the awareness, whereas, for the well-established brand, a higher-frequency reminder message will be more effective.

Don't forget to consider your competition, too. You might set as your objective that within the first six months of your new campaign, awareness levels for your Trek mountain bike will be equal to or greater than those of your closest competitor. Geography is another factor. If your bike is the number-one brand in the category with the highest awareness levels in the Northeast and the Pacific Northwest but falls to number two or three in the South, then you might set different objectives in different parts of the country, broadening your reach in areas where awareness levels are currently lower.

There are three factors to consider when developing communication objectives: campaign timing, category and brand dynamics, and media reach and frequency.

Campaign Timing

Here you should consider what stage your campaign is at—are you launching a new product or changing the strategy for selling it, or is this the third or fourth or twentieth year of an ongoing campaign? Also think about the specific timing of the campaign. Are you trying to communicate a seasonal message to warn young adults about drinking and driving during the holidays? Or maybe it's April and people are starting to think about summer vacation, so it's the perfect time to begin promoting your park district's swimming pool. Thinking of your communications objectives within a specific time frame will help to ensure that your media plan stays focused on that period.

Category and Brand Dynamics

If you study the trends for your brand in particular, as well as trends within the category overall, your communication objectives will be firmly fixed in reality. That is, if research shows that users of lawn-care products are extremely brand loyal, it makes little sense to say the objective for Scotts weed killer is to gain 15 market share points from their competitors in the next 12 months. Related to loyalty, you should also think about what degree of consumer involvement with the category can be reasonably expected. It's hard to get people excited about staplers or canned tomatoes, no matter how wonderful your creative message or media plan. Try to be objective about your brand's positioning, too. Is your advertising message really very different from your competitors', or is it just another version of the same idea? If you look at the advertising for most products, you'll see that the latter is far more common than the former. Almost all banks tout their low financing rates, while beer companies talk about great taste, and garbage bag makers emphasize their strength. None of this should be too surprising; you wouldn't want to buy a beer that didn't taste good or a garbage bag that wasn't strong.

Reach and Frequency

Having stated earlier that communication objectives tend to be more subjective than objective, more art than science, there is still a role for some numbers. But they should only be included if you will have some way of measuring them. The two key concepts to consider here are *reach* and *frequency*. These are the two most commonly used media terms in the overall planning process. The *reach* of the plan refers to the number (or percentage) of the target audience that will be reached by the brand's advertising in the media. As we shall learn in Chapter 4, this number is determined by calculating what percentage of the target audience will be exposed to the media in which your ad appears. Along with knowing how many people will have the opportunity to see or hear your ad, you also need to state how many times they need to do so for the message to have some effect. This is the concept of *effective frequency*. You should identify some reach and frequency goals as a way of measuring whether your communication objectives were achieved. If the communication goal is to increase awareness of the brand by 10 percent among the key consumer target, then that can be measured by establishing what percentage of the target was actually reached with the message, how many times they saw or heard it, and whether brand awareness levels did in fact go up. More will be said on this topic in Chapter 4.

Creative Requirements

The last area that should be considered in preplanning discussions is any special creative requirement that will affect the media selected. As noted previously, this should be made evident in the creative brief, and it provides another reason why it is critical for media specialists to be exposed to that document. If, for example, you are introducing a new hybrid car and want to talk about its advanced engineering and environmental benefits in detail, you will have to think in terms of the media that can allow you to do that. If your task is to promote the Florida Keys as a vacation destination for families, then the creative aspect will likely require media that enable the ad to feature many different sights or sounds from that area, such as print or digital, TV, or radio. The message will, in part, determine where you choose to place it. Yet another example might be introducing a new Pillsbury pie crust. Your ads will showcase the delicious results of using the product, so the visual element is going to be particularly important. Immediately, this leads you in a certain direction when starting to consider your media plan strategies and tactics.

Summary

For a media plan to be successful, it must be tied directly to the broad marketing objectives for the brand, usually defined in terms of sales and market share. The goals for media should also be derived from the advertising objectives, which show where the advertising fits in to the consumer journey, such as increasing awareness or improving customer satisfaction or generating additional use of the product. Both marketing and advertising objectives are tied to the media objectives by considering the relationship that exists between consumers, brands, and media. Media objectives should be developed with a consideration of how they might tie to the brand or company's return on investment, demonstrating how each media dollar spent contributes to sales. The media objectives state to whom the message will be delivered (the target audience); when it will be distributed (timing specifics); and how many times a given proportion of the target will, ideally, be exposed (media reach and frequency). Special creative requirements for the brand's communications should also be considered, in part by ensuring that media specialists are able to review the creative brief.

Notes

1. ANA Report, "KPIs That Matter," as found on https://www.ana.net/miccontent/show/id/rr-2021-media-kpis.
2. Jennifer Lee Burton, Jan Gollins, Linda E. McNeely, and Danielle M. Walls, "Revisiting the Relationship between Ad Frequency and Purchase Intentions: How Affect and Cognition Mediate Outcomes at Different Levels of Advertising Frequency," *Journal of Advertising Research*, vol. 59, no. 1, March 2019, 27–39.

Chapter 3

From Consumers to Audiences

Learning Outcomes: In this chapter you will learn how to:

- Define a target audience
- Interpret survey data on potential targets
- Determine the right balance between context and audience

When you buy a new pair of running shoes, you are most likely thinking about their durability, their style, and how well they fit. From the perspective of Adidas or Nike or New Balance, however, they want to know who is buying their shoes. Are they more likely to be male or female, young or old, urban or suburban? Are they dedicated marathoners or people who visit the gym once a week? Do they like other athletic activities? Do they watch sports online or read about their favorite athletes on ESPN.com?

At this point in the media planning process, you have a good general knowledge of how media fits within the broader advertising and marketing ecosystem, as well as an understanding of how to develop your plan objectives and strategies. The next major step is to get to know your target audience. Without knowing who your target is—their demographics, lifestyle, attitudes, interests, and, most importantly, their media preferences—the media plan would likely fail to deliver on its objectives of reaching the right people at the right time and place.

Defining the Target Audience

As far as media definitions of targets are concerned, the syndicated data sources of audience information are usually the first port of call. Depending on the target, these resources may provide armloads of information, or they may offer up next to nothing. In particular, if you are dealing with a non-consumer target, such as retailers or dealers, you may find yourself without much syndicated information at all, relying more on your experience and

DOI: 10.4324/9781003175704-3

judgment. You can assume, for example, that if you are trying to promote your refrigeration equipment to restaurants, one place to put your message would be RestaurantNews.com.

An important consideration for defining your media target is whether it should be broad or narrow. Because everyone in the country uses laundry detergent, does that mean your media plan should be aimed at all adults in the United States who use laundry detergent? Increasingly, the answer will be no. Today's brands are becoming more and more segmented. We don't just have one box of Tide on the store shelf but 57 of them, including liquid Tide or PODS, Tide HE Turbo Clean Liquid, Tide plus Febreze Sport, or Tide Simply Clean and Fresh. There are six different sizes of liquid Tide Plus Bleach Alternative and four in powder form, aiming to suit the needs of diverse groups, from singles living alone to large families. Each of these groups is likely to have different media habits and preferences, so to try to create a media plan that would reach everyone would ignore the needs of different population groups in terms of both product benefits and media usage. There might be one plan aimed at mothers with young children, another for those with large families, another with an environmental slant, and a fourth promoting the smaller size for urban apartment dwellers. Each plan has a different target audience.

There is also the opposite danger, however. That is, you might define your target audience so narrowly that it would be almost impossible to reach them. You might, from previous research into who owns a massaging shower head, find that they are more likely to be aged 50 years or older, live in the South, have household incomes of $100,000+, read the editorial page in the daily newspaper (in print or online), listen to Classic Hits on the radio, and watch the early evening news (Exhibit 3.1). But there may only be a few thousand of them!

Exhibit 3.1 Profile of Those Who Own a Massaging Shower Head

People who own a massaging shower head are more likely to	People who own a massaging shower head are less likely to
Be aged 50+ years	Be aged under 35 years
Be college educated	Have graduated high school
Have household incomes of $100,000+	Have household incomes less than $50,000
Live in the South	Live in the West or North East
Be White	Be Black or Hispanic
Live in D counties	Live in C counties
Own home worth $500,000+	Have lived at present address less than one year

People who own a massaging shower head are more likely to	People who own a massaging shower head are less likely to
Read	**Read**
Editorial page in weekday newspaper	Women's Fashion magazines
International/national news in weekday newspaper	Science/Technology magazines
Listen to	**Listen to**
Classic Hits	Contemporary Hit Radio
Amazon Music	Soundcloud
Watch	**Watch**
Late-night talk shows	Adult Swim
Early evening news	MTV

Source: 2020 Doublebase MRI-Simmons.

There are two major problems to note here. First, most traditional media will not only present your message to *your* target but also to many others for whom the product is probably irrelevant. This is a problem that currently can only be alleviated by careful consideration of exactly who your target should be and which media will best reach that audience. As noted in Chapter 2, digital advertising allows marketers to send messages to a more selective and relevant group of individuals, delivering ads dynamically based on where the user has been online. That approach is increasingly being applied to digital forms of other media, such as streaming TV or digital audio like Spotify.

Collecting Information on Consumers

So how do advertisers learn about consumers? One of the simplest and most effective ways to do that is by asking them. Companies such as MRI-Simmons and GWI in the U.S., or TGI and Nielsen in many other markets, run largescale surveys of the population to ask them questions about who they are, what they think and do, and what they buy. In many countries, these surveys have been conducted completely, or in part, through in-person surveys. But increasingly, and especially following the global COVID-19 pandemic, the studies are done online. The premise is similar, however. The sample of people responding to the survey is designed to represent the total population. Questions are asked for the individual as well as for the household. Results are released on a quarterly or semi-annual basis so that the data can be trended over time. That is, KraftHeinz will want to see whether its ketchup is being purchased more or less over time by people who are older or African-American or have children.

A food delivery service such as UberEats might want to look at the trend in older people using their offering.

One of the keys with these surveys is that they rely on people reporting on themselves and their own behavior. That is, respondents might say that they use Colgate Total toothpaste, when in fact, they buy the brand's Enamel Health tube instead. Or when asked how often they drink Coca-Cola, they might say two or three times per week, when in fact it is almost daily. So, there could be some error due to inaccurate recall. Other questions might be considered sensitive by some groups, such as their income or race/ethnicity or gender. Sometimes the questions can be so complex or lengthy that it is difficult for people to answer. For instance, imagine you took a survey that asked you to remember all the steps you undertook the last time you purchased a laptop computer, including all the brands you considered and why. If you haven't bought one in the last three years, how much would you remember? How much of the detail on brands could you still accurately report? Researchers spend a lot of time figuring out how to ask the questions in ways that people are willing and able to answer.

Yet despite all the data now readily available that can track actual online behavior or purchase activity, advertisers still look to surveys to understand more about what drove that behavior—the "why" behind the "what." That understanding helps give direction on both the media channels to include and on the creative message. Figure 3.2 gives an example of survey information about people who shop online at beauty retailer Sephora. While the company can track all the details of the website or app visits, the survey data gives them a richer understanding of their online shopper.

Exhibit 3.2 Profile of the Sephora.com shopper

Profile of the Sephora.com shopper	
People who bought from Sephora.com in the past 12 months are more likely to	*People who bought from Sephora.com in the past 12 months are less likely to*
Be	**Be**
Women 18–49	Men 25–54
Hispanic or Asian	Lived at present address 5+ years
In a household income of $150,000+	Live in smaller (C or D) counties
Live in West region	Live in South region
Do	**Do**
Karaoke	Play chess
Attend dance performances	Fly a drone
Paint & draw	Play video console games
Visit online blog in past 30 days	Traded stocks online

Profile of the Sephora.com shopper

People who bought from Sephora.com in the past 12 months are more likely to	People who bought from Sephora.com in the past 12 months are less likely to
Watch/Listen/Read	**Watch/Listen/Read**
TV online	Read Sports Illustrated
Watch Netflix	Listen to Classic Hits on radio
Watch Bravo network	Watch Fox News Channel

Source: MRI Survey of the American Consumer, 2020 Doublebase. Courtesy of MRI-Simmons.

Reading Survey Crosstabs

There are many companies that conduct consumer surveys, asking people about their demographics and lifestyle, attitudes and opinions, and product purchase or intent. While they may differ in how they undertake the survey—in-person, via phone, or today, primarily online—what is common among most of them is how the results are presented. The basic format is a crosstabulation, showing the percentage of "this group" who "did that" (or "agreed with that"). Exhibit 3.3 shows an example of how the data appear for the Sephora.com shoppers shown in Exhibit 3.2.

There are two columns. The first, All Adults, represents the base population, which in this case is the total number of adults. The second is the target group, which in this example are people who ordered from Sephora.com in the past 90 days. Now, looking at the rows, there are two items here selected from Exhibit 3.2: those who said they live in the West, and those who said they live in the South. Looking at each row, the *unweighted* row is the actual number of survey respondents who answered the question. There are 338 people in the survey who ordered from Sephora.com and live in the West, while there are 409 respondents who ordered from Sephora.com and live in the South. The next row, *weighted (000)*, shows those segments projected to the total population. These numbers must be read with an additional thousand added, so that, for the U.S. overall, there are 1,896,000 Sephora.com users living in the West and 2,178,000 of those users living in the South.

The next two rows represent percentages. The *horizontal percent* shows the composition of the left-hand column. Here, 3.26 percent of people living in the West have shopped on Sephora.com, compared to the 2.29 percent of people living in the South who have done so. The *vertical percent* on the next row provides insight into the target column group. In this example, 30.02 percent of those who ordered from Sephora.com live in the West, and 34.49 percent of the Sephora online users live in the South.

Exhibit 3.3 Examining a Crosstab

		All Adults	Ordered From: Sephora.com
Census Region: West	Unweighted	11,162	338
	Weighted (000)	58,139	1,896
	Horz %	100.00	3.26
	Vert %	23.24	30.02
	Index	100	129
Census Region: South	Unweighted	19,418	409
	Weighted (000)	95,318	2,178
	Horz %	100.00	2.29
	Vert %	38.11	34.49
	Index	100	91

Source: MRI Survey of the American Consumer, 2020 Doublebase. Courtesy of MRI-Simmons.

The final row is one of the most useful. It provides the comparison between the target segment and a total population (in this example, All Adults). As shown in Exhibit 3.3., the index for the All Adults column is always 100. Sephora.com users are 29 percent <u>more likely</u> than All Adults to live in the West, with an index of 129. In contrast, this segment is 9 percent *less likely* than All Adults to live in the South (index of 91). The calculation for the index is quite simple: it is the horizontal percent for the target divided by that percentage for the base: 30.02 / 23.24 = 129.

Tracking Consumer Behavior

The rapid growth of digital advertising occurred, in large part, because it enabled advertisers to track consumers online through the dropping of a digital cookie that could "follow" a specific device (laptop or mobile phone) wherever it went on the internet. That included purchases made online, enabling the advertiser to answer the age-old question attributed to Lord Leverhulme in the UK and John Wanamaker in the U.S.: I know half of my advertising dollars are wasted; I just don't know which half. The arrival of digital advertising meant that companies such as Hewlett Packard (HP) could see how many people who clicked on a specific ad for their Laserjet printer then went ahead and bought the item.

It did not take that long for advertisers to move significant portions of their budgets from non-digital to digital media, in the ongoing quest to quantify the impact of their ad dollars, and deliver short-term results to shareholders or other stakeholders. A debate ensued about whether and how advertising can build long-term value as well as short-term results. Some companies noted that while the digital ads could be shown to help drive sales, they appeared to be less effective at creating or sustaining brand awareness, preference, or loyalty.

Nonetheless, the behavioral data race was on. It mattered less whether the target audience for Kit Kat bars was more likely to be children aged 3+ or be women aged between 18 and 49. More importantly, people who bought those chocolate bars could be tracked to Facebook or hulu.com or YouTube. The masses of data created from all the tracking could be owned by the advertiser, purchased from companies working on the advertiser's behalf, or acquired from companies whose primary purpose was to gather consumer data to sell to companies.

The information that a company collects itself is called *first-party data*. It could be collected by Procter & Gamble when you go to Tide.com or Gillette.com. It is also captured by any website or app you visit, helping them to enhance their site or app. When another company gathers that type of information and sells it to the advertiser, this is known as *second-party data*. Rewards programs commonly belong here. If you belong to Southwest Airlines' frequent flyer program, then Southwest could sell the data it has collected on its travelers to other marketers who might be interested in targeting them, such as Samsonite (luggage) or Marriott Hotels. Websites can package up the data they collect on people who visit to sell to companies wishing to reach that type, or segment, of the population. *Third-party data* is the most widely available, gathered by companies expressly to offer targets to marketers. Companies such as Experian, Acxiom, and Epsilon, all of which began as credit-checkers of consumers, now gather thousands of data points about nearly every individual in the U.S. Some of it comes from government sources (including financial health, household income, or auto registrations). Some comes from largescale custom consumer surveys these companies run. And some is gathered from purchase activity to loyalty programs or direct purchases online. All of it is combined and linked to individual names and addresses, in a privacy-protected way so that when an advertiser wants to buy a target of people who have shopped three or more times at an auto repair shop in the past six months, there is no sharing of any personally identifiable information (PII).

One of the biggest sources of third-party data comes from the supermarket. Every time someone scans the barcode on an item, data are recorded for the store, the manufacturer, and the supply chain. If you have a loyalty card at that store, then the purchases are directly linked to a name and address, and hey presto! You now have someone who can be targeted by ads based on what they bought in the store. This is not a new phenomenon; for decades, coupons at the checkout were given with the receipt to encourage you to buy either more of the brand you just purchased or its competitor. Today, companies such as 84.51 or IRI will sell audience segments based on that supermarket (and other store) activity.

A more recent type of trackable consumer data comes via the mobile phone. When you download many apps, buried in the fine print that you need to accept in order to use the app is the right of the company to use the phone's location data to see where you (technically, your phone) is going. While this may not seem as interesting or valuable as your online behavior or purchase activity in-store, for many companies it provides an important signal of your purchase interest or intent. An Audi car dealer, for example, wants to target ads to people who have visited the BMW or Acura dealers in the vicinity. Starbucks is interested in seeing how many people are in the area of each store, and what proportion come in to buy a Venti coffee. Perhaps they will send mobile ads to those who are nearby to remind them of a special offer "today only" on its seasonal Pumpkin Spice Latte.

Context and Audience

As the amount of data on consumers kept growing and, especially, as it became increasingly digital, advertisers began to look for media to deliver ads to those precise audiences regardless of where the ad appeared. That is, instead of seeking to place a message announcing a new pain reliever in a health magazine or in a TV newsmagazine show, it was now possible (and preferable) to send that ad to any digital media channel that could reach the target defined as "active women with children under 12 who visit parenting websites or spend 3+ hours/ week on social channels." The ad might appear anywhere from wnba.com to Pandora to a streamed episode of *Jeopardy* viewed on the Xfinity app.

By mid-2021, however, as the prospect of the end of digital tracking via cookies loomed, advertisers began reconsidering the value of ad context. As research has shown, consumers who see ads in an appropriate context are more likely to respond to those messages.[1] This is, in part, the rationale for influencer marketing and brand integration (discussed in Chapter 8). When you see Simone Biles talking positively about Athleta on Instagram, there is a contextual relevance to that person speaking about that brand. Similarly, the integration of Lucy Pet Products into Brandon McMillan's YouTube show about dog rescues makes total sense from the context.

Turning Consumers into Audiences

For media planners, knowing something about the consumer who likes or prefers or buys the client's brand of coffee or cookie or car is an important first step. But, of course, that is not enough information to determine where the advertiser's messages should be placed. The missing piece of the puzzle is understanding how the sports-loving, adventurous, eco-friendly, urban-living 25–34-year-old women who buy Lululemon leggings use media. Do they watch a lot of streaming TV? Listen to podcasts? Are they heavy social media users? Light magazine readers? In their active lives, are they likely to see a lot of billboards? Creating target audiences out of all the consumer information we can compile requires audience measurement. While this is covered in greater detail in Chapters 5, 6, and 7, we take a brief look at this topic now, in the context of building our targets.

Audience Measurement

Our knowledge of media audiences depends on a wide variety of methods. Some audiences are measured passively, while others require active consent and input. Some approaches capture individual, person-level information, while others are effectively measuring what is occurring on a device. And some rely on a sample of individuals that are then projected to larger populations, while others collect data on everyone to measure a census of a given group. The point here is that no single audience measurement system is perfect (even though some measurement companies would like us to believe that they are). But they each provide the mechanism for media planners and buyers to decide where to place their ads in order to achieve their reach and frequency objectives, which in turn help marketers attain their sales, or other goals.

Television measurement for the past several decades has been done in most countries through some kind of metering system. Typically, this involves a set meter attached to the TV set to capture tuning, along with a people meter remote-control that a representative sample of individuals agree to use to record when each person in a household starts and stops watching. The audiences are defined primarily in terms of age and gender. In the U.S., Nielsen operates a panel of about 40,000 households to collect TV viewing in this way. More recently, several countries (including the U.S., Canada, and the UK) have added in passively collected tuning data from set-top boxes and/or smart (internet-connected) TVs. This approach can greatly expand the volume of data collected, and its granularity, but cannot—on its own—show *who* is watching. The person-level information may be attributed in various ways, such as combining the tuning data with a traditional TV panel; or the data can be modeled probabilistically based on other data known about a given household.

In a world where TV viewing has moved increasingly online, it becomes digital video, where the viewing behavior is captured passively. Now, instead of smaller panels of age-gender audiences, we can expand the audience definitions to include all that is captured on digital audiences through first-, second-, or third-party datasets. There are also digital measurement companies such as Comscore and Pathmatics that run largescale panels of people who have agreed to have all their digital activity monitored and collected, along with providing their individual demographics or lifestyle information so that planners can define and find audiences based on both behavioral and individual characteristics.

Print audiences have historically been created through surveys that probed in detail on reading habits at the individual title level. By combining readership with all the other survey responses, planners could easily find out that the Corn Chex cereal buyer liked to read *Good Housekeeping* and *Reader's Digest* magazines. Today, with a greater interest in many countries in reaching print audiences online, digital audiences are relied upon more. For radio, where audiences were first measured using weekly radio diaries, today's methods include that, together with pager-like meters worn by representative panels of people, and passively collected digital audio behavior.

Audience-First Approach

In recent years, as more data about consumers became available, an approach to marketing and media developed called an *audience-first* strategy. In some ways, this is not new; that is, marketers are always trying to think about the audience they want to reach with their messages. The difference here is the idea that a campaign should be created based on what the brand wants the audience to do, rather than what the company thinks they should do. This approach requires a deeper understanding of what problems the target may want solved, or what issues they care most about. The financial services company, TD Ameritrade, created an online publication called thinkMoney to help its audience better understand financial markets, and saw that subscribers traded five times more than non-subscribers. In the UK, the supermarket chain Sainsbury's created a print magazine with information about its new items. Subsequently, eight in ten readers purchased a product in the store after they had read about it in the magazine. In adopting this audience-first approach, marketers hope to show their customers that they are focusing on them, rather than on the company itself, to serve the audience instead of simply selling to them.

In order to develop fuller understanding of customer needs, brands may undertake extensive consumer research that enables them to create *segmentations* to differentiate the needs and preferences of their buyers or prospects. One outcome, as noted earlier in the chapter, is that the marketer creates new flavors or new line extensions to meet those various needs (such as the numerous kinds

Exhibit 3.4 Example of a Persona

Hannah is 40 years old and lives in Bar Harbor, Maine. She works as an art teacher at Washington Elementary School, where her husband, John, teaches English. They have two young children, Daniel and Sofia, who are 11 and 9 years old, respectively. The family enjoys spending time outdoors, whether hiking in the Acadia National Park during the summer or enjoying the snow during winter months. Hannah likes cooking, experimenting with new recipes that she has seen on her favorite TV channel, Food Network. While she doesn't like her family to spend too much time in front of their screens, she acknowledges that she finds many ideas for her classroom on Instagram and education-oriented websites.

of Tide detergent). A hotel chain may, for example, find that there is a segment of Seeking Adventure travelers who are looking for new or less commonly visited places, while the segment of Familiar Comfort likes to return to the same places but explore their surroundings in new ways.

One way that these targets can be brought to life is through the creation of a *persona*. This is a fictional composite portrait of the person the brand is trying to reach through media. Rather than describing the target as a woman aged between 35 and 54 with two or more children, a household income of $150,000+ and a professional or managerial job, the persona presents that same information in a concise narrative. Exhibit 3.4 provides one example.

With a clear idea of who the brand should be targeting, the task of creating the media plan becomes easier. Before embarking on that, however, it is important to understand the key terms and calculations that are used in media. This is covered next, in Chapter 4.

Summary

Once you know what your media plan is aiming to achieve, the next step is defining who it is the media will reach. Creating the target audience requires a careful analysis of available information on who buys (or wants to buy) your brand, and how they use media. Consumer surveys provide a wealth of data here, so it is important to know how to read a crosstab. Additionally, today's digital behavior provides marketers with useful insight to enrich a target audience profile. It is helpful to find the right media balance between selecting the media where your desired target can be found and choosing the best fitting context for your ad messages. The ongoing art and science of media planning extends to audience measurement. By keeping a clear focus on the audience for brand messages, the planner is better equipped to create a successful media campaign.

Note

1 Eun Sook-Kwon, Karen Whitehill King, Greg Nyilasy, and Leonard N. Reid, "Impact of Media Context on Advertising Memory: A Meta-Analysis of Advertising Effectiveness," *Journal of Advertising Research*, vol. 59, no. 1, March 2019, 99–128. Aachyut Telang and Debajani Sahoo, The Effects of Context Congruity on Ad Persuasiveness on e-Magazines, *Journal of Advertising Research*, vol. 61, no. 3, September 2021.

Chapter 4

Media Terms and Calculations

Learning Outcomes: In this chapter you will learn how to:

- Demonstrate the importance of reach and frequency
- Explain the difference between ratings and reach
- Understand the key cost measures (CPM, CPP)

Defining Key Media Terms

Just as artificial intelligence experts talk about natural language processing (NLP) and machine learning (ML) and car enthusiasts dwell on RPM, jerk, and lateral acceleration, so do media specialists converse in their own language. Now that you have a broad understanding of the landscape in which media operates, it's time to start learning more about the foundations you need to create the media plan. This chapter will review some of these terms and their definitions.

Understanding Ratings

Most of you are probably already familiar with the release of the Nielsen ratings that show which are the most popular television programs. The size of the audience is usually given in two ways: absolute terms (i.e., millions of people) and as a percentage of the population. It is this latter figure, known as the *rating*, that has traditionally been used as the baseline measure for all media concepts.

Rating Point

One rating point equals 1 percent of a particular target group. That audience can be defined in various ways: by household; by geographic market; by a given demographic group, such as men aged between 18 to 49 or women aged

DOI: 10.4324/9781003175704-4

between 25 to 54; or by product usage or ownership, such as people who own a dog. The television program *The Bachelor* might receive a household rating of 8.5 in Detroit, which means that 8.5 percent of homes in that city watched the show. The magazine *US Weekly* might get a rating of 9.6 among females ages 18 to 34, meaning that 9.6 percent of all women in that age group read an average issue of the magazine. In television, the "currency" rating on which national ads are bought and sold is called C3, which stands for the percent of the audience tuned to the average commercial in the program when it airs (live) and for the following three days (delayed or time-shifted).

Gross Rating Points

By adding up all the rating points we wish to achieve, we end up with a concept known as *gross rating points*, or GRPs. For media planning purposes, we set as our goal a given number of total, or gross, rating points to achieve and then figure out which media vehicles to use to obtain that number. We might want our plan to have a total of 100 gross rating points each week against our target of women with children. These could come from any media.

The reason these rating points are considered gross is that they do not take into account any duplication of exposure. That is, there are probably many people within our target for Fruitola who see our ad on Instagram and also hear the same message on the local talk radio show. While our total number of rating points placed in the media each week is set at 100, each person will be exposed to a different number of them and in different vehicles. This is shown in Exhibit 4.1.

Exhibit 4.1 Diagram of GRPs and Duplication

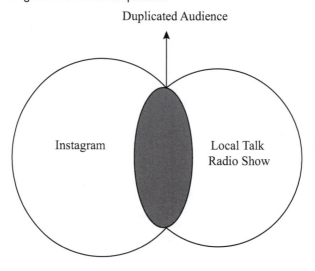

In today's media world, where our targets are more and more narrowly defined, the term GRP is often altered to TRP, or *target rating point*. This makes explicit the fact that we are planning our ratings against a specific *target* rather than the whole world. The concept is the same, however.

Gross Impressions

This term simply converts the gross rating points into a number by dividing the number of rating points by 100 and multiplying that figure by the size of the target audience. If our plan calls for obtaining 200 GRPs against a target audience of 500,000 people, then we are aiming to achieve 1 million gross impressions (200 / 100 × 500,000). Impressions can also be calculated using the cost of the media channel divided by the cost of reaching 1,000 of your target audience in that channel. That is then multiplied out by 1,000. Increasingly, media plans are being based on gross impressions rather than ratings, reflecting the fact that digital exposures are measured this way. So in order to have a consistent metric for all media channels, and given the ongoing importance of digital channels, and the growth of digital forms of traditional media, the impression has begun to replace the rating as the basis for trading and reporting.

Reach and Frequency

Although many would argue that advertising is more art than science, we still need some way to assess whether the messages we place in the media are having any impact. It is not enough to know how many impressions are made with one ad or what percentage of the target audience is exposed to a given online video or paid social ad. As media specialists, we also need an estimate of the cumulative effect of our media plan. That is provided by the concepts of reach and frequency, which are typically the key measures used to define and deliver the media objectives of a plan.

Reach

Reach refers to the number or percentage of people in the target audience who will be exposed to the medium where the message appears. You should note that we often need to estimate exposure to the *media vehicle*, not to the ad itself. If you think about your own media habits, there are many intervening variables that easily prevent you from seeing or hearing an ad. You might deliberately ignore it, such as by swiping past an ad on your smartphone, fast-forwarding through the TV ad when watching it in a time-shifted mode, or avoiding the ad that appears at the top of your search results. You could be doing something else at the same time, such as messaging a friend on Snapchat or cooking dinner, and not be paying attention to the message. Or you could find the ad boring, irrelevant, or uninteresting and see or hear it but not really absorb the contents. When we talk about the reach of a plan, we are usually talking about the *opportunity for exposure* (sometimes called opportunity to see, or OTS).

Of course, we should also emphasize that *reach*, like all media terms, is merely an estimate. We rarely know exactly how many people were reached or how they reacted. Even with the more precise metrics of digital media, where we can "know" how many devices clicked on an ad, we still don't know how that message was received. Perhaps they clicked by accident and ignored the message. But if we are trying to reach women ages 25 to 54 to persuade them to try our new brand of body wash, then, using syndicated data sources, we can find out how many women of that age watch *The View*, read *Marie Claire*, or go to Pinterest boards focused on skincare. To reach a target audience of men aged between 18 to 49 to increase the number of inquiries for Fidelity Investment's pamphlet on investing wisely, we can learn how many men of that age go to FT Online or watch CNN.

The critical difference between reach and GRPs is that reach concerns the number of *different* people in the audience you are trying to communicate with through advertising. For media schedules that try to maximize reach, you would place ads in several different media vehicles to reach different people through each one. Complicated formulas are used to calculate the numbers, requiring computer software. Here, we look at a simple example.

If the rating for *Black-ish* against our target of 18–49-year-olds is 5 and for *Grown-ish* it is 6, then one ad placed in each TV show will deliver a total of 11 GRPs (5 + 6). However, if we know from research that 3 percent of the target audience will see both ads (the duplicated audience), then the reach, or *unduplicated* audience, for this schedule is 11–3, or 8 percent. That is, 8 percent of our target of adults between 18 and 49 will be exposed to our ad in *Black-ish* and/or our ad in *Grown-ish*. Even if they see both ads, they will only be counted in our audience one time. Therefore, reach equals GRPs minus duplication. Exhibit 4.2 depicts this.

Frequency

It is not enough to know whom our media plan is intended to reach. We must also set goals of *how many times* we wish to reach them with our message.

As with the concept of reach, the notion of frequency, while ultimately referring to *message frequency*, in reality is based on the frequency of exposure to the *media vehicle* rather than to the advertisement. A media plan will typically establish the desired number of times that the audience should be exposed to the message, based on past experience, judgment, or previous research into how long it takes for the audience to comprehend and remember the message.

Exhibit 4.2 Example of Duplication

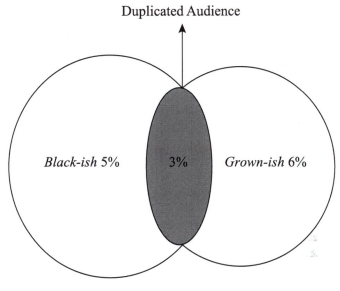

Duplicated Audience

Black-ish 5%   3%   *Grown-ish* 6%

Reach = 5% + 6% −3% = 8%

In some media, especially digital, the number of messages delivered to each consumer can have a limit placed on it through the practice of *frequency capping* to ensure that one person is not bombarded with the same ad 50 times.

A simple way to back into the frequency number is from the following equation:

Reach × Frequency = Gross Rating Points

If you know your reach goal and have established the number of GRPs you will be buying, then it only requires simple mathematical division (GRPs/Reach) to figure out how many times, on average, the target will be exposed to the media vehicle(s).

Random Duplication

One of the questions that media specialists are often asked is what the reach will be of a complete media plan. The answer today is typically calculated by software, but there is a very basic formula that can give you a rough estimate to guide you. It is known as the *random duplication formula*, and it assumes that the probability of reaching the audience in one medium (or media vehicle) is independent of the likelihood of reaching them in a different one. In reality, this is not generally the case. For example, if your media plan includes food sites such as Epicurious and cooking shows on The Food Network, the odds are probably greater than average that your target is going to be exposed to both.

The random duplication formula assumes, however, that the reach of two media is the reach of one added to the reach of the other minus the product of the two. All figures are calculated as decimals. That is:

Combined Reach = Reach A + Reach B − (Reach A × Reach B)

As an example, if your TV schedule has a total reach of 65 percent and your digital schedule has a reach of 25 percent, then the combined reach will be:

$$0.65 + 0.25 - (0.65 \times 0.25) = 0.90 - 0.1625 = 0.7375 = 73.75 \text{ percent}$$

If there are more than two media involved, then you simply take that initial product and use it as your first medium in the formula to combine with the third medium's reach number.

Beyond Reach and Frequency

If you think about the commercials that you can remember, the ones that are most likely to come to mind are those that you have seen or heard more than once. That is, for a message to be truly *effective* in terms of communicating with the target audience, it generally has to be conveyed more than one time. Of course, this is not a hard-and-fast rule. If your bathroom drain gets blocked, then you only need one exposure to an ad for Drano drain cleaner at the right moment for the message to be extremely effective. For the most part, given the limited attention we pay to commercial messages, we need to see or hear them several times before the information is properly absorbed. Even then, it is most likely filed away somewhere in memory for use on a future occasion.

Effective Frequency

The key here is to determine *how many times* an ad has to be received for it to be deemed effective. What we mean by *effective* is that the target receives the desired communication message. A considerable amount of research was done on this topic during the 1970s and 1980s, following a landmark study by Colin MacDonald, a British researcher. After looking at the relationship between opportunities to see ads for laundry detergent and sales of the product, he concluded that the optimal number of exposure opportunities was three.

This was later explained by breaking down what happens with each exposure. The first time someone sees an ad, his reaction is "What is it?" On the second exposure, he asks "What of it?" or "So what?" It is only on the third occasion that the person will start to process the information and decide if the message is relevant and interesting or not.[1]

Since those early research studies were released, there has been much discussion about their accuracy. Many have argued that it is impossible to set an arbitrary number for effective frequency. Some believe that rather than having a single figure, the most effective frequency lies within a range, typically set between three and ten. Others claim that only one exposure is needed, as long as it is placed at the right time (see the following section). The answer, probably, is "it depends." As with the drain cleaner example, sometimes a single exposure is sufficient. On the other hand, you might need to see an ad for a breakfast cereal 15 times before it has any real impact. What it ultimately depends on is the relevancy and impact of the message. There has been considerable research in this area to better understand the purchase process and how advertising impacts that.[2] Today, with so much of the ad exposure occurring in digital channels, there are questions over whether the optimal frequency levels should be reconsidered.

The key point to remember is that when establishing your media objectives and deciding on the strategy to fulfill them, you must keep in mind that your message should probably be heard, read, or viewed several times for it to have an effect on the audience.

Exposure Distribution

Most media plans involve placing multiple ads in many different media vehicles, so it is important to know how many people are reached how many times (once, twice, three times, and so on). We find this by creating an *exposure distribution*, which shows the percentage of the target exposed to a given schedule at each level of frequency. The method used to calculate it is fairly complex, based on mathematical theories of probability; today it is done by special software. At a basic level, a media model estimates the likelihood of being exposed to a given number of ads together with the number of different ways you can be exposed to those messages.

For example, if you placed one ad in *Black-ish* and one in *Grown-ish*, the viewer might see anywhere from zero to two ads total—they might not see either ad, or they could see one of the two, or they might see both. Looking at Exhibit 4.2, we already know the percentage of the target exposed two times (the duplication figure) is 3 percent. In addition, we can easily figure out those not exposed at all (the total, or 100 percent, minus those exposed one or more times): $100 - 8 = 92$ percent. To estimate what percentage is reached exactly

Exhibit 4.3 Exposure Distribution

Frequency (f)	Percentage Reached (%)
0	92
1	5
2	3
Total	100

once, you subtract the duplication figure from the number reached one or more times (reach 1+): 8 − 3 = 5. You should notice that the final exposure distribution must account for everyone in the target audience and therefore sum to 100 percent. The final exposure distribution is shown in Exhibit 4.3.

Frequency Planning

In the late 1990s, research evidence became available that suggested that reach was a more important determinant of media effectiveness than frequency. Based largely on the work of John Philip Jones and Erwin Ephron, the analysis of sales and TV viewing data from the same households suggested that short-term advertising sales were driven largely by exposure to a TV commercial within seven days prior to purchase. Since we as media specialists never know precisely when that sale might occur, this suggests that it is more important to maintain a lower level of media weight across more weeks than to place sporadic, albeit larger, flights of advertising throughout the year.[3] We revisit this in Chapter 9.[4]

A couple of decades later, the theories of Byron Sharp around *How Brands Grow* expanded on this idea further. He posited that, since most brands' buyers are only making a purchase occasionally, it is critical for marketers to strive to reach all category buyers on a continuous basis so that your brand is top of mind whenever someone is ready to buy.[5]

Calculating Costs

It is highly unlikely that you will be able to spend however much money you want to execute your plan. You will have to provide a clear rationale of how efficiently your plan will spend your client's money. Two concepts can help with that.

Cost per Thousand (CPM)

Since different media are bought in different ways—a 15-second spot on TV, a digital video ad on a social media site, or a poster for a billboard—we need some way to compare media in terms of cost. To do so, media specialists turn to the cost per thousand, or CPM. This shows the cost of reaching 1,000 of the target audience either with an individual media vehicle or the complete media schedule. It puts all media on a level playing field and is calculated as follows:

CPM = Total Schedule Cost / Gross Impressions divided by 1,000

Let's use an example of 68,000,000 women aged between 18 to 49 and assume that an ad in *Real Simple* (3 rating) costs $275,000, while one in *Food Network Magazine* (7 rating) costs $90,000. A total of 6,800,000 impressions would be generated (10 TRPs / 100 × 68 million women). At a total cost of $365,000, the cost per thousand would be $53.68. This means it costs $53.68 to reach 1,000 women ages 18 to 49 with one ad in *Real Simple* and one in *Food Network Magazine* in a given month. By using this formula, you can compare the cost efficiency of one vehicle, media category, or schedule against another.

Cost per Point

Another useful media concept is the cost per rating point (CPP), which offers a different way of comparing media schedules. Here, you find the cost of one rating point for each media vehicle against your target by dividing the total schedule cost by gross rating points:

CPP = Total Schedule Cost / Gross Rating Points

With our total cost of $365,000 and total rating points of 10, the cost per point comes out to be $36,500. It therefore costs $36,500 to obtain one rating point against women ages 18 to 49 using one ad in *Real Simple* and one in *Food Network Magazine*. If you know the cost per point against a particular target group and the approximate number of rating points you wish to buy, you can then calculate an approximate total schedule cost using the same formula.

Note that the CPM and CPP are interrelated. That is, if you know the size of your target audience, you can calculate a CPP from a CPM, or vice versa.

CPM = CPP / 1% of target audience × 1,000

CPP = (CPM / 1,000) × 1% of target audience

Gross Versus Net

One of the traditions of the media business that remains in place today is the use of gross versus net costs. This was how agencies traditionally made money—they bought the media time or space at one price and charged their advertiser clients a 15 percent margin (gross up) on the cost. Today, most agencies and advertisers have different cost structures in place. Many now have a flat fee arrangement, where the two companies set a fixed price for how much the advertiser will pay the agency for their service, or they may pay based on how well the ads perform, paying the agency more if the ads are shown to have generated more revenue. In all these cases, the agency will pay the net costs to media companies and charge that same amount to the advertiser. It is important as a media specialist to understand the relationship between gross and net.

Using the previous example of a one-page ad in *Real Simple* and a one-page ad in *Food Network Magazine*, where the gross cost is $365,000, you simply multiply that gross cost by 0.85:

$$\$365,000 \times 0.85 = \$310,250$$

This would be the net amount the agency would pay.

Summary

In this chapter, we covered the basic terms and calculations of media planning. To understand media, it is essential that the media specialist be familiar with the concepts of reach, frequency, gross rating points, and gross impressions. Beyond these, it is also helpful to understand the notion of effective frequency, which assumes that for an ad to be effective, the target audience has to be exposed to it more than one time. Frequency planning forces you to think about exposure within the purchase cycle. An exposure distribution lets you know the number of people who are exposed a given number of times to an individual vehicle or a complete media schedule. Media costs are accounted for by calculating the cost per thousand and cost per rating point. The difference between net and gross price reflects how some media forms are still purchased.

Notes

1 Herbert E. Krugman, "Memory Without Recall, Exposure Without Perception," *Journal of Advertising Research*, vol. 40, no. 6, November/December 2000, 49–54.
2 Michael J. Naples, "Effective Frequency—Then and Now," *Journal of Advertising Research*, vol. 37, no. 4, July/August 1997, 7–13. Kenneth A. Longman, "If Not Effective Frequency, Then What?" *Journal of Advertising Research*, vol. 37, no. 4, July/August 1997, 44–50. Lawrence D. Gibson, "What Can One Exposure Do?" *Journal of Advertising Research*, vol. 36, no. 1, March/April 1996, 9–18. Byron Sharp, *How Brands Grow*, Oxford: Oxford University Press, 2010.
3 Gerard Tellis, "Effective Frequency: One Exposure or Three Factors," *Journal of Advertising Research*, vol. 37, no. 4, July/August 1997, 75–80. Hugh M. Cannon and Edward A. Riordan, "Effective Reach and Frequency: Does It Really Make

Sense?" *Journal of Advertising Research*, vol. 34, no. 1, March/April 1994, 19–28. John Philip Jones, *The Ultimate Secrets of Advertising*, New York: Sage Publications, 2002. John Philip Jones, *When Ads Work*, New York: Lexington Books, 1995. Erwin Ephron, "Recency Planning," *Journal of Advertising Research*, vol. 37, no. 4, July/August 1997, 61–65. John Philip Jones, "Single Source Research Begins to Fulfill Its Promise," *Journal of Advertising Research*, vol. 35, no. 3, May/June 1995, 9–17.
4 Erwin Ephron, "More Weeks, Less Weight: The Shelf Space Model of Advertising," *Journal of Advertising Research*, vol. 35, no. 3, May/June 1995, 18–24.
5 Byron Sharp, *How Brands Grow*, Oxford: Oxford University Press, 2010.

Chapter 5

Planning and Buying for Television

Learning Outcomes: In this chapter you will learn how to:

- Differentiate the various forms of television
- Understand how each one is planned and bought
- Compare and contrast the benefits and disadvantages offered by TV

After you have clearly defined media objectives and strategies for attaining those objectives, defined your target audience, and have a good understanding of the terms used in planning media, the next step is to decide which media types, and vehicles within those types, are best suited to reaching the target audience.

The next three chapters will explore these in detail. As a point of reference, Exhibit 5.1 shows how much was spent on advertising in each major paid media form in 2020.

Exhibit 5.1 Ad Spend by Medium in 2020

Medium	Amount (Billions of Dollars)
Television	$67.7
Digital	$52.6
Magazines	$8.9
Radio	$6.0
Newspapers	$4.8
Outdoor	$4.1
Cinema	$0.7
Total Paid Media	**$144.8**

Source: Kantar Media, 2021. *Note:* Total U.S. 2020 Adspend: $144,294,539,598; total in table higher due to rounding.

DOI: 10.4324/9781003175704-5

From TV to Video

When you visit your grandparents, there is a good chance they will talk about watching last Tuesday's episode of "The Voice" on NBC, or Sunday's "60 Minutes" on CBS. Your parents moved on to recording the programs they liked, via DVR, watching them *on demand* within the next seven days. Today's generations simply stream the video content they want to see, from wherever and whenever. That could be a 5 minute *Trevor Noah* YouTube video, the 30-minute situation comedy, *Ramy*, on Hulu, or a full-length movie on Netflix. For advertisers wanting to reach their target audiences through video channels, how they do so will depend on how the content is being delivered and consumed. This chapter will explore the ways that marketers can plan and buy all forms of television, including traditional broadcast TV, and newer offerings such as connected TV and over the top (OTT).

The task of today's media planners has become much broader than in times past. Instead of just considering *television*, planners must think more about how to use various types of video media to deliver brand experiences to consumers in numerous ways. Should Kraft macaroni and cheese pay for an integration into *Masterchef Junior*? Could Tide detergent create a YouTube channel to share stain removal tips? Should the characters in *The Goldbergs* be seen eating Kellogg's cereals? How can Fancy Feast send its ads for cat treats to homes that are known to have cats? The key with all these different types of video communications is that they are designed to provide the target consumers with a relevant brand experience through media. At the same time, they all need to be part of a coordinated effort we call the *media plan*. That is, the message that Kraft conveys in its TV ads about providing moms and kids with healthy, fun meals should be consistent in its sponsorship, in all digital formats, and on TV. As with all media planning elements, the communications platforms that are used should all relate to and work toward the brand's marketing and media objectives.

A Television in Every Home

Almost every household in America has a television set. Eight in ten adults (83 percent) have two or more. The average household has three sets. According to Nielsen, about half (56 percent) have three or more sets.[1] Television historically has been the largest mass medium available for advertisers. In 2020, about $68 billion was spent promoting goods and services this way, still slightly more than the total spent by advertisers on digital channels. Households in the United States have their TV sets tuned, on average, 8.1 hours each day, which is one of the highest viewing figures of anywhere in the world. More than half of all homes (56 percent) have a smart TV set that is connected to the internet.[2] People are spending almost 6 hours with video each day.[3]

Traditional broadcast television programming is divided up in two ways: by daypart and by format. *Daypart* refers to the time of day the program airs. There are nine standard dayparts, which are shown in Exhibit 5.2. Costs are still tied to the relative audience size for each daypart, with prime time enjoying the largest viewership and, therefore, the highest cost. Program formats are also standardized into numerous types, which are shown in Exhibit 5.3.

It is worth emphasizing that these breakdowns are really only the concern of the programmers and advertisers; you don't choose to watch situation comedies

Exhibit 5.2 Television Dayparts

Early morning	M–F	7:00–9:00 a.m.
Daytime	M–F	9:00 a.m.–4:30 p.m.
Early fringe	M–F	4:30–7:30 p.m.
Prime access	M–F	7:30–8:00 p.m.
Prime time	M–Sat	8:00–11:00 p.m.
	Sun	7:00–11:00 p.m.
Late news	M–Sun	11:00–11:30 p.m.
Late night	M–Sun	11:30 p.m.–1:00 a.m.
Saturday morning	Sat	8:00 a.m.–1:00 p.m.
Weekend afternoons	Sat–Sun	1:00–7:00 p.m.

Source: Nielsen, 2002.

Exhibit 5.3 Television Program Formats

Animation/Children
Daytime serials
Drama/Adventure
Game shows
Late-night talk
Movies
News
News magazines
Reality-based
Sitcoms
Specials
Sports

Source: Nielsen, 2002.

or reality-based programs; rather, you decide to watch *Dancing with the Stars* on ABC or *Manifest* on NBC.

The cost to create a program genre directly affects how much an advertiser will pay to appear in it. Dramas and sitcoms are more expensive to make, in contrast to the less expensive reality shows. Today, the reality genre is a staple of the prime time TV lineup, although general drama still accounts for about 40 percent of prime time hours.

One challenge for media specialists is to predict which shows will be popular several months or even one year from now, buying them at lower costs and enjoying higher-than-predicted ratings. At the same time, fewer people are watching the live broadcast, while more are viewing that same program on demand or streamed or via apps, so there is an increasing need to consider the *total* audience. This varies considerably by who is watching. Among older (55+) consumers, more than half of the time they spend with media is with Live + Time-shifted TV. That drops precipitously with younger viewers; those aged between 18–34 spend only 16 percent of their recorded media time with this type of TV. In contrast, that younger group spends nearly 40 percent of their media time using apps or the Web on their smartphones.[4]

Indeed, television has moved from a passive medium where viewers watch what is shown at the time it first airs to a much more active experience where people can watch whatever they want whenever they wish to do so. This is reflected in the industry by using the term *linear* TV when talking about traditional viewing. The rapid expansion of streaming forms of TV—whether through smart, *connected* TVs or viewed *over the top* on laptops, TVs, or phones—have resulted in viewers wanting and expecting that they can choose whatever they want to watch at any place or time. Currently, nearly eight in ten (78 percent) of all households have one or more internet-enabled devices to access a streaming service. One large consumer survey estimated that the average viewer in the U.S. watches their content across about six different sources, including broadcast, cable, and streaming services.[5]

What people watch can also be impacted by who owns the various TV networks. For example, Disney's ownership of ABC, ESPN networks, Freeform, and Disney Theme Parks is seen in ESPN announcers appearing on ABC sports programming or the creation of a Phineas and Ferb attraction at Disney World. Media ownership is constantly changing. The merger of WarnerMedia and the Discovery Networks in May 2021 brought together a large number of networks, from HBO and CNN to the Food Network and Discovery. While viewers might not notice too much difference, at least in the short term, ad buyers faced a reduction in the number of companies with which to negotiate.

There are four main types of traditional television to consider: network, syndication, spot (local), and cable.

Network Television

Network television consists of four major broadcast networks: ABC, CBS, NBC, and FOX, and two Spanish-language broadcast networks, Univision and Telemundo. There is also one smaller network: The CW, owned jointly by CBS and WarnerMedia (now Warner Bros. Discovery). A "network" is actually made up of hundreds of local stations that become affiliates of the national organization. A small proportion of them are owned outright by the parent network; these are called the *owned and operated stations*, or O&Os. For example, ABC owns and operates eight TV network stations, while FOX has 18 stations airing that network's content. More than 1,000 of the total 1,761 commercial TV stations in the United States are network owned or affiliated. Each station receives a set amount of money every year from the network in return for agreeing to air national programs for a given number of hours every week, although the networks have attempted to reduce or eliminate these payments and have looked for ways to cut their costs in recent years. Network programs air at the same time in every market within a given time zone. The east and west coasts are differentiated from everywhere in between. CBS's *60 Minutes* appears at 7:00 p.m. on Sunday night in the Eastern and Pacific time zone but at 6:00 p.m. in Central and Mountain markets.

Network shows come with several minutes of commercial time both within and between programs that are sold by the network. The local station is then able to sell an additional one to three minutes of commercial time in the hour to local or regional advertisers, depending on the daypart. Originally, local commercials always had to appear between programs, but now local or regional advertising occurs within the program, too. The local station also decides what to air when it is not showing network programs. This might include locally produced shows, such as local news or current affairs programs, or programs purchased from independent producers, known as syndicated programming (discussed next).

Stations not affiliated with a network are known as *independents*. Today, there are a dwindling number of stations in the United States that are not affiliated with any broadcast network. Several hundred others are non-commercial or are broadcasting on locally based UHF signals. Each one decides which programs to air throughout the broadcast day and is responsible for selling its own commercial time.

In Exhibit 5.4, the top-rated broadcast TV programs in prime time are shown. As explained in Chapter 4, programs are evaluated in terms of their rating, the percentage of a given target group that watched the show. Currently, the official U.S. trading currency for national TV is the C3 rating, which includes the audience for those watching the average commercial in the program as it airs plus any viewership of that program in the 72 hours following the original telecast. Here, we show the rating, share and PUT for Live viewing + three days

Exhibit 5.4 Top Ten Prime Time Broadcast Programs: Ratings, PUT, Share

Rank	Network	Program	Adult 18–49 Rating (C3)	A18–49 Rating (Live +3)	A18–49 Persons Using Television	A18–49 Share (Live +3)
1	CBS	The Equalizer	1.70	2.07	16.26	12.56
2	FOX	The Masked Singer	1.47	1.94	16.06	12.03
3	ABC	The Bachelor	1.27	1.69	16.72	10.14
4	FOX	911	1.26	1.64	16.31	10.08
5	ABC	The Bachelorette	1.26	1.69	17.14	9.83
6	ABC	Grey's Anatomy	1.23	1.77	15.94	11.08
7	NBC	This Is Us	1.22	1.78	16.24	10.89
8	NBC	Law & Order: Organized Crime	1.22	1.52	13.63	11.11
9	CBS	60 Minutes	1.18	1.27	17.44	7.13
10	NBC	Chicago PD	1.12	1.47	14.19	10.37

Source: Nielsen Npower for Regularly Scheduled Broadcast Prime Time (from September 21, 2020 – April 25, 2021)

beyond (Live + 3). Planners can also look at how many people in the target were using TV at all (PUT), and the share of that viewing that the individual program received.

Syndication

One of the major sources of programs for TV stations is syndicated programming. Here, an individual program (or a package of several programs) is sold on a station-by-station basis, regardless of that station's affiliation. The programs may be of any type or length. There are two main types—original shows and off-network fare. The former are filled with game shows, such as *Wheel of Fortune*, and talk shows, such as *Live with Kelly and Ryan*. They are sold either by the program's producers or by syndication companies that put together packages of properties. All the major broadcast networks operate syndication divisions or companies. The distinction between syndication and network shows is that syndicated programs can air at different times in different markets as well as on different networks. This leads to syndicated shows having to be cleared by each local station that chooses to buy them. The *clearance* figure refers to the percentage of markets across the country that can view that particular show. So, for example, if a syndicated talk show is cleared in 70 percent of the United States, it means that broadcast TV stations seen by

70 percent of all TV viewers have purchased that program. Syndication clearances generally range between 70 percent and 99 percent. It is worth noting, too, that some network programs do not have total (100 percent) clearance because an affiliate station may refuse to air them or will put them on at a different time than the rest of the network. For example, some stations pulled syndicated episodes of *The Cosby Show* after its former lead actor, Bill Cosby, was found guilty of indecent assault in 2018.

The goal of many network programs is to produce enough episodes to go into the syndicated marketplace (usually 85 or more episodes). This is known as *off-network programming*, and it helps fill up the hours of airtime that stations have when network shows aren't running. Programs that have been popular on the networks can continue to air for many years in syndication. Hits from the 1970s, 1980s, and 1990s, such as *M*A*S*H*, *Seinfeld*, and *Friends*, can still be seen on TV during the early evening or late-night hours in syndication. Today, there are more than 100 daily or weekly shows offering several hundred hours of content. Exhibit 5.5 shows the top programs in syndication among adults aged 25 to 54 years.

Spot Television

Spot television is another way to purchase television time. Here, instead of contracting with the network to distribute a commercial to all of that network's affiliate stations across the country, an advertiser can pick and choose which programs and stations to use, placing the message in various spots across the country. As noted previously, very few commercial TV stations are not

Exhibit 5.5 Top 10 Syndicated TV Programs Among Adults Aged Between 25–54

		Rating (%)
1	*Family Feud*	1.82
2	*Judge Judy*	1.54
3	*Wheel of Fortune*	1.44
4	*Jeopardy*	1.38
5	*Dateline (Weekly)*	1.33
6	*Big Bang Theory*	1.06
7	*Weekend Adventure*	0.96
8	*Modern Family*	0.88
9	*Law & Order: SVU*	0.76
10	*Last Man Standing (M–F)*	0.72

Source: Nielsen, September 21, 2020–February 14, 2021. Excludes sports, specials, breakouts, and programs less than 5 minutes.

affiliated at least part of the time with a network. The spot TV buy could be as small as a single station in one market to a couple of hundred stations across a region. While the actual cost of placing spots on local stations is lower than a total network buy, once you start including a large number of markets, it can become quite expensive.

Ownership of television stations has become increasingly consolidated in the past several years. The largest owner, Sinclair Broadcasting, which started in 1971 with one Baltimore FM radio station, now owns 294 TV stations across the country. From a viewer's standpoint, the impact of this may be minimal; for buyers, it means fewer companies to negotiate with.

Spot TV time is sold either by the individual station and/or by station representative firms, or *rep firms*. These firms put together packages of stations known as *unwired networks* (because they are not physically linked together, or wired). Rep firms can usually customize buys, allowing the buyers to pick only those stations in which they are interested in a given number of markets. It provides a way for advertisers who cannot afford to buy nationally to reach their target more efficiently through local buys.

Viewership can vary quite considerably from market to market. In September 2020, NBC's *America's Got Talent* reported a national (Total U.S.) rating among persons 2+ of 5.69 percent, which means that 5.69 percent of that population group watched the show, but in Dayton, Ohio, that program's rating was 11.5 percent and in Phoenix, Arizona, it was 2.07 percent.[6]

Cable Television

Cable television has existed as a means of conveying television signals since 1948. Because it does not depend on over-the-air signals but comes into the home via wires laid underground (or sometimes on poles on the street), reception is much clearer in many areas. This was the original reason behind its growth—so that people in Eugene, Oregon, or Lancaster, Pennsylvania, could receive the signals of the broadcast networks more clearly. While the broadcast networks distribute their programs from a central location to each of their affiliates, cable programs are sent via satellite from the cable network to individual cable operators (franchises) within each market, who then distribute the signals to the subscribers' homes. There are thousands of separate cable systems operating today, although the majority belong to one of the large multiple system operators (MSOs) that have cable systems in numerous markets. In 2020, there were a total of 450 cable operators, the largest being Comcast and Charter Spectrum. Together, these two operators can reach about two-thirds (65 percent) of the U.S. population.

Another difference between broadcast TV and cable TV, from the consumers' standpoint, is that they must pay a monthly subscription fee to receive cable services. The average monthly cost of cable in 2020 was about $60—or even more to receive a pay cable network, such as Home Box Office (HBO) or Showtime, where there are no ads. Much of that access has moved to premium streaming subscriptions, however.

Cable TV is made up of a wide variety of different networks, many of which specialize in certain kinds of programs or appeal to certain types of people. For example, ESPN airs sports all the time, and Comedy Central has 24 hours of comedy programming. There are several cable networks, such as USA Network and TBS, which are more similar to the broadcast networks in their programming, airing a variety of shows, from adventures to situation comedies to movies and dramas. Most cable networks also produce their own original programming, which attracts larger audiences; those, in turn, allow the cable networks to charge advertisers higher prices. The third season of Paramount Network's *Yellowstone*, which aired during the summer of 2020 on Sundays at 9:00 p.m., generated a 2.37 household rating across its ten original airings, outperforming the average prime time rating of the five major broadcast networks during that same time period, at 2.17. Cable networks will sell aggregated ratings, combining the individual ratings for the same episode that airs multiple times. The season three finale of *Yellowstone* in 2020 generated a cumulative 3.97 household rating over its multiple airings. Despite having hundreds of channels to watch (200 on average), the average U.S. household tunes in to about 15.[7]

Today, nearly $29 billion of total TV advertising dollars go to cable television, representing about one-third of the total amount advertisers spend in television. Most of cable's ad dollars are purchased on a national basis, although the medium exists at the local level, too, with about $5 billion in advertiser spending in 2020. If you manage a local restaurant or a bank, you can run your commercials throughout the market, or you can confine your messages to a particular cable system's area. Both national and local advertisers use cable TV to buy certain zones within the coverage area of the operator. Advertisers can purchase time on several systems at once by going through a central sales office, known as an *interconnect*. This is similar to a rep firm: You select the cable systems on which your ad will appear. Most interconnects operate on a metropolitan or regional basis, such as Greater Chicago or the Bay Area.

Another way that consumers receive hundreds of cable (and broadcast) channels is via *satellite* TV. With this distribution platform, the TV signals go directly from the satellite to small dishes sitting on rooftops of houses or apartment buildings. The two major satellite providers are Dish Network and DirecTV. According to eMarketer, about 17 percent of the country receives television via satellite.[8] It is projected that both cable and satellite penetration will decline, leading to fewer than half of all homes subscribing to either service by 2024 down from about 60 percent of households doing so in 2020.[9]

As noted in Chapter 3, advertisers can send different TV ads to individual households, depending on the characteristics of each home. This practice, known as *addressable advertising*, allows companies selling home furnishings to send ads to new homeowners, while makers of diapers can deliver ads just to the households with infants and toddlers. As the technology has been deployed in larger numbers, across nearly 70 million cable and satellite TV homes, it is now possible for advertisers to pay only to send ads to homes they care about, rather than having to bear the cost of sending ads to all households. In this way, television can become a far more targeted, less "mass" medium, and its impact can be accurately measured in terms of consumer response or product sales. In addition to using addressable TV for better audience targeting and measuring outcomes from exposure, this type of advertising can also be deployed to find those homes that have not seen (or seen too few) traditional TV ads, and thereby replace that "lost" reach. As TV ratings to regular broadcast and cable programs continue to decline, addressable ads provide one way to recoup those lost impressions.

Viewing on Demand

The development of video on demand (VOD) through technology that created two-way systems between the cable operator and each household, enabled cable subscribers to watch "on demand." Programs could cost as little as a few dollars for an old TV series or movie or as much as $100 for a special boxing match, for example. Today, we think of VOD more in terms of subscription streaming services such as Netflix, Prime Video, or Hulu. About three-quarters (74 percent) of all homes are paying for this kind of service, while nearly one-quarter (24 percent) use three such services in a month.[10] Ad-supported VOD offers *dynamic ad insertion* where ads are inserted right before the program content plays, so those ads are not only timelier but can be targeted to the household viewing. Currently, the two largest subscription VOD (*SVOD*) companies, Netflix and Prime Video, do not offer ad opportunities. As more such services are introduced, however, several are at least partially ad-supported (*AVOD*), including Peacock (NBC Universal), Paramount+ (Viacom), and Tubi.

The ability for viewers to watch content whenever they want has largely replaced digital video recorders, or DVRs. Today, DVRs are in about half (51 percent) of all U.S. households. In many ways, this technology "trained" consumers to avoid commercials, with estimates that viewers who watch programs recorded on a DVR typically skip about 60 percent of the commercials.

The implications of these changes in how people watch TV for advertising are potentially huge, especially for buyers. What happens when there is no such thing as prime time television anymore? And what if the viewership of a program no longer occurs simultaneously because large numbers of people are streaming it or recording for later use? At what point does the rating get replaced by the impression so that a cross-channel (digital + TV) metric becomes the new standard? There has been much deliberation in the industry over these questions, driven by the World Federation of Advertisers (WFA), and with strong support from Google and Meta.

Connected TV

As the cost of cable and satellite subscription packages grew, more and more viewing households chose to *cut the cord* and watch television through connected devices such as gaming consoles, smart TVs, and external add-ons like a Roku or Chromecast that attaches to the set. All these forms of television *connect* the TV set to the internet, opening up a vast array of content to watch, and letting the viewer choose what (if any) subscriptions to pay for. Today, about eight in ten TV households in the United States are connected. Although the majority of what is viewed is still traditional broadcast or cable programming, it is estimated that this will decline as consumers (especially younger ones) move more of their viewing to streamed original content. Today, according to Nielsen, adults aged 18–34 spend 71 percent of their media time with apps or websites, TV-connected devices, or internet on the computer. This compares to just 42 percent of the media time spent by adults 50–64.[11] Nielsen reported that in June 2021, people were watching streaming services for about one-quarter (26 percent) of their TV viewing time.[12]

For advertisers, reaching their target audiences via connected TV opens up the opportunity to do so in the same way they do with other digital channels. From a planning perspective, this means the ability to define the desired audience based on their digital behavior (search activity or websites visited or purchases made online). While Lowe's Hardware Stores might target men aged 25–54 on traditional TV, they could refine that considerably with connected TV to "adults who have watched YouTube woodworking videos in the past 3 months, and visited the Lowe's or Home Depot websites in the past 30 days." For connected TV buying, about one-quarter is done *programmatically*, in an automated manner. More is said on this in Chapter 7.

Over the Top Television

Connected TV has been a big driver of the idea that television is really just video, and, as such, it is no longer confined to the television set. When video can be streamed to any device, it is referred to as *over the top*, or *OTT*, because it bypasses the traditional forms of TV distribution and lets viewers watch the content on a TV, computer, or mobile device. As of 2020, it was estimated that about one-quarter of TV usage goes to streamed content in homes that have that ability.[13] More and more households are paying to view streamed content from services such as Netflix, Hulu, or Prime Video, thereby going "over the top" of the traditional TV access methods. According to Comscore, 69.2 million homes used OTT in 2020, with the average OTT home watching 95 hours of that type of content in a month, across 18.5 different days.[14]

When consumers choose to watch OTT, it is often to catch up on missed episodes or prior seasons or to take advantage of the convenience of "anytime, anywhere" viewing. For example, the most streamed content in the U.S. in 2020 was old episodes of *The Office* on Netflix. Indeed, the most-viewed original series, Netflix's *Ozark*, ranked in fourth place in terms of hours viewed.[15] For advertisers, these streaming TV viewers are particularly desirable because they tend to be light viewers of traditional TV programs. According to Nielsen, 10.4 percent of the audience for the Netflix original, *Cobra Kai*, did not watch any traditional TV during the same week they watched the martial arts comedy-drama.[16]

In addition to watching TV programs this way, viewers are also consuming large quantities of short-form programming, whether on sites such as YouTube or on social media platforms like TikTok. This type of content, whether professionally produced or created by individuals and then posted online for OTT viewing, is especially popular with teens and young adults.

How Television is Bought: Broadcast

There are three ways that national television is bought, for both broadcast, cable, and syndication—long term, short term ("scatter"), and opportunistic. The first, and most intense, is what is generally known as the *upfront marketplace*. For broadcast TV, this usually takes place in late May after the networks present their new programming slate to advertisers, while for cable, it runs from May to July. With either television form, the media specialist negotiates time with the major networks well in advance of the actual air dates. Most typically, these fall during the following TV season that starts in September and runs through the next 12 months. The time purchased is usually over four-quarters of the year.

When TV advertising was initiated in the late 1940s, all commercial time was, in effect, bought upfront. That is because programs were fully sponsored by advertisers, so the negotiations for which companies would put their names in front of new programs' names occurred as those same programs were being developed (e.g., the Philco Theater Hour). After quiz show scandals in the late 1950s, where contestants were secretly fed the right answers in order to maintain viewer suspense, the networks took back control of programming from advertisers (who had sponsored those unfair quiz shows). In 1962, ABC became the first TV network to air all of its new programming in one week, right after Labor Day, and the "new fall season" was created. From then on, the annual schedule was born. The network marketplace is a modified version of supply and demand, with TV ratings (viewers) acting as the supply and advertiser budgets providing the demand. However, given that the networks have certain profit goals to meet, they will only offer programs at prices that are in line with those goals, therefore diminishing the dynamics of a true supply-and-demand market. In 1967, ABC also became the first network to offer the *guaranteed* program rating to advertisers who agreed to buy upfront. Although this meant the advertiser had to commit to a buy in advance, the advantage was that hit programs might be purchased at a relatively inexpensive cost.[17] Today, upfront buys account for 80 to 85 percent of all network prime time sales. In 2021, nearly $20 billion worth of network and cable TV ad time was sold this way. Today's upfront buys include both traditional (linear) TV programs or dayparts and streamed content.

When you buy *long term*, you receive a guaranteed rating, along with the opportunity to set up cancellation options. Typically, the options decelerate over the future quarters. For instance, in the first quarter you might buy all of the spots confirmed; in the second quarter, three-quarters or 75 percent might be firm, with the option to cancel the remaining 25 percent by an agreed-upon date. Then for the third or subsequent quarters, only half of the spots you negotiate are firm and half are cancellable by a certain date. One advantage of buying time this way is that more favorable rates may be offered, as the networks like to lock in the advertisers to their shows (both new and returning series). Also, advertisers are more likely to get a better mix of programs and to be ensured of spots in the time periods and/or shows they want. The disadvantage, from the buyer's standpoint, is that there may be less room for negotiation because everyone is trying to buy from a limited amount of inventory. That is, the networks can choose how much of the available airtime they wish to sell upfront, manipulating the demand for that time. The buyers also don't know how well the new programs will perform, basing their judgment on brief promotional excerpts the networks release, along with their historical experience of similar shows from the past.

The commercial minutes the networks hold back or don't sell then form the bulk of the second type of national television time, which is known as the *scatter* market because it is scattered throughout the broadcast day across months. Buyers typically purchase this type of commercial time on a quarterly basis, though it does not need to be bought at the beginning of a calendar quarter. It used to be purchased several months in advance, but now buys are more commonly made two to four weeks before airdate. Prices in scatter will vary, depending on the supply and demand, and what happens in scatter tends to impact the long-term or upfront marketplace, too. In boom years when the economy is thriving, advertiser demand during the upfront period is high, but when a recession hits, advertisers are loath to commit large funds in advance, so upfront deals tend to decrease while scatter buys rise.

Advertisers who purchase spots in the scatter market may or may not get guaranteed ratings, depending on the supply and demand. Those spots are usually purchased by advertisers who are unable or unwilling to commit to a schedule a year in advance. If demand for scatter time is high, the network can close a particular daypart on very short notice, pulling it out of the sale and then repricing it for future buyers. Advertisers who do not move quickly enough may find themselves shut out of the daypart completely.

The third way to buy time on national television is the *opportunistic* buy. Here, the advertiser chooses to purchase at the last minute, picking up what-ever remains available. While there is less flexibility in this kind of buy, the costs are lower. However, as ratings have continued to fall, this kind of buy has become increasingly rare because the networks do not have inventory available as they need to give spots back to advertisers whose guaranteed ratings were not met (see below).

Deciding how to purchase TV time depends on many factors, not the least of which is the size of the advertising budget. The number of quarters in which the commercial is to run also plays a key role, as does the type of programming mix desired. First and foremost, however, should be strategic considerations regarding the impact of the decision on the marketing, advertising, and media goals.

Buying Television: The Process

The process of buying television time is as follows. The buyer requests a pack-age of programs from the seller (broadcast, syndication, or cable). The package may be based on costs or on ratings, but it is ultimately based on the goals of the plan. The sellers submit their inventory, and the buyer chooses the package that best meets the client's needs and negotiates the price. Instead of purchasing them immediately, however, the buyer "goes to hold," which means the buyer is almost certain he or she will buy that time but has not fully committed to it yet. Both sides agree on how long that hold will last; generally, it is up to two weeks in the scatter market and four to eight weeks in the long-term market. After that period, the buyer will either purchase the time or drop out. Once the deal is finalized, however, the buyer effectively owns that time. If, later on, the buyer wants to get rid of the commercial time he or she bought, the network may try to sell it to a different advertiser if the marketplace demand is strong. If for some reason the spot does not run as promised, the buyer is given the option of a comparable spot on the program schedule. This is known as a *make-good*. That might mean moving with a program to another day or time, if the network decides to reschedule it, or staying in the same daypart but switching programs. When programs do not achieve the audience rating that the network had guaranteed to the advertiser, the network will then provide, over the course of the contract term, *audience deficiency units*, or ADUs. Sometimes these have to be delivered in the advertiser's next flight of commercials due to lack of inventory or client needs. Sometimes these are referred to as under-delivery weight, or UDW. These no-charge units are provided in the same or comparable programs to the advertiser.

All national television time is priced based on a 30-second spot. For advertisers wishing to buy more or less time than that, the rates are adjusted accordingly. Hence, a 60-second spot costs twice as much, while a 15-second spot is 50 percent of the full rate. Negotiations are typically conducted based on CPMs for the target, defined in terms of age and sex. For example, it could be the CPM for reaching women 18 to 49 or adults 25 to 54.

With the introduction of newer forms of television (connected TV, addressable TV) that enable the viewing data to be matched to other information about each household through companies such as Experian or Epsilon, it has allowed for buys to be made against more granular targets. Now, the buyer can start to buy programs that are more likely to reach households with infants (for Huggies diapers) or high-income households (for Lexus). In an addressable advertising environment, those are the only homes that would see the ads, while other forms of advanced TV by several TV networks and technology companies can deliver ads to all homes but skew the buy to those households, which are more likely to have that granular target within them.

TV buys today increasingly include connected or OTT viewing. Broadcast networks include these kinds of views as part of the packages they offer to buyers, to account for all the ways that their content is being consumed. In particular, they are eager to strike more fluid deals with advertisers, allowing them to make up for under-delivery in traditional (linear) TV with digitally delivered spots instead. While this makes sense from the perspective of the audience, who like to watch what they want on any screen, it is harder for the buyers because measurement systems are not yet integrated to provide robust "cross screen" ratings.

As noted, the U.S. TV marketplace operates based on the laws of supply and demand. The more people who watch a particular show, the more expensive it is to advertise within it. The ranges are enormous. You might pay $600,000 or more for a 30-second commercial on network television during prime time, but only a few hundred dollars to have your ad appear on your local TV station during the night. That cost will correspond to the number of people exposed to your ad—millions versus a few hundred.

Considerations in TV Buying

In addition to looking at ratings, another important measure for television trading is the *share*. That is, of all those watching television at a given time, what percentage are tuned to the program of interest? The share can be looked at as a percentage of all households using TV (HUT) or, more commonly, as a percent of all of your desired target group (persons using TV, or PUT).

The viewers per viewing (or tuning) household, or *VPVH*, numbers (sometimes called VPTH) provides an assessment of the concentration of a given demographic group in a program's audience, showing how many people in every thousand viewers fall into that particular category. If the VPVH among women aged between 25 to 54 for *The Bachelor* is 535 and for the *Masters Golf Championship* is 155, that indicates you will reach more than three times as many women aged between 25 to 54 with an ad placed in the reality show than you will with the golf tournament.

One way that the VPVH can usefully be applied is in the conversion of household rating points to target audience ratings. This is done by creating a *conversion factor* that is then applied to the household rating. For example, if you know that there are 420 viewers per viewing household for your men aged between 18 to 49 target watching *NCIS*, and the total population size of that group is 66 million while the total number of households is 110 million, then your steps would be as follows:

$$(420 \times 110{,}000{,}000) / (66{,}000{,}000 / 1000) = 0.7$$

$$= \text{Conversion Factor (CF)}$$

$$14.3 \text{ Household Rating} \times 0.70 \text{ CF} = 10.01 \text{ (M18} - 49 \text{ Rating)}$$

What you should be most interested in, as a media specialist, is finding which programs are going to best reach your target audience. As discussed in Chapter 3, although you may have a fairly detailed description of your customer, when it comes to getting data on TV audiences, the industry has traditionally only been able to look at age and gender, which were thought to be powerful determinants of product purchase and behavior. Today, with the ready availability of more detailed and precise person-level and household-level data on people's purchase activity or interests or lifestyles, media planners and buyers look at it more the same way they look at digital. An analysis of viewing behavior based on category, brand consumption, or intent, may well be a better way to demonstrate how TV advertising works. While the trading currency for TV today remains the Nielsen rating, more advertisers are using product usage-based (or other targeted) ratings as measures for planning and buying television advertising.

TV ratings data can be combined with lifestyle and other media use information from another source through *data fusion*. This process, successfully used in many countries, including the United States, involves "matching" respondents from two different databases, linking them on a number of common variables (gender, age, geographic location, ethnicity, etc.) known as *hooks*, and then "fusing" the data so that the information that is unique to one dataset can be used to describe or explain the behavior of all the respondents in both datasets. It is a complex and intricate process that requires statistical expertise and understanding but is quite commonly applied to television data to understand viewership beyond just age and gender.

In selecting TV programs, the buyer must keep in mind that the list may be changed when the commercial time is bought. The plan is just that—a *plan* of which media vehicles are desired. When negotiations take place, it may be that other programs are included, or some of your recommendations are rejected, based on other considerations such as cost and availability. What may be emphasized, however, is the *daypart* in which the ads should appear because, although people do tend to watch individual programs rather than time periods, there is more similarity in the kinds of programs watched within time periods than across them. Alternatively, you may wish to specify the *program type* or genre so that the buy focuses on comedies or news programming, for example, regardless of when it airs. TV has become more digital-like in its targeting capabilities, which enables more audience-based buying where there is less (or no) emphasis on the specific programs but more on delivering impressions against a very specific audience, such as people in the market for a new Hyundai SUV or frequent travelers who have stayed at a Marriott hotel three+ times in the past year. As TV goes OTT and is consumed across all video screens (TV, PC, mobile, gaming device), TV networks are negotiating to sell their ad time on screens beyond the TV set. In today's marketplace, where about one-quarter of all homes are watching streaming video, and about one in five households watch via broadband-only, TV measurement is changing. Streamed content is mostly reported by a number of viewers, while local TV is transitioning to impressions from ratings.

Buying Time on Syndication and Cable

Buying national television time on syndication and cable is not that different from the broadcast network marketplace. There are long-term, scatter, and opportunistic buys available in each television form. Additional considerations need to be given, however, to the individual buys. With syndication, for example, *coverage* is critical. Because syndicated programs are sold to individual stations in each market, they may not be seen in every market across the country. The buyer therefore has to know what percent of stations in the U.S. will air a given program. It may be as low as 60 percent or as high as 99 percent. The day and/or time of airing will also vary by town or city, and although people do watch programs rather than dayparts, it may make a difference to the effectiveness of a media schedule if you are trying to reach women 25 to 54 with *The Kelly Clarkson Show* and find that it airs at 9:00 a.m. in

Chattanooga, Tennessee, but at 3:00 p.m. in Gary, Indiana. The audience delivery and composition could be quite different in those markets because of that airtime variation.

Syndicated programs are guaranteed, but the syndicator will often overstate the ratings estimate. That means the buyer then has to be given make-goods, either in the form of bonus units or cashback. While this might seem an inefficient way to operate, the syndication marketplace has operated this way since its inception, despite a decline in ratings beginning in the late 1990s. Many packaged-goods advertisers still rely on syndication to reach their "average" American consumers.

Cable television also sells a good deal of its commercial time in advance, usually with guaranteed ratings. Cable is mostly bought by daypart rotations, except for select original programs or popular off-network reruns. While this might appear to be a big problem for advertisers, it is less critical on cable networks, where the programming is considered "vertical," offering similar content all day, so an advertiser knows that his spot will air, for example, within news content on CNN or in classic sitcoms on Nick at Nite. Most networks, however, have moved to program-based buys as they have built up their individual brand images based on their well-known personalities or, increasingly, their original programming. Examples here include Comedy Central's *The Daily Show* and ESPN's *Sports Center*.

Another consideration for cable is the distribution of the network. That is, some of the smaller networks are not available for viewing in all U.S. households, which often leads the networks themselves to sell their audiences based on a *coverage-area rating* (a national rating that has been adjusted for the area covered by the distribution). For instance, if Cable Network X is only available in half of the country, its 2.0 nationally reported rating is really a 4.0 since only half of the population is watching it (2.0/50%). Many buyers do not like to adjust for the coverage since it makes it harder to draw apples-to-apples comparisons.

How Local TV is Bought

The purchase of time on spot television has both similarities and differences to the network process. Local television buyers usually buy time on shorter notice than for national television. They work with individual stations in each market, rather than buying a complete network, unless they make a buy across various stations that are linked together into an ad sales network. The stations are focused on selling their reach within a given market and many excel in specific dayparts, often promoting themselves as the "Number 1 News Station." Keep in mind that everyone is number one at something! The planner provides the buyer with the details of the specifications, which include the marketing and media objectives, a demographic and psychographic description of the target, the desired dayparts and flights, the number of ratings or impressions per market and/or time period, the total budget, and the mix of commercial lengths (15, 30, and 60 seconds).

Local TV is purchased by geographic areas called the *designated market area*, or DMA. This is defined as the viewing area in which the counties that have the stations of the originating market get the largest share of household viewing or listening. Every county in the United States is assigned to just one DMA. For large cities such as Los Angeles or New York, they are individual DMAs, but smaller markets may consist of several cities, such as the DMA of Albany-Schenectady-Troy in upstate New York or Harlingen-Weslaco-Brownsville-McAllen in Texas.

Once the DMAs are selected, the buyer can then start negotiating with stations in those markets. Until recently, local buyers negotiated the cost per rating point, or CPP, with the goal of ensuring they ended up buying the appropriate number of rating points for the budget. Today, however, local broadcast is shifting to impression-based buying, which makes the channel more akin to digital buys. The negotiating process involves a collaboration between buyer and seller, with the TV station working hard to price the available local time on their station to meet the advertiser's needs. The buyer will usually talk to all stations in the market that have programs or formats appropriate for the target in the desired daypart and ask each of them to submit prices. For a few advertisers, price is the most important criterion, so the buyer looks to purchase "tonnage"—lots of media weight at the lowest price available. But today, with more information available on local TV audiences, the program or format is key; they may be willing to pay slightly more to get a closer fit between target and vehicle. The challenge is finding the right balance between cost efficiency and desirable program content.

Once the buyer has received submissions from each station, he or she can then start negotiating to see if any of the sellers are willing to lower their price any further. Once final prices and terms are agreed to, then the buy is made, and an electronic confirmation of the order is sent from seller to buyer.

In theory, local television buys are fixed; that is, the time is bought on a given daypart and/or program (unless the buyer purchases run-of-schedule, or ROS, which means that the station can air the spot at any time). In practice, however, stations may pre-empt a spot if another advertiser comes in who is willing to pay more for that time slot. If this happens, the first advertiser will usually request a make-good or compensation if the station airs their spot at a less favorable time. The make-good is supposed to be of equal or greater value.

Viewers will see many familiar national companies and brand names appear during local programming; for most TV stations outside of the largest markets, their revenues come primarily from local businesses who are eager to get their message out to as many of that local population as possible.

Benefits of Television to Advertisers

Whichever type of television advertising you choose, you will enjoy a number of benefits unavailable from any other medium. Among these benefits, television's ability to imitate real-life situations, its pervasiveness, and its broad reach are most noteworthy. The digital forms of TV also enable more sophisticated targeting.

True to Life

The most obvious advantage of television advertising is the opportunity to use sight, sound, color, and motion in commercials. This form of advertising is generally considered the most lifelike, recreating scenes and showing people in situations with which we can all identify. That does not mean we don't see cartoons or animated commercials or fantasies on the screen; they can include everything imaginable. But of all the media available, TV comes closest to showing us products in our everyday lives and summons our emotions most effectively.[18] This is not only important for packaged-goods advertisers—firms such as Kellogg's, Anheuser-Busch, or Unilever, who are able to show us what their products look like and how they are used or enjoyed—but also for service companies such as Marriott Hotels or American Express, which can offer us ways to use their amenities. Many 15-second TV ads are shown as *pre-roll* ads in digital video or paid social.

Most Pervasive

Television advertising is the most pervasive media form available, given that the average American is watching about five hours or so of TV every day and spending more time with TV than all other major paid media. Several slogans from TV commercials have entered the mainstream of conversation, such as Bud Light's "Whassup?" or Wisk detergent's infamous "ring around the collar" line. Characters in commercials have also become part of our lives, such as Flo for Progressive Insurance or Tony the Tiger for Kellogg's Frosted Flakes. Today, many of these ad characters have large followings on social media, perhaps reflecting how they have become a part of people's everyday lives.

Reaching the Masses

Another important advantage of television from an advertising perspective is the wide *reach* of people it offers at any one time. Even in programs with Adult 18+ ratings below five, you are reaching about 12 million individuals! While there is generally a smaller audience for the commercials than for the programs themselves, television remains a truly mass medium. More than 3 billion people worldwide watched some of the 2016 Olympic Games. On average, Nielsen reports that TV reaches 87 percent of all persons aged 2 and older each week.[19] Furthermore, by buying time on several different programs shown at different times and/or on different days, it is possible to reach a wide *variety* of individuals. And although each ad appears for a short time (usually 15 or 30 seconds), if it is repeated on several occasions, more people are likely to be exposed to it, often more than once. This helps build brand awareness, which in turn may lead to the formation of favorable attitudes or intentions to purchase that brand. Perhaps one testament to the powerful reach of TV is that some of the biggest spenders on the medium are large digital companies such as Google, Amazon, and Facebook!

Digital Targets

Once TV is viewed in a connected or OTT way, it has the potential to let advertisers define target audiences more precisely than simply the age and gender variables used in linear TV. That means that Chase Bank can deliver its video ads via Hulu or Roku (as well as on YouTube or Pandora) to households with incomes of $100,000+ to inform them about its high-yield savings plans. United Airlines can reach people who have a frequent flyer card with its video ad offering the latest rewards available to Mileage Plus participants. More and more advertisers today want to utilize the same target audience definitions across both TV and digital and manage their campaigns in a fully cross-platform way.

Drawbacks of Television Advertising

Unfortunately, television advertising has particular drawbacks as well as the unique benefits just discussed. Four of the most commonly encountered drawbacks are high cost, cluttered airwaves, limited exposure time, and where best to place spots.

Dollars and Sense

Perhaps the biggest disadvantage of advertising on TV, particularly at the national level, is the high cost. The average 30-second commercial during prime time on the six main broadcast networks in the 2020/2021 TV season cost about $115,000, with a wide range from about $10,500 at the low end to $780,000 at the top.[20]

Even that cost pales in comparison to television's most expensive ad opportunity. A single 30-second ad in the 2021 Super Bowl cost about $5.5 million. For many advertisers, this is far beyond their budget, leading them to shift more dollars into digital channels.

Cluttering the Airwaves

A related factor that is a major concern for advertisers is the sheer number of ads appearing on TV. This leads to a clutter of spots, again believed to reduce the effectiveness of individual commercials.[21] There is evidence to support this fear. From 2010 to 2020, the number of spots shown on prime time network TV grew by 66 percent. Part of the explanation for this is the increase in the number of TV networks. But another major reason is the growth in the number of shorter-length commercials. For many years, the standard television spot lasted a full minute. Then, in the mid-1960s, more and more advertisers started using 30-second commercials, finding them more cost-efficient and no less effective. As costs continued to increase during the 1970s and early 1980s, advertisers tried the same tactic, shifting to even shorter commercial lengths. Today, according to Nielsen, the 15-second spot accounts for 57 percent of all prime time broadcast TV commercials. Exhibit 5.6 shows the trend in TV ad clutter in prime time, while Exhibit 5.7 displays the expansion of 15-second commercials. The result of clutter on consumers is questionable, but research suggests that it hinders the communication, sometimes considerably.[22]

Quick Cuts

Another drawback to this medium is its brief exposure time. Although many ads are seen several times within a short period of time, unless the commercial is particularly inventive or unusual, it is likely the viewer will ignore it or be irritated by seeing it after the first few occasions and will deliberately try to avoid the message.[23] Controversy remains over just how many times people can be exposed to spots without getting bored or annoyed, a phenomenon referred to as *commercial wearout*. This drawback may be mitigated somewhat through addressable or connected TV, where viewers receive ads considered more relevant to their needs and/or they select the kinds of messages they are more interested in, finding out more about a specific brand or product in detail. The key here is that this self-selected audience is more interested and involved in the message.

Placing Spots

One area that has provoked a good deal of discussion is where commercials should be placed for optimal effectiveness. For network TV, you can buy time either within the program (*in-program*) or between two shows (*break*). While some believe there is no difference in viewer attention between these two options, others feel that you are likely to lose more viewers during the breaks than within the program itself. On spot TV, the break position used to be the only time slot available, although that is no longer the case, particularly as

Exhibit 5.6 Commercial Clutter Trend: Prime Time

	Number of Commercials	Percent Change	Number of Minutes	Percent Change
1990	4,990		2,059	
1995	7,609	52.5%	3,177	54.3%
2000	11,202	47.2%	4,751	49.5%
2005	11,742	4.8%	5,300	11.6%
2010	13,129	11.8%	5,615	5.9%
2013	16,338	24.4%	6,976	24.2%
2016	21,773	33.3%	10,312	47.8%
2020	39,718	82.4%	18,601	80.4%

Source: Nielsen Media Research 2006, 2011, 2014, 2017, 2021. Copyrighted information © 2021, of The Nielsen Company, licensed for use herein.

Note: Networks included for November 2020: ABC, BOU, CBS, CHG, COM, COZ, CW, FOX, GRT, HI, ION, LAF, MET, MYS, NBC, NLX, STV, TBD

Exhibit 5.7 Growth of 15-Second Commercials in Prime Time

Percent of Commercials That Are:	1990	1995	2000	2005	2010	2016	2020
:15	36%	34%	35%	35%	40%	45%	57%
:30	62%	64%	62%	58%	55%	43%	30%
:60	1%	1%	2%	5%	3%	8%	8%
Other	1%	1%	1%	2%	2%	4%	5%
	100%	100%	100%	100%	100%	100%	100%

Source: Nielsen 2011, 2015, 2017, 2020. Copyrighted information © 2021, of The Nielsen Company, licensed for use herein.

Note: Networks included for November 2020: ABC, BOU, CBS, CHG, COM, COZ, CW, FOX, GRT, HI, ION, LAF, MET, MYS, NBC, NLX, STV, TBD

commercial breaks have slid a few minutes into the program rather than only at the top or bottom of each hour.

Related to this placement issue is where to position your commercial within the series, or *pod* of spots being shown. Evidence suggests that the first ad to appear will receive the most attention, followed by the last one; those in the middle are likely to suffer from viewers switching channels, not looking at the screen, or leaving the room. The advertiser, however, does not routinely get the choice of where in the pod to air the ad. Some advertisers will pay a premium to ensure their ads appear first, but this is not always permitted.

Research on Television

Much of the research literature on television has focused on two key issues: the impact of a lifelike message and the effects of the program environment. Buchholz and Smith found that the more "involved" consumers are in the medium, the stronger their cognitive responses to ad messages.[24] Kamins and colleagues examined how TV ads are evaluated depending on the mood created by the program in which the ads appear.[25] Barwise, Bellman and Beal explored the emotional response to video viewing, finding through brainwave analysis that it helps people feel relaxed.[26] More recently, research has focused on the combined impact of social media or multitasking on TV ad effectiveness.[27] Several other research articles are also available.[28]

Summary

In order to decide which paid media might best be suited to achieving your plan objectives, it is important to understand how consumers use each one, how to plan and buy each channel, and consider the advantages and disadvantages that each can offer. Television remains a significant ad medium, even as it moves from traditional linear broadcast and cable to digital viewing through connected TV, and streaming offerings. The TV buying process is morphing from standard person age-gender ratings to more targeted impressions that are more comparable to digital media. As you analyze the various TV options, consider the benefits and drawbacks to help determine whether—and in which formats—TV should be included in the final plan.

Notes

1 Nielsen TV Audience Series Universe Estimates, February 2017.
2 Nielsen, February 2021.
3 Nielsen Total Audience Report, Q2 2020.
4 Nielsen Total Audience Report, Q2 2020.
5 Hub Entertainment Research study, as reported in Advanced TV Insider, found at www.mediapost.com, May 14, 2021.
6 Nielsen NPower Report, National-Local ratings, April 2021.
7 Nielsen Average Channels Tuned, February 2017.
8 As reported on www.eMarketer.com, 2021.
9 Ibid.
10 Nielsen Streaming Video Ratings Report, January, 2021.
11 Nielsen Total Audience Report, Q2 2020.
12 "Nielsen Tool May Solve A Streaming Mystery," John Koblin, *The New York Times*, June 18, 2021, B1/B5.

13 Nielsen Beyond SVOD Report, 2020.

14 Comscore Digital and CTV Trends to Watch in 2021.

15 "Finding Comfort in Some Old Familiar TV Faces," John Koblin, *New York Times*, January 13, 2021, B3.

16 "Branded Integrations Come of Age in a Streaming World," Nielsen 2021.

17 "How the TV Nets Got the Upfront," Erwin Ephron, Ad Age Special Report on TV's Upfront, May 14, 2001, S2/22, *Advertising Age*, June 2005.

18 Feng Shen and Jon D. Morris, "Decoding Neural Responses to Emotion in Television Commercials: An Integrative Study of Self-Reporting and fMRI Measures," *Journal of Advertising Research*, vol. 56, no. 2, June 2016, 193–204.

19 Nielsen Media Research, Total Audience Report, Q2 2020.

20 "How Much for a 30-Second Spot?" *Advertising Age*, October 2020.

21 Louisa Ha and Barry R. Litman, "Does Advertising Clutter Have Diminishing and Negative Returns?" *Journal of Advertising*, vol. 26, no. 1, Spring 1997, 31–42.

22 Michael T. Elliott and Paul Surgi Speck, "Consumer Perceptions of Advertising Clutter and Its Impact Across Various Media," *Journal of Advertising Research*, vol. 35, no. 3, May/June 1995, 29–42. Paul Surgi Speck and Michael T. Elliott, "The Antecedents and Consequences of Perceived Advertising Clutter," *Journal of Current Issues and Research in Advertising*, vol. 19, no. 2, 1997, 39–54. Yongick Jeong, "The Impact of the Length of Preceding and Succeeding Ads on Television Advertising Effectiveness," *Journal of Marketing Communications*, vol. 23, no. 4, 2017, 385–399.

23 Paul Surgi Speck and Michael T. Elliott, "Predictors of Advertising Avoidance in Print and Broadcast Media," *Journal of Advertising*, vol. 26, no. 2, Summer 1997, 61–76.

24 Laura M. Buchholz and Robert E. Smith, "The Role of Consumer Involvement in Determining Cognitive Response to Broadcast Advertising," *Journal of Advertising*, vol. 20, no. 1, 1991, 4–17.

25 Tiffany Venmahavong, Sukki Yoon, Kacy K. Kim, and Chan Yun Yoo, "Five Seconds to the Ad: How Program-Induced Mood Affects Ad Countdown Effects," *Journal of Advertising*, vol. 48, no. 2, 2019, 232–241. Michael A. Kamins, Lawrence J. Marks, and Deborah Skinner, "Television Commercial Evaluation in the Context of Program Induced Mood: Congruency Versus Consistency Effects," *Journal of Advertising*, vol. 20, no. 2, June 1991, 1–14.

26 Patrick Barwise, Steven Bellman, and Virginia Beal, Why Do People Watch So Much Television and Video? Implications for the Future of Viewing and Advertising, *Journal of Advertising Research*, June 2020, 60 (2), 121–134.

27 Claire M. Segijn and Martin Eisend, "A Meta-Analysis into Multiscreening and Advertising Effectiveness: Direct Effects, Moderators, and Underlying Mechanisms," *Journal of Advertising*, vol. 48, no. 3, 2019, 313–332. Steven Bellman, Jennifer A. Robinson, Brooke Wooley, and Duane Varan, "The Effects of Social TV on Television Advertising Effectiveness," *Journal of Marketing Communications*, vol. 23, no. 1, 2017, 73–91.

28 Lianlian Song, Peng Zhou, Geoffrey Tso, and Hingpo Lo, "Converting People-Meter Data from Per-Minute to Per-Second Analysis: A Statistical Model Offers a Closer Look at TV Ad Avoidance and Effectiveness," *Journal of Advertising Research*, vol. 59, no. 1, March 2019, 53–72. Nazrul I. Shaikh, Mahima Hada, and Niva Shrestha, "Allocating Spending on Digital-Video Advertising: A Longitudinal Analysis across Digital and Television," *Journal of Advertising Research*, vol. 59, no. 1, March 2019, 14–26. Charles Young, Brian Gillespie, and Christian Otto, "The Impact of Rational, Emotional, and Physiological Advertising Images

On Purchase Intention: How TV Ads Influence Brand Memory," *Journal of Advertising Research*, vol. 59, no. 3, September 2019, 329–341. Steven Bellman, Magda Nenycz-Thiel, Rachel Kennedy, Nicole Hartnett, and Duane Varan, "Best Measures of Attention to Creative Tactics in TV Advertising: When Do Attention-Getting Devices Capture or Reduce Attention? *Journal of Advertising Research*," vol. 59, no. 3, September 2019, 295–311. Duane Varan, Magda Nenycz-Thiel, Rachel Kennedy, and Steven Bellman, "The Effects of Commercial Length on Advertising Impact: What Short Advertisements Can and Cannot Deliver," *Journal of Advertising Research*, vol. 60, no. 1, March 2020, 54–70. Robert E. Smith and Laura M. Buchholz, "Multiple Resource Theory and Consumer Processing of Broadcast Advertisements: An Involvement Perspective," *Journal of Advertising*, vol. 20, no. 3, September 1991, 1–8. V. Carter Broach, Jr., Thomas R. Page, Jr., and R. Dale Wilson, "Television Programming and Its Influence on Viewers' Perceptions of Commercials: The Role of Program Arousal and Pleasantness," *Journal of Advertising*, vol. 24, no. 4, Winter 1995, 45–54. Andrew B. Aylesworth and Scott B. MacKenzie, "Context Is Key: The Effect of Program-Induced Mood on Thoughts about the Ad," *Journal of Advertising*, vol. 27, no. 2, Summer 1997, 17–32. Donald Miller Dennis and David Michael Gray, "An Episode-by-Episode Examination: What Drives Television-Viewer Behavior: Digging Down into Audience Satisfaction with Television Dramas," *Journal of Advertising Research*, vol. 53, no. 2, June 2013, 166–174. Leslie A. Wood and David F. Poltrack, "Measuring the Long-term Effects of Television Advertising. Nielsen-CBS Study Uses Single-Source Data to Reassess the 'Two-Times' Multiplier," *Journal of Advertising Research*, vol. 55, no. 2, June 2015, 123–131. Fred K. Beard, "Comparative Television Advertising in the United States: A Thirty-Year Update," *Journal of Current Issues & Research in Advertising*, vol. 37, no. 2, 2016, 183–195.

Chapter 6

Planning and Buying for Audio, Print, and Out-of-Home

Learning Outcomes: In this chapter you will learn how to:

- Differentiate the various forms of audio, print, and out-of-home channels
- Understand how each one is planned and bought
- Compare and contrast the benefits and disadvantages offered by audio, print, and out-of-home

When a friend asks you if you saw the latest Budweiser ad (or Coca-Cola or Athleta), there is a good chance they are referring to seeing that brand on TV or on social media platforms. Yet, for many brands, there are important reasons for appearing in other media channels. Whether to drive awareness, consideration, or actual sales, audio, print, and outdoor provide valued avenues for advertisers to reach their target audiences. In this chapter, we look at the value propositions for each one, in both their traditional forms and their digital offerings.

Radio: The "Everywhere" Medium

Radio is the oldest electronic advertising medium. It first became popular in America in the early 1920s, and since that time it has managed to hold its own against all other media forms. Although families no longer sit around their radios as they once did to listen to the most popular programs of the day, they still rely on this medium for both information and entertainment. Indeed, almost every home in America has at least one radio, and most have several. The number of radios per household has been dropping (the mean number is now 1.5), most likely due to the increase in audio listening via digital devices.[1] Nonetheless, radio reaches about 92 percent of adults 18 and older each week—more than any other medium. According to Nielsen, radio is the third most-used medium each day, at 1 hour 34 minutes, behind live/DVR TV and smartphone usage.[2] Radio listening is highest between 10:00 a.m. and 7:00 p.m. About seven in ten (69 percent) of adults are listening to the radio outside the home, much of it in the car.[3]

There are 15,451 commercial radio stations across the country. Of those, about one in four operate on the AM (amplitude modulation) wavelength,

DOI: 10.4324/9781003175704-6

while the remainder are FM (frequency modulation) stations. The primary differences between them are in reception area and audience. AM stations can broadcast over a wider distance, but because the soundwaves are impeded by any kind of obstruction (hills, tall buildings), the sound quality is inferior to FM stations, which broadcast in a narrower listening area. AM tends to be listened to more by older adults, reflecting the fact that more AM stations offer news and talk programs rather than the music formats that dominate the FM wavelength. Radio stations are either commercial, accepting advertising as their chief source of revenue, or non-commercial, funded by public monies and/or audience sponsorships. Commercial stations will air, on average, about 10 minutes of advertising per hour, in blocks of about three and a half minutes.

As with television, radio is classified by both daypart and format. The different formats that are available for the advertiser are not defined the same way by the listener. Radio dayparts and formats are shown in Exhibits 6.1 and 6.2.

Exhibit 6.1 Radio Dayparts

Day of Week	Time Period
Monday–Friday	6:00 a.m.–10:00 a.m.
Monday–Friday	10:00 a.m.–3:00 p.m.
Monday–Friday	3:00 p.m.–7:00 p.m.
Monday–Friday	7:00 p.m.–midnight
Saturday–Sunday	6:00 a.m.–midnight
Monday–Sunday	6:00 a.m.–midnight

Source: Nielsen 2002.

Exhibit 6.2 Top Ten Radio Formats

	Format	Share of Total Listening
1	Country	13.2%
2	News/Talk (Commercial + Non-Commercial)	12.0%
3	Adult Contemporary	8.6%
4	News/Talk (Commercial)	8.3%
5	Pop Contemporary Hit Radio	7.3%
6	Classic Rock	6.1%
7	Classic Hits	5.8%
8	Hot Adult Contemporary	4.7%
9	Urban Adult Contemporary	4.1%
10	Contemporary Christian	3.9%
	Share of all radio listening in the United States	74%

Source: Nielsen Audio, Audio Today Q2 2019.

The two main types of radio advertising are network (national) and spot (local). The way programs and ads are distributed is similar to that of network and spot (local) TV. Today, radio represents about 4 percent of all advertising expenditures, with about $6 billion spent in these two traditional ways (not including digital audio).

Network Radio

Unlike television, network radio is less important to advertisers than is local radio. It currently receives about 13 percent of all radio dollars and reaches about 94 percent of people 12 and older each week. Like TV, however, a message placed on network radio is distributed via satellite to each network's affiliate stations. These stations are paid an annual sum to take, or clear, the network's programs. Almost all radio stations are affiliated with one network or another. The kinds of programs they receive from the network may be aired every day, such as the Westwood One newscast, or weekly, such as Weekends with the Breakfast Club. There are presently seven major radio networks, each of which offers subnetworks based on the programming and the demographic makeup of their listeners. Westwood One News provides hourly newscasts to affiliate stations around the clock, reaching listeners of all ages, while the stations that are part of United Stations' Country network include stations playing that format across the country. Exhibit 6.3 lists the major Nielsen-measured networks. Additional networks are available.

From an advertiser's perspective, one key benefit of using network radio is that you can go through a single source to place your ads across a region or across the country. The downside of this form of radio, however, is that you have less flexibility in choosing the stations you wish to be in. If you buy the Westwood One News Network, you may get the number-one station in Biloxi, Mississippi, but a distant fourth station in Little Rock, Arkansas.

Exhibit 6.3 Major Measured Radio Networks

AdLarge Media
American Urban
Crystal Media
Premiere
Sun Broadcast Group
United Stations
Westwood One

Source: Nielsen Audio, 2020.

Spot Radio

Nearly 90 percent of radio's advertising dollars are spent in spot markets, where you buy time on individual stations on a market-by-market basis. Here, if you were placing the advertising for Coldwell Banker realtors, you could buy time on individual stations in a market, regardless of which network they belong to, and choose which markets you wished to target. The advantage of purchasing radio in this way is that you can select the exact stations and/or markets in which you wish to advertise your product. This also allows you to customize the message to each location so that Home Depot stores can mention the address of different locations in each market's ad.

Some stations are linked together only for the purpose of selling advertising time. They constitute an "unwired" network, allowing you to select which stations within the group you wish to use based on your demographic or geographic preferences. Typically, an advertiser buys time through a representative, or rep firm, rather than dealing with every station individually. If you are trying to target teens with the Nintendo Switch, you could go to a rep firm that offers you stations that do well against that group. Examples of unwired networks include the Entercom Audio Network, which helps advertisers buy across the 230+ stations owned by that company, providing more efficiency. But, as with wired network radio, you may end up buying time on less-attractive stations as part of the package deal.

Satellite Radio

In 2001, satellite radio services were introduced to the U.S. marketplace. The original two companies, XM Radio and Sirius Radio, merged in 2008 to create SiriusXM, which today has 34 million subscribers in the United States. Consumers need special receivers in order to tune in to these services, and they must also pay a monthly subscription (about $15/month). One incentive for them to pay is that about half of the 150 stations air without commercials. Even on those channels that include advertising, the amount will be far less than on regular radio stations—6 minutes per hour, compared to 15 to 20 minutes on terrestrial stations.

The content offered by satellite radio ranges from niche forms of music to all kinds of sports to news and politics across the spectrum of views to syndicated talk shows such as "Mad Dog" Russo, Howard Stern, or Andy Cohen. This type of radio resembles cable TV in that there are so many channels that they can afford to be highly specialized (e.g., a NASCAR channel, several baseball channels, or a channel offering bluegrass music). The SiriusXM company has deals with the major U.S. auto manufacturers, who have built satellite radio capability into their models and offer it as a standard piece of equipment in many vehicles. The service is also available for subscription via an app.

Digital Audio

Another competitor to satellite and terrestrial radio is streaming or online radio, where radio signals are digitized and then available via mobile or laptop devices. Many traditional, land-based stations offer simultaneous signals on the Web, while other stations have been created solely online. Today, there are thousands of streaming radio stations, and 60 percent of persons 12 years of age and older listen to radio online in an average week. Those people spend, on average, 15 hours 12 minutes tuned in.[4] The ongoing popularity of streaming audio is due to two factors: ease of use via digital devices and the ability to stream stations through voice assistants such as Google Home or Amazon Echo.

In addition to local stations that stream digitally, there are several significant *pure-play* digital audio offerings. The largest is Pandora, which about one-quarter of the 12+ population say they have listened to in the past month, followed by Spotify (also one in four listening monthly).[5] Others in this space include Apple Music, iHeartRadio, and Amazon Music, all of whom are seeing continued growth in audiences and, as a result, ad dollars. Together, digital audio is estimated to be approaching about one-third of radio ad dollars. As with other digital media forms, the audio offering can enhance creativity in how brands reach consumers. In Italy, pasta company Barilla developed eight music playlists on Spotify that people could listen to while cooking their pasta. Each combined a popular genre of music with a pasta shape.

One slightly less commercialized form of digital audio is the podcast. These are audio programs or series that people can download and listen to whenever they want. They may be developed as podcasts or be rebroadcasts of content that has already aired. It is estimated that more than one in three (37 percent) listen to a podcast each month.[6] The average number of podcasts that people listen to is six per week, but most do not come with traditional radio commercials. Instead, advertisers can sponsor them and will often have the podcast narrator read the copy, giving the listener the feeling that there is an implied endorsement of the product. The amount invested here is growing rapidly, with nearly $800,000 spent on the medium in the United States in 2020, according to eMarketer.

Buying Local Radio

While buying local radio is similar in many respects to buying local television (explained in Chapter 5), there are two opportunities for advertisers that are commonly made available in the audio medium. The first is merchandising and promotions. This has become an extremely important consideration for many companies that use spot radio, particularly national advertisers. Local radio stations may be willing, as part of the deal, to run special contests for listeners, allow sponsorship of a commercial-free hour, set up a remote site broadcast, or hold a special event for the trade, for example. The Scion car dealership could offer a new car as the grand prize in an on-air contest, the afternoon music show could be aired from the dealer's showroom, or a cocktail reception for all new Scion owners could be held at the radio station one evening. Such promotions need to be negotiated as part of the buy, but they may add considerably to the efficiency of the purchase.

The second difference that local radio can offer advertisers is the chance for live commercials. In the earliest days of radio, all commercials were spoken live by announcers on the air. Today, this is only possible at the local market level. As noted above for podcasts, some believe that having a local radio personality deliver the message adds greater authority and integrity to the product. While the advertiser may have to pay a premium for this, and even though the station never officially endorses any individual brand, it can be beneficial because of the DJ's credibility in that market. In addition, because relatively few commercials are presented this way anymore, it offers another way to stand out from the crowd. The standard commercial length in local radio used to be 60 seconds, but today, with audience attention decreasing, there is a greater use of 30-second radio ads.

When buyers work with local rep firms in radio, they will send out an *avail* request that includes markets and dayparts; the two sides will then negotiate based on an overall cost per point and typically go back and forth to agree on terms, often focusing on the share of the buy being given to a specific station in a market.

In contrast to local TV, radio has historically been considered more of a lifestyle medium thanks to stations offering content based on format. That has made it easier in some ways for radio to make a transition to an audience-based, digitally driven world since they had been more audience focused and their content migrated online earlier. Today, stations are taking the additional information they have learned about their digital listeners and applying it to their traditional broadcasts.

Buying Digital Audio

While the digital version of a magazine or newspaper is often negotiated into the print buy, digital audio is usually handled separately from terrestrial. Advertisers can buy digital impressions on radio station websites. But the greater interest is in the pure-play digital audio companies such as Pandora or Spotify. Audio buyers at larger agencies will typically buy any digital audio inventory that is not programmatic. Some radio stations are pushing for all audio measurement to move the way of digital and be based on impressions.

Considerations for Radio Advertising

Radio uses the same principal term as television for planning and buying purposes. You purchase time based on audience ratings. The main difference here is that the rating is based on a time period rather than on a program. For the most part, you plan radio by dayparts, although it is possible, for an additional cost, to specify selected, narrower time periods. For example, if you operate a number of McDonald's franchises and only want to advertise in the hour before lunch (which technically falls in morning drive), you could request the noon to 1:00 p.m. hour; most stations will sell that time to you, although perhaps at a premium.

Radio audiences are measured by Nielsen Audio and reported on a quarter-hour basis, so you can look at the average quarter-hour (AQH) rating for each station in a market. This is the average number of people listening to an individual station for at least 5 minutes within the quarter-hour period, expressed as a percentage.

The radio market can be defined (and measured) in several ways. In addition to the standard measure of the DMA, a smaller geography for radio is the *total survey area*, which consists of the metropolitan area plus outlying additional counties that listen to the major metro stations. In Chicago, the total survey area would not only include the Chicago metropolitan area but the rest of Cook, Lake, and DuPage counties, which can also receive Chicago radio station signals. The most narrowly defined measure is the *metro survey area*. This is defined by the government and includes the city and surrounding counties that are closely linked economically to the central city area.

The total radio listening figure is provided in the persons using radio (PUR) measure, which is equivalent to TV's PUT number. This tells you what percentage of a given audience listens to radio at a particular time. Another measure to consider is the *time spent listening*, or TSL. This gives an indication of how much time people are spending with an individual station in a daypart, day, or week. The calculation is as follows:

$$TSL = \frac{\text{Number of quarter-hours in daypart} \times AQH}{\text{Total Listening } (\textit{Audience})}$$

The more time people spend listening to that particular station, the greater the chance of reaching them with your message. On the other hand, if your goal is to reach as many *different* people as possible, then the TSL may be of less concern.

Two more radio-specific measures are the *cume rating*, which is the total number of people listening to a particular daypart, expressed as a percentage, and the audience *turnover*, which is the ratio of total number of people listening to a particular station in a daypart to the average number listening to that station in a quarter-hour. If the turnover is high, meaning that people don't listen to the station for very long at any one time, then that would suggest you would need to air your ad fairly frequently to reach more people.

Radio audience measurement occurs in two ways. Historically, it relied on samples of people in each market to complete a seven-day listening diary; in the 1990s, a new methodology was developed to collect radio listening activity passively. The portable people meter, or PPM, has been the currency measurement in more than 50 markets. The PPM is a pager-size device, soon to become a wearable watch, worn by a sample of about 70,000 people wherever they go during the day. The meter passively picks up inaudible codes that have been inserted within the radio signals. These codes are used to identify which station was being listened to, by whom, and for how long. In effect, the PPM measures *listening* activity and does so with far greater accuracy for radio than the listening diary, which requires people to actively remember and write down everything they were tuned to. The technology can collect codes from anywhere, including television, sports arenas, or retail stores. The data collected can also be used to monitor the duplication of audiences to TV, radio, and digital media, providing person-level information that can be applied to household-level set-top boxes or digital media.

For digital audio, whether the streamed version of terrestrial radio or the pure-play content from Pandora or Spotify, audiences are measured in terms of impressions served. The digital pure-play streams are still not included in radio's currency measurement, but as more media channels shift to digital impressions, it seems likely that the industry will move to "total audio" measurement.

Benefits of Radio to Advertisers

As an advertiser, you cannot afford to ignore the many benefits of radio advertising. Although it does not offer the visual power of television advertising, it does provide the opportunity to reach targeted audiences frequently and at a reasonable cost. These and other benefits of this medium are discussed here.

Local Appeal

As mentioned earlier, most advertising dollars in radio are spent at the local or regional level rather than on the networks. Radio is therefore listened to primarily as a local medium, allowing you the opportunity to connect to local events, news, or celebrities. According to one survey, nearly half (46 percent) of those who listen to AM/FM radio said they had considered a new company, product, or service after hearing a radio ad.[7] It also plays a critical role during natural disasters, when people turn to local radio stations for news and weather updates. The local appeal also includes the on-air personalities with whom listeners build a relationship. In some ways, these radio hosts are an early version of influencers!

Format-Driven Audience

Because of the way radio stations are formatted, the medium provides you with targeted, specific audiences. If you run a local health club, you can reach women aged between 25 to 54 by placing your message on light rock stations. As the owner of a religious bookstore, you can promote your store by advertising on the local religious radio station. Radio also offers good opportunities for reaching diverse ethnic groups. In areas with sizable Black or Hispanic populations, you are likely to find at least one station that appeals to each of these audiences. It will generally have a very loyal following. For a baby-clothing manufacturer, for example, advertising to Hispanics may turn out to be very profitable because they tend to have larger families than non-Hispanic households. And with digital audio, the opportunities to reach even more defined targets based on the type of content is even greater. Those who are listening to classical music on Pandora, for example, could be assumed to be older and hence targeted with more ads for life insurance or over-the-counter medications than the people who are listening to rap music, where one would expect them to be younger and more urban, meaning ads for electronics or fashion retailers might be more appropriate.

Imagery Transfer

For many advertisers, radio is seen as a secondary medium, used in conjunction with a major digital or television campaign. The good news here is that research has shown the power of radio ads to create a visual image in listeners' minds from the TV commercials they have seen for that same brand.[8] This process, known as imagery transfer, gives radio ads far more impact than the auditory stimulus alone and, therefore, greater potential influence on consumer response.

Keeping Costs Down

Compared with television, radio is an extremely inexpensive ad medium. A 30-second spot in prime time on a broadcast TV network may cost more than $600,000, while the price for that same length commercial on a local radio station could be as low as a few hundred dollars. Of course, these costs are linked to the number of people you will be reaching. For digital audio, the costs are based on the number of digital impressions, but still are affordable compared to other types of digital.

Frequency Builder

With a TV buy, you are usually looking for high reach numbers. In order to gain frequency, you need either a very large budget or inexpensive dayparts. On radio, however, because the costs are so low, it is practical to buy a lot of time and build up frequency against your target audience. It also makes sense to do this for strategic reasons; people tend to listen to a particular station for a fairly brief period of time, so you want to ensure you reach them while they are listening. You should keep in mind that listening habits are not seasonal, so frequency can be built up year-round.

Radio and ROI

Research shows that radio provides a strong return on the advertiser's investment. In a large-scale study that linked the ad exposure of 40,000 Nielsen panel members to their expenditures across six major categories, the results showed that for every $1 spent on radio, the advertiser would get more than $6 back in additional sales.[9] In the United Kingdom, the industry group supporting commercial radio, Radiocentre, reported on a study of more than 500 radio campaigns that demonstrated for every £1 spent on radio, the advertiser received a seven-times greater return.[10]

Flexible Messages

Compared to the high production costs and long lead times of television, radio is extremely flexible. If your ad is read live on the air, as is often the case, you can change the message at very short notice without much difficulty. You can vary the ad creative for different dayparts or station formats, perhaps changing the music backgrounds depending on the type of music played on that station. With digital audio, as noted previously, ads can be distributed dynamically in the same way as other digital formats. For all types of radio, there is the flexibility of tie-ins to local retailers or other promotional opportunities, such as local contests or events.

Drawbacks of Radio Advertising

In addition to the numerous benefits of radio advertising, there are a few drawbacks to keep in mind as well. Each of these can be seen as a challenge; most can be overcome with some planning and creativity.

In the Background

When we listen to the radio, we are usually doing something else at the same time, making it a background medium. Ads on radio must therefore work a lot harder to grab—and keep—our attention.

Sound Only

Radio in its terrestrial form can only offer sound, rather than the sight and motion of television or digital video. However, the medium can still be used to great effect because it offers the possibility of inspiring the listener's imagination. You can hear the waves crashing against rocks, breaking glass, or party chatter and conjure up images in your mind of what the scene looks like. Radio advertisements also tend to feature humor, both as a way to get attention and because the audience is less likely to be distracted by any visuals and can listen to the words. As noted previously, if used in conjunction with similar TV commercials, listeners will often transfer the video images to the radio spot.

Short Message Life

Because we listen to radio in the background, for the most part, ads on this medium have a very short message life. Like TV or digital, and unlike newspapers and magazines, once the ad has aired, the opportunity for exposure has disappeared. This makes it all the more critical to grab the audience's attention right away with a message that is relevant, involving, and interesting.

Fragmentation

One drawback for radio is the fragmentation of the medium. We no longer just have rock stations; we have active rock, classic rock, and album-oriented rock formats, among others. Each one appeals to slightly different kinds of people, so if you wanted to reach them all, you would have to buy each type of rock station in a market. Audience shares, particularly in major markets, may be very small, which makes it harder to use the medium as a reach vehicle. With pure-play digital audio such as Pandora and Spotify, each listener is effectively creating their own station that plays the specific artists or type of music that he or she prefers. Advertisers then need to rely on digital targeting approaches to effectively reach the right listeners.

Research on Radio

Although radio is considered a "second cousin" to other media, research has been done to compare the channel, particularly to television and digital media. In addition, the power of sound, and of music in particular, has been studied to see how that impacts radio ad effectiveness.[11]

All the News That's Fit to Print: Newspapers

Newspapers are one of the oldest media forms in this country and perhaps one of the most troubled in the early part of the 21st century. They were one of the earliest media to accept advertising. In fact, the first advertising agencies were established to handle the purchase of space in this medium. Some of the earliest ads were for "medicinal" remedies, such as Lydia Pinkham's Compound.

In contrast to many other countries that have national newspapers, the majority of newspapers in the United States are written for and distributed primarily to a local audience. As a result, most of the advertising is placed on a market-by-market basis. You can also choose which section of the paper the ad will appear in, such as news (local, national or international), sports, entertainment, business, fashion, food, home, and travel, among others.

There are more than 2,000 newspapers published in the United States. This figure includes both weekday and Sunday editions. That number has remained relatively stable over time. In 1970, for example, there were 2,334 papers published. Newspaper audiences are measured in terms of *circulation*, or the number of people who subscribe to or purchase the newspaper. Exhibit 6.4 shows the top ten papers across the country based on their circulation.

The past decade has witnessed a significant decline in the percentage of the adult population that says they read a printed paper. Currently, about 15 percent claim they do so daily, in contrast to the 78 percent who read a paper back in 1970. What is perhaps more worrying for the newspaper industry is that the readership figure is even lower among younger people, who constitute the medium's future readers (among 18- to 34-year-olds, only 8 percent

Exhibit 6.4 Top Ten Daily Newspapers by Circulation

Rank	Newspaper	Total Average Circulation (in Thousands)
1	USA Today	970,030
2	Wall Street Journal	894,176
3	New York Times	861,267
4	Los Angeles Times	660,116
5	New York Post	480,970
6	Chicago Tribune	438,228
7	Boston Globe	387,312
8	Minneapolis Star Tribune	342,959
9	The Washington Post	320,576
10	The Philadelphia Inquirer	278,717

Source: Alliance for Audited Media, Q1 2021. Total circulation includes print, digital replica, and digital non-replica editions. Figures do not include affiliated publications of the main title. Quarterly data as filed with the Alliance for Audited Media, subject to audit.

read a daily paper). The future looks brighter for the digital versions. About 45 percent of all adults say they have read or looked into the digital edition of a newspaper; among 18- to 34-year-olds, that rises to more than half (53 percent).[12] Some newspapers have attempted to adapt their content to be more appealing to younger readers. The *Wall Street Journal*, for example, launched a monthly digital magazine called *Noted*. However, the venture did not appear too successful, and quickly moved to a more practical "how-to" content that might attract people of all ages.[13]

Circulation, especially at large newspapers, continues to decline. From 2016 to 2020, the total number of readers for the country's ten largest weekday and Sunday papers fell about 30 percent.[14] What is keeping circulation from falling further are the digital editions of the paper. Among the top newspapers, these generate an increasing proportion of the total circulation, although the newspaper companies are not recouping lost print revenues from digital sales.

An added problem the industry faces is the demise of the two-newspaper town. Most large cities used to have at least two competing newspapers; today, due to the high costs of running a newspaper, this is the exception rather than the rule. Only in the largest cities (New York, Los Angeles, Chicago) are there still two or more daily papers. This not only harms the newspaper industry, but it is not particularly good news for advertisers either. Without competition, the paper can set its advertising rates wherever it wants them, as long as it can still compete with other media alternatives.

A more recent trend in U.S. newspaper ownership has seen wealthy Americans buying up local newspapers to help them survive. One of the first to do so was Jeff Bezos, founder of Amazon, who bought *The Washington Post* in 2013. That alone will not save the industry. In 2020, a report from the University of North Carolina at Chapel Hill stated more than 25 percent of U.S. newspapers had gone out of business since 2005.[15] As major cities dropped competing papers, some of the readership moved to suburban or weekly newspapers. The focus of these titles is far more local, writing about high school sports scores or local ordinances rather than national or regional news. During the COVID-19 pandemic, it was college newspapers that found themselves on the frontlines of reporting.[16] Some small towns have supported the creation of a digital news outlet to fill the need for local news as traditional daily papers either go out of business or are greatly reduced in size and scope.[17] For advertisers, local papers offer the opportunity to bring the message down to the truly local level. National advertisers such as Gap stores can announce the opening of a new store in Arlington Heights, Illinois, in the *Arlington Heights Post* instead of in a zoned or regional edition of the *Chicago Tribune*.

As noted earlier, the one bright spot for newspapers is growth in their digital readership. All newspapers have a digital version, and many have tried to make money from that audience by charging readers to read the stories digitally.

In 2020, digital subscriptions to newspapers in the U.S. grew by 36 percent, reaching more than 11 million people. It is expected that in 2021, newspaper revenues from these subscribers will surpass $1 billion. A leading indicator is that in the second quarter of 2020, *The New York Times* reported it generated higher revenues from digital subscribers than from print, for the first time.

Social media platforms have become an increasingly important destination for news content. According to a Pew Research study conducted in mid-2020, at least half of all U.S. adults said that they got their news from social media *often* or *sometimes*.[18] This became a contentious topic during the 2020 presidential election, with concerns over the amount of misinformation being spread through these channels.

How newspapers manage their digital content may be starting to change. In 2021, the Australian print conglomerate, News Corporation, claiming that they should receive payment for having their content appear on the major digital platforms, helped support legislation to make that happen. The News Media Bargaining Code encourages digital companies to negotiate fair agreements with media companies. As a result, Facebook agreed to new terms with News Corp.

Newspaper Advertising Revenue

Total newspaper ad revenue continues to fall (in line with the drop in overall readership). In 2020, it was about $4.7 billion, down by one-third since 2017. The COVID-19 pandemic hit newspapers especially hard, seeing a 42 percent drop in ad revenue between the second quarter of 2019 and a year later.[19] The largest categories of advertisers now are retail, financial, and telecom. This includes large companies—from major national department stores like Macy's and Nordstrom to regional banks such as Fifth Third or First National to local stores for T-Mobile or Verizon.

The other type of newspaper advertising is that which is placed on a national basis so that it appears in all (or most) papers across the country. This type of advertising represents about one-quarter (24 percent) of total advertising revenues for the medium, despite the efforts of many newspapers to position themselves as valuable national vehicles in the face of increased competition with other local media, such as spot TV and radio, regional magazines, or billboards. The main problem that advertisers have with using newspapers on a national basis is the considerable premium that it costs to run their ads in all markets. Most are reluctant to pay that premium, which can cost up to 75 percent more than a local or regional ad.

Digital advertising revenues are growing. They account for about four in ten (42 percent) of the total, with forecasts that by 2022 they will be more than half of newspaper ad dollars. Increasingly, advertisers are choosing to put their messages solely in the digital version, known as *pure-play digital* similar to digital audio or connected TV. One of the unintended consequences of advertisers moving to the digital format is that it enables them to be more selective about the context of their messages. The concept of brand safety was developed to ensure that ads for Mazda or Citibank did not appear next to deceptive or unpleasant content. During the COVID-19 pandemic, many marketers became particularly sensitive to that topic, leading them to block their ads from the topic, which exacerbated the drop in ad revenues for digital news providers.

Newspapers also offer a medium within a medium, in the form of *pre-print inserts*, sometimes known as *free-standing inserts* or FSIs. These are pre-printed sheets that are usually distributed within the Sunday paper and often include coupons. However, with the decline in printed copies, the funding for the FSIs that came from the manufacturers shifted into digital channels. Consumers are more likely to seek out coupons on specific websites (e.g., coupons. com or fatwallet.com), or get them via their mobile phones for the products they want.

Newspaper advertisers used to have to consider an invisible "sacred" line between the advertising and editorial departments. Today, with native advertising or sponsored content, there really is much less obvious distinction between what content has been produced or paid for by the advertiser and what the editorial staff of the paper has developed.

Buying Newspapers

The purchase process for newspapers is as follows. First, the buyer must analyze all possible newspapers available based upon an advertiser's geographic criteria such as DMA, markets, or zip codes, while also taking into account factors such as the newspaper's circulation, coverage, waste (distribution outside the advertiser's areas or audiences of greatest interest), audience composition, and zoning options (the ability to customize ads to different areas of the paper's coverage area or only appear in selected editions). The newspaper buyer will typically only handle the print portion of the buy (which includes the digital replica that a newspaper's subscriber can access online). Digital buys are usually handled by the digital programmatic team.

As newspaper publishers experienced a drastic reduction in advertising revenues, they have been increasing their ad rates. Today, if an advertiser decreases its spend in a newspaper it is more likely to see a higher increase in cost than in prior years; publishers are now resetting their pricing based on actual spend rather than looking back at an advertiser's historical spend. They are also looking to bring ad rates to parity across advertisers based upon spend or frequency. Consolidation of ownership within the newspaper industry and newspapers ceasing operations due to COVID-19 has meant that there are now fewer titles or publishers for buyers to negotiate with, reducing their leverage further.

Nonetheless, the buyer must still negotiate with each newspaper to obtain the best rate. Newspapers are typically purchased as standard ad unit sizes, or SAUs; although the size of the newspaper itself may vary, its ad sizes are standardized. Sizes such as full-page, half-page, quarter-page, are examples of SAUs. Buying SAUs has allowed buyers to move to a cost per thousand (CPM) negotiation model, which allows for more consistent comparisons across publications and media channels.

The newspaper buyer will usually want to specify where in the paper the ad will appear—an ad for Hidden Valley salad dressing in the food section, an ad for Universal Studios' latest movie in the entertainment section, and an Ethan Allen furniture store ad in the home section. Sometimes, that decision is made based on what the target audience is more likely to read, so an ad for Verizon cellular phone service might appear in the business section to reach professionals who are more likely to be interested in that item. Advertisers have become warier of appearing in the Main News section of a paper, not wanting to inadvertently be placed next to controversial topics.

The agency will issue a newspaper authorization to the client that sets out all of the specifications for the campaign, such as publication list, ad type (ROP or pre-printed insert), whether it will be black and white or color (run of press), page count (pre-printed insert), and any special instructions. Then all the details must be confirmed, including the insertion dates, space and material closing dates, ad size, negotiated net flat rate, insertion order and production contact information, and desired position in the newspaper. This is done for every newspaper in which the ad will appear. After the buyer receives advertiser approval, the buy is made by executing insertion orders to the publications. Follow up to obtain complete acceptance of the insertion orders from the publications is critical to ensuring a successful campaign run.

Considerations for Newspaper Advertising

In looking at individual markets, the media specialist needs to have a clear understanding of the product's distribution within those areas. Is it available primarily within certain parts of the market, or DMA? Is it found more in the metro area or the suburbs? Are there any major ethnic areas of the market that could play a role in product or media usage?

Once you have determined which markets to use, the media specialist looks at the number of copies distributed, or the newspaper *circulation*. This figure is used to compare one paper with another. Circulation is often broken out into counties or city zones, depending on the size of the market. While one newspaper might have a larger overall circulation, another might deliver more readers in the particular zone where your retail outlet is located and therefore be a more appropriate vehicle to use.

The *coverage* number, also called the *newspaper penetration*, is the print equivalent of a TV rating. That is, it shows the percentage of households reached by a given newspaper. As with the circulation figure, the numbers might look different depending on how the coverage is defined. Taking Boston as an example, if you only consider the overall market, or DMA household penetration, you might choose the *Boston Globe*, but if you are interested in reaching singles or African Americans, the *Boston Herald* has greater coverage.

Last but not least, newspaper *readership* figures provide more detailed information about the paper's readers according to standard demographic breaks or, where available, product usage data. This helps the media specialist find out, for example, what proportion of the readership is aged between 18 to 49 years or how many readers are working women. One newspaper may reach more men than women or younger adults more than older ones. As noted earlier, a critical consideration for newspaper advertisers today is to look at what proportion of readership is digital.

Benefits of Newspapers to Advertisers

Although newspapers have struggled in recent years, they continue to offer several benefits to advertisers, including wide reach, timeliness, desirable audiences, editorial impact, and local or regional possibilities.

Wide Reach

As Exhibit 6.4 illustrated, the top ten newspapers in the United States reach more than five and a half million consumers every day. Nearly half (45 percent) say they have read a digital newspaper in the past month.[20] Add to that the circulations of the other, smaller newspapers in the country, and you'll begin to see just what kind of exposure is possible with newspaper advertisements.

Timeliness

During the stock market crash of 2008, ads appeared in many newspapers each day, reassuring consumers and stockholders that everything was still all right at financial institutions. In 2018, amidst all the news stories about the U.S. opioid addiction crisis, Purdue Pharma, which makes and distributes OxyContin, one of the drugs cited as part of the problem, took out full-page ads in major U.S. newspapers reinforcing their corporate commitment to helping solve the prescription drug crisis.

Unlike magazines or even television, newspapers are by their very nature filled with news. People turn to them for the latest information on products, prices, and availability. The role that newspaper advertisements play in purchase decisions may be critical. A Canadian study conducted on behalf of that country's newspapers found that newspapers play a vital role throughout the purchase process and more so when the actual item is bought.[21]

In addition, electronic scanner devices in most supermarkets and retail stores can assess the link between advertising and sales more directly and rapidly. Data suggest that newspaper ads can triple the sales volume for items that are advertised at reduced prices.

Desirable Audience

In the battle to attract advertisers, newspapers can offer highly desirable audiences. A newspaper reader is more likely to be better educated, have a higher income, and be more involved in upscale activities than non-readers. People with higher household incomes are more likely to be newspaper readers. This is true for both the print edition and the digitally distributed content. Exhibit 6.5 gives a profile of the newspaper audience, comparing print and digital editions.

In contrast to other media, readers spend a considerable amount of time with the newspaper, with readers of *The New York Times* taking, on average, about 43 minutes with each issue and more than an hour (62 minutes) with the Sunday edition.[22]

Another consequence of the time readers spend with the paper is that it offers the media specialist more opportunity to provide detailed information. If you are trying to sell a new home equity loan program, you need the space to provide details on the terms of the deal, as well as on bank locations so interested consumers can find you. While you might worry that so much fine print will be boring or encourage page-turning, those people who are in your target audience

Exhibit 6.5 Profile of the Newspaper Reader

Read Printed Copy	Read Digital Copy
More likely to be ...	More likely to be ...
Graduated college/postgraduate	Graduated college/postgraduate
Age 55+	Age 18–54
Household income $250,000+	Household income $250,000+
Live in North East or Midwest	Live in West
County size C (more suburban)	County size A (more urban)
Lived at present address 5+ years	Asian
Boomer generation	Gen Z or Millennial generations
Retired/not employed	Working full-time

Source: 2020 Doublebase MRI-Simmons.

will probably be interested enough to read through the entire ad (assuming the copy is inviting and attention-grabbing).

Impact of Editorial Context

An obvious advantage of newspaper advertising is that you can choose which section of the paper or website your ad is placed in, putting food ads in the food section or offering investment advice in business content, for example. This effectively narrows your reach to those consumers most likely to be interested in your product or service.

Local and Regional Possibilities

Although advertisers are reluctant to use newspapers on a national basis, they rely on them heavily for local or regional marketing. If Unilever wishes to test a new shampoo in Peoria, Illinois, it can advertise in the *Peoria Journal Star* and feel confident that the message will only reach those people able to buy the product, thereby creating awareness for the new item. They might also test the effects of advertising on sales this way. For regional operators, such as Friendly Restaurants—located only in the eastern part of the country—ads can be placed in newspapers in the selected markets where the restaurant is found.

Even within a market, an advertiser can buy space in only those papers being sold in a certain area. The *Chicago Tribune*, for example, offers eight different zones to advertisers within the Chicago area.

Drawbacks of Newspaper Advertising

As with every medium, newspapers have several drawbacks. The three most critical are short issue life, the challenge of grabbing the readers' attention, and the constraints of using a largely black and white medium.

Today or Never

While magazines can often prolong their issue life and reach more people by being passed around or picked up on several occasions, at the end of each day, the printed newspaper is usually discarded. If the reader misses your ad that day, you are not given a second chance. So, although printed newspapers are available every day, their issue life is very short. This is less of a drawback for digital editions, where the ads are delivered in near-real-time and can therefore remain timely.

Active Readers

The issue life of the newspaper is closely linked to how people read it. Although more than half of all pages are likely to be opened, it is up to the reader to actively choose what to look at. If your headline doesn't attract the readers' attention, they won't look at it at all; if the copy isn't intriguing and relevant, readers can simply turn to another article or piece of content. It is crucial that newspaper advertisements get the readers' attention. Today, there are so many distractions for consumers, and they are now used to taking full control over all their media behaviors.

Black and White

In the 1980s, it was rare to find a color ad in a newspaper. Then along came Gannett's national newspaper, *USA Today*, which offered full-color capabilities. The quality of newspaper color reproduction has been improving ever since, although it is still a long way from looking as sharp as the digital image. Even so, newspapers charge a premium for the use of color, generally about 17 percent extra for a one-page four-color ad. For many advertisers, particularly those who wish to show "lifelike" qualities, such as food manufacturers, it remains more effective to use magazine, television, or digital ads. Newspapers have become increasingly creative, however, to attract advertisers, offering "glow in the dark" or scented ad pages within the paper or attention-getting features surrounding the paper when it is delivered. For the digital editions, the color is prominent and of the same quality as all digital ads.

Research on Newspapers

While the amount of research on newspapers has been fairly static in recent years, there appears to be an upswing in interest in the role of newspapers, in a world where fake news has damaged the reputation of social media. Academic research has examined the impact of ad size on consumer responses, as well as the economics of increasing costs but declining readership.[23]

Magazines: An Explosion of Choice

Although magazines have a long history in the United States, with the earliest publications appearing in the middle of the 18th century, they are also a medium that may be said to have had two very distinct life stages. Originally, most magazines catered to a very general audience, offering a mixture of news, stories, and features aimed either at the total population or, in the case of titles such as *Ladies' Home Journal* and *Good Housekeeping*, at women. The strength of publications such as *Life*, *Look*, and the *Saturday Evening Post* is reflected in the fact that an ad placed in those magazines in the 1950s would be likely to reach about 60 percent of the total population.

But with the rise of television in the 1950s, general interest magazines found they could not compete effectively either for advertising dollars or for readers. Rather than simply disappearing, magazines began to move toward greater specialization in their targeting and their editorial content. This trend continues today, with extremely narrowly focused magazines devoted to topics such as tropical fish (*Tropical Fish Hobbyist*), cross-stitching (*Just Cross Stitch*), or aircraft (*Plane & Pilot Magazine*). And while there are still some general offerings, such as *Atlantic Monthly* or the *New Yorker*, their readership is considerably smaller than the audience of their general interest forebears. Because of this increased specialization, there are today 7,216 different consumer magazines available, most of which also have digital editions. In 2020, despite the economic downturn due to the COVID-19 pandemic, 60 new titles were introduced.

Magazines Today

While magazines have grown more specialized over time, the medium reaches a broad range of the population. Indeed, 91 percent of all adults say they read magazines in the previous six months, reading on average about nine issues in a month.

There are three main types of magazines available: consumer, farm, and business-to-business. Consumer magazines are usually categorized according to their editorial content, such as business, men's, women's, sports, news, and entertainment. This category includes titles enjoyed by all segments of the population, from *Time* to *Sports Illustrated* to *Cosmopolitan*. Farm magazines are geared toward that particular industry. Some may be crop-specific, such as *Corn & Soybean Digest*, while others deal with the technical aspects of agriculture. The third type, business-to-business, covers all titles aimed at the industrial user, everything from *Chemical Age* to *Hotel Business* to *Information Week*.

Taken together, magazines account for 6 percent of all ad dollars spent in the United States. Most magazines are considered as national vehicles for advertising, although city or regional publications are also classified within the consumer segment, such as *Milwaukee* or *Southern Living*. Many national magazines offer geographic breakouts of their circulation, allowing an advertiser to place a message that will, for example, only reach southerners or people who live in the northeastern states or in the Los Angeles metropolitan area. They also offer demographic "splits" so that Fidelity Investments can advertise its mutual funds in the edition of *Bloomberg's Business Week* that is read by people earning $75,000 or more per year.

Magazines are sold in one of two ways—at the newsstand or by subscription. For most titles, it is the latter that generates the most sales, accounting for over 95 percent of total magazine copies sold. As with newspapers, magazines are assessed in terms of their circulation (number of copies distributed) and audience (number of people who read the circulated copies). Today's top ten magazines in terms of audience size are shown in Exhibit 6.6.

Digital is the brightest spot for magazine companies. About 7 percent of all adults say they only read the digital version of a magazine, but among those aged between 18 and 24, the figure is over 11 percent. There is clearly an audience for digital magazines, although currently digital versions of magazines account for about 2 percent of total circulation. Compared to the print version, readers of the digital edition spend about the same time with the latter (52 minutes versus 49 minutes on average).[24]

Magazines have taken advantage of the growth of digital consumption and devised many creative ways to attract both audiences and advertisers. That includes inserting QR codes in ads that can be activated by mobile phones, making the ads shoppable with direct links to e-commerce sites to buy what you see in the digitally viewed magazine, or bringing content (and ads) to voice-assistant devices, such as food tips from *Allrecipes* on Google Home or entertainment updates from *People* magazine on Amazon's Alexa.

Similar to audio, publishers have become more data-driven, taking their knowledge learned from their digital readers and using it to enhance their overall offering. Indeed, magazines have an advantage here, in that they are largely subscription-based, which provides them with valuable basic information (name and address) about their readers that can be combined with other data to enhance their ad offerings.

Exhibit 6.6 Top Ten Magazines by Audience (Print + Digital)

Rank	Title	Audience
1	AARP The Magazine	36,104,000
2	People	27,472,000
3	Better Homes & Gardens	25,571,000
4	National Geographic	25,532,000
5	Time	13,681,000
6	Good Housekeeping	13,229,000
7	Southern Living	12,654,000
8	Sports Illustrated	12,189,000
9	Food Network Magazine	11,483,000
10	Woman's Day	11,363,000

Source: Alliance for Audited Media, Magazine Media 360, December 2020.

Another growth area for magazines is in events and experiences. This helps move a magazine from being a printed publication to being seen as a brand in its own right. *Food & Wine* magazine is known for the Aspen Food & Wine Festival, while *Vanity Fair* has become synonymous with awards parties. During the COVID-19 pandemic, several magazines successfully pivoted to virtual versions of these experiences. *Vogue* magazine moved its Forces of Fashion event fully online, while its publisher, Conde Nast, sponsored a virtual prom for high school seniors who had lost that rite of passage.

Taking this approach one step further, and in an effort to stem circulation declines, publishers have been testing new models of subscription that are promoted to consumers as memberships, with different tiers of content or access. *Oprah Magazine*, for example, has its Oprah Insider membership, which not only includes the print publication, but also early access to exclusive digital content, and an opportunity to watch a livestream event with Oprah and Gayle King.

Buying Magazines

It is fairly common in many smaller or midsize advertising agencies for media planners to be responsible for magazine buys, although at larger agencies there is usually a specialized staff of print buyers who focus solely on the negotiations. Magazines used to only work off a *rate card*, listing the cost of buying various page sizes with or without color or other special features. Additional charges were also made for preferred positions, such as the inside front or back covers and the back cover itself, which are believed to be read by more people.

While the extra costs remain, today's magazine buys require negotiating. That is, the rate card is usually the starting point, but then it is up to the media specialist and the magazine's representative (or rep) to discuss the final cost for the client. Discounts may be offered for volume buys if, for example, the client purchases ads in multiple issues, buys several pages in one issue, or, given how consolidated the industry has become, buys space in several magazines owned by the same publisher. The standard ad size in magazines is the one-page, four-color (full-color) and bleed, meaning the ad goes to the edge of the page (P4CB).

The cost of a magazine ad will depend on the size and nature of the magazine's readership. Obviously, you will pay more to reach more people. It would cost you about $731,000 for one full-page, four-color ad in *Better Homes and Gardens*, which reaches about 9.7 percent of the adult population, whereas the same ad placed in *Allrecipes*, which reaches 2.6 percent, will cost only $137,000.

At the other end of the spectrum, however, you may also have to pay more to reach a highly specialized audience. Although both *Taste of Home* and *Food Network* magazine have similar-sized audiences of around 10 million, the one-page ad will cost $60,000 in the former and $109,000 in the latter because it is assumed that the more practical material of articles and recipes is reaching a more interested, involved audience that is more likely to pay attention to the ads in that publication. There have been research studies both supporting and rejecting this hypothesis, with the dissenters claiming that if the reader is more involved in the subject matter, he or she is in fact *less* likely to pay attention to the ads. For the media specialist, the main focus should be on the suitability of each individual magazine to the media objectives and how efficiently and effectively each vehicle can be used.

When the magazine space is negotiated, the specialist will usually request certain positioning preferences. As noted, for some of these a premium must be paid. Aside from covers, the specialist may want a Hellman's mayonnaise ad, for example, placed near or within the food editorial or a Cover Girl cosmetics ad to appear in the beauty section of the magazine. Sometimes it is enough to simply request that the ad is in the first third of the issue, under the assumption that those far forward pages are more likely to be seen, although research from magazine publishers indicates that ads are noted and consumers say they have taken subsequent action regardless of which quartile of the publication the ad appeared in.[25] The power of contextual relevance for magazines is as important online as it is in print. That is, if you are reading the latest on a celebrity such as Kim Kardashian or Jennifer Aniston, it is likely you will be more interested in seeing ads for Kylie Skincare or Aveeno. Buyers will take this into consideration when placing ads in digital magazine content.

The willingness and ability of the magazine to fulfill these kinds of requests will vary depending on who the client is and how many ad pages it needs to fill. One of the important things to remember about magazines is that, unlike TV or radio, which have a finite amount of airtime, printed media (including newspapers) can simply add pages if they can attract enough additional advertisers.

In addition to the practice of magazines negotiating off the rate card, many publications also offer further benefits to their advertisers. These might include special promotions, bonus circulation, digital ads, or trade deals. While these may be offered at little or no extra charge, the cost is built into the amount the specialist pays for the ad pages. These extras reflect the extremely competitive media landscape, with an increasingly fragmented marketplace not only within the magazine industry, but also across different media. *Good Housekeeping* not only competes with the other women's titles (such as *Better Homes and Gardens*, and *Real Simple*), but it must also fight for dollars with television, radio, newspapers, outdoor billboards, and social platforms—the list is almost endless.

Once the magazine space has been agreed on, including the price of special features and positioning, it is time to make the actual buy. At larger agencies, this is accomplished through an insertion order, which sets out the terms of the contract to which both parties must agree. Some clients may like to see this first, to be sure they know what they are getting. If everyone accepts these terms, the media specialist can go ahead and place the order for the buy.

Considerations for Magazine Advertising

In today's print world, the main focus for media specialists is the *audience*, indicating the total number of people who read an average issue of a particular magazine. It includes both the primary readers who subscribe to or bought an issue of the magazine, as well as the secondary readers (sometimes called the *passalong* audience) who read an issue that someone else in their household bought, or that they saw in a public place such as a doctor's office.

The print term for a rating is typically referred to as *coverage*. It tells you the proportion of a given target group that saw (were "covered" by) the publication in the past month (or whatever is the relevant publication period). To determine how well a publication will reach your particular audience in terms of how concentrated its audience is with a particular target group, the media specialist looks at a publication's *composition*. If you are advertising a backpack designed for trekking through the rainforest, it would be important to know what proportion of the readers of *National Geographic Traveler* and *Travel + Leisure* are planning to go to Latin America or Asia, for example. While the one-page cost or the CPM may be cheaper in *National Geographic Traveler* than in *Travel & Leisure*, you may reach more prospective tourists in *Travel + Leisure*, making the cost of reaching 1,000 of *those* individuals less expensive.

Another key measure is how many copies of the magazine are distributed for each issue. This *circulation* number is provided by the magazine itself in an audit report or can be obtained from the Alliance for Audited Media, the premier U.S. source for circulation data. The media specialist should also find out what proportion of that figure is *controlled*—that is, distributed free of charge to potentially interested parties. They are usually not the main target audience for the publication and, therefore, would be less interested in seeing the ads that appear. In addition, the *net paid* circulation figure shows the number of copies sold at no less than half of the basic newsstand or subscription price. Circulation is usually broken out by geographic area, which can be very helpful, particularly for products that have regional skews.

The growth of digital copies of magazines created the need for a new measure. That "total readership" measurement across all platforms shows that more than half (52 percent) of total monthly magazine readership occurs only via a digital platform (desktop or laptop, mobile, or digital video).[26]

One last key measure of a publication's health is its *rate base*. This is the guaranteed average circulation on which prices are based, indicating how many copies the publisher guarantees the advertiser he will sell. Although the advertiser does not get anything back if that number is not reached, a magazine that consistently fails to meet its rate base is probably one to be avoided. In addition to reporting circulation, the Alliance for Audited Media discloses how many times in the past six months or one year the publisher has not met the guaranteed audience.

Benefits of Magazines to Advertisers

To an advertiser, three of the most attractive qualities of magazines are their high-end audiences, the enthusiasm of those audiences, and the long issue life of the medium.

Upscale and Niche Audiences

One of the incentives to using magazines for your advertising message is the favorable demographic profile of magazine readers. Similar to newspaper readers, the heaviest user of this medium is in the age range of between 18 to 44 years, has a college education and a household income over $75,000, and is employed in a professional or managerial job. At the same time, given the fragmented and targeted nature of magazine titles, they are able to reach a variety of audiences, from youth to multicultural segments to people at different life stages (parents, seniors, etc.).

Getting Engagement

Another benefit of placing ads in magazines is reader involvement. While this concept is rather difficult to define (and even harder to measure), it generally refers to the interest that the reader has in the material, both editorial and advertising. Since most magazines today focus on a particular subject or interest, they can tie in more readily with the personal needs and lifestyles of the audience, enabling advertisers to do so as well. In this way, automakers can target car enthusiasts or prospective buyers in *Car and Driver* or *Road and Track*; detergent manufacturers can promote their new or improved products in magazines aimed at homemakers (*Better Homes and Gardens*, *Good Housekeeping*, *Real Simple*), while financial services companies can offer their mutual funds to interested investors in *Fortune* or *Fast Company*.

Consumers also seem less resistant to seeing ads in magazines. One study conducted in 2019 found that respondents were more likely to pay attention to or notice the magazine ads relative to websites or TV and similarly said they had greater trust in magazine advertising compared to those other media. These findings are in part due to the fact that, as a reader, you get to select what ads you read, whereas television ads are embedded in the programming. Digital advertising is seen, by most users, as mere "clutter" on the screen.

Hanging Around

Another important and unique feature of magazines is their *long issue life.* While the television program is over in half an hour and the newspaper is thrown out after one day, you will probably keep a monthly magazine in your home for four weeks or longer. This not only helps to reach more of your audience, with opportunities for additional or repeat exposures to the advertising, but it is also likely that other people, known as the *secondary audience,* may see the issue, too.

Drawbacks of Magazine Advertising

Magazines do have their drawbacks. Among the most significant obstacles to keep in mind is the considerable lead time necessary and the move from print to digital readership.

Long Planning Cycle

For most printed publications, ads have to be completed and at the printer well in advance of their publishing date, a factor known as the *lead time.* This makes it difficult for advertisers to create particularly timely or newsworthy ads such as those seen in newspapers. The closing date for a monthly magazine is typically two months prior to the date it goes on sale. With digital editions, these drawbacks are partially overcome because the ads can change very quickly and there are numerous types of ad units available, including video.

Digital Downsizing

As more of the magazine readership moves to a digital platform, advertisers are shifting their traditional print dollars to digital. While some of that spending may still be with magazine content, it is all too easy to be attracted by the notion of reaching those same kinds of audiences wherever they are found, via display or video ads on platforms such as Facebook and YouTube. As a result, many print publications have lost so much circulation and ad revenue that they have either reduced their publication frequency (*Time, Sports Illustrated,* and *Men's Journal*) or stopped the print version altogether (*Teen Vogue* and *Playboy*).

Research on Magazines

Studies on magazines as a medium have focused on similar areas as broadcast research. The value of the context in which an ad is seen was found, by Norris and Colman, to impact consumer recall and recognition of the ad. The same topic was explored further by Yi to see what happened when readers were given additional information prior to seeing the magazine ad in its context. More recently, researchers have looked at ways to enhance consumers' attention to magazine ads.[27] Meanwhile, the magazine industry has itself sponsored several studies showing the impact of magazines on sales.[28]

Out-of-Home: From Billboards to Everywhere Advertising

There are some in the outdoor industry who like to claim that billboards are the oldest medium in existence. They date it back to Egyptian times, when hieroglyphics were written on roadside stones to give people directions to the nearest town or village. Whether you agree with that or not, outdoor billboards are certainly well established, having been in the United States since the 1800s. At that time, companies began leasing space on boards for bills to be pasted (hence the term *billboard*). There are two main types of billboards: posters and bulletins. Posters come in several sizes; they can be identified by the frame around them. Posters are found mostly in populated areas in or near cities and towns. Bulletins are larger boards situated along highways and major roads. Nearly half (45 percent) of the $4.1 billion spent on out-of-home advertising goes to billboards.

Putting messages on outdoor boards used to be extremely labor-intensive. The sheets that made up each poster were pasted onto the board, and bulletins were hand painted. Both were created either at the board site or at a central location within the market or region. Since this had to be done in each market, differences resulted in how the message appeared from one market to another (and even one site to another within the market). Today, poster messages are created electronically and then shipped either in one piece or in sections to the board site. Bulletins may occasionally be hand painted, but computers make sure that the finished product looks identical across boards. Today, bulletins are mostly created using other materials, such as lithography or special stretch vinyl. Increasingly, the message is delivered digitally and in rotation with several ads on one board. There are about 9,600 digital billboards available today. Overall, digital out-of-home accounts for about one in five (18 percent) of the media channel's expenditure.

In the past 75 years, the industry has come under criticism from environmentalists who claim that the boards are a blight on the scenery. Many cities and several states have introduced bans on putting up new boards and, in certain cases, demanded the removal of existing structures. You won't see any billboards in Hawaii or Vermont, for example.

Unlike other media that have editorial material too, outdoor billboards exist solely for advertising messages. They are primarily a local medium, bought on a market-by-market basis, but they are used by both national and local advertisers. The type of business using the medium has changed considerably in the past 30 years. For many years, the biggest category of advertiser was the tobacco industry, but in 1999, legislation banned advertising tobacco messages on any outdoor billboards. This not only had a significant impact on the tobacco industry, but it freed up many high-profile and well-positioned billboards across the country for other advertisers who had never been able to buy that space because the tobacco companies had long-term deals with the billboard companies. Today, you are far more likely to see billboards from local retailers, the travel industry, or healthcare providers than you would have even five years ago. Exhibit 6.7 shows the top categories that spend on outdoor advertising.

The outdoor industry has moved far beyond billboards and become an *out-of-home* (OOH) industry instead. The reason for that is simple. Ads are now prevalent in many places outside, from bus shelters and subways to "street furniture" such as newsstands or benches or kiosks. There are always new ideas for where to place an out-of-home message. As a result of the COVID-19 pandemic, many businesses installed hand sanitizers; ad messages are starting to appear on those. Indeed, the out-of-home industry, while suffering like other media during economic downturns, does tend to bounce back sooner because as soon as people resume their normal activities and are moving around outside, companies return to outdoor advertising to reach them.

For many years, outdoor billboard audiences were calculated from manual traffic counts conducted by each system operator of how many cars passed by a given billboard, multiplied by government statistics on how many people were present in the average car. That became the estimated audience viewing a billboard. Today, Geopath, the out-of-home industry's organization, oversees

Exhibit 6.7 Top Outdoor Advertising Categories in 2020

Rank	Category	Dollars in Thousands
1	Beauty, health, and medical services	$411,916.5
2	Miscellaneous services	$259,729.9
3	National restaurants	$235,070.4
4	Financial products and services	$182,299.1
5	Resorts and travel accommodation	$173,302.6
6	Government (non-political)	$159,424.7
7	Amusements and events	$157,974.1
8	Television and cable television	$149,894.6
9	Home and building services	$128,306.8
10	Food and beverage retailers	$122,167.9

Source: Kantar Media, 2021.

a range of more sophisticated audience measurement that combines circulation counts with visibility research, demographics, and reach/frequency calculations. They have enhanced their capabilities for the industry to provide advertisers with a better way to understand not just where potential target audiences are located, but how they move around a city or state.[29] Anonymous location data from phones and cars are used to track who is actually passing by which board or sign. All of these data are combined through statistical modeling techniques into a system that can provide estimated audiences to the ads on every outdoor board across the country.[30] In 2021, a new out-of-home measurement system was proposed by the U.S. outdoor trade association, with a lesser standard for ads of "opportunity to see" rather than "likelihood to see."

As noted previously, outdoor billboards are increasingly digital. They offer advertisers the opportunity to create messages that can change by the touch of a button from a central location, altering the ad based on conditions outside, for example, or simply to create a more engaging environment. These boards also allow the outdoor company to sell ads to multiple marketers at one time, with different messages appearing in rotation on the same site. The targeting for digital out-of-home is more sophisticated than the traditional billboard, using location data collected from mobile phones, for example, or delivering messages based on the behaviors of the desired audience. Anheuser-Busch placed billboard ads in several cities with real-time trackers that displayed the proportion of adults in each location that had received the COVID-19 vaccine.[31] Indeed, the digital element even allows marketers to send personalized messages. Mini Cooper, for example, created a promotion that involved sending owners of the vehicle a special key fob. After the recipients answered a few questions on a special website, when they drove by specially enhanced outdoor billboards, individual messages would appear on the sign, such as "Motor on Jim!"[32]

The biggest outdoor advertising location in the United States is in Times Square in New York City. Before the COVID-19 pandemic shut down tourism, an estimated 340,000 people were going through there each day and spending on average 81 minutes in that location, of which one-tenth (8 minutes) was spent looking at the vast array of billboards. The added appeal for advertisers, and one reason why they are willing to spend over $1 million per year to place their messages in this location, is that the median age of the Times Square visitor is young, at 32, and more than half are likely to post about their visit to a social media channel, helping the advertisers earn additional impressions.[33]

Buying The Great Outdoors

Because outdoor billboards are bought on a market-by-market basis, the buying process is, in some ways, akin to local TV and radio buying. Here, instead of dealing with individual TV or radio stations (or rep firms that put stations together into a network), the media buyer must either work with individual outdoor plant operators or with networks of plants that are available through large outdoor companies such as Clear Channel, JC Decaux, or Outfront Media.

The primary factor in negotiations for outdoor billboards is location. While cost and poster size matter too, advertisers care most about where their messages will appear. Different boards are purchased for different time frames, with posters typically being sold on a 30-day basis and bulletins sold in much longer-term deals, such as six months or one year.

For certain products, such as a local restaurant, you might want to be on smaller posters in the city to remind people of your address; for hotels or gas stations, highways would make more sense, to reach drivers as they are passing through the area. And today, many advertisers place their billboards strategically close to their competitors' locations. CVS, for example, looks for boards that are near its key competitor, Walgreens, reminding consumers as they get close to Walgreens why they might want to reconsider that decision.

It is important, too, to know which side of the street the board is located (in the U.S., the right side is preferable) and whether there are any potential blockages that could get in the line of sight for the board, such as a tall building or tree. This kind of information can best be gained by actually going to the location to look at the board. The operator can provide a complete inventory of addresses for both bulletins and poster panels. In the case of posters, the buyer can also find out if the poster is in an ethnic neighborhood and/or in a restricted location (no alcohol) and whether it is on a wall or a pole.

While billboards used to be bought by *showing*, or the number of daily exposures on the number of boards to generate the desired reach, today outdoor advertising is purchased based on ratings, similar to other media, with costs based on the CPM. Once all of the negotiations have taken place, and the units have been chosen, the buyer should request that the specific locations are mapped to verify that they are properly distributed throughout the market, and that there is no duplicate coverage of boards (or posters) that are within sight of each other. After that, the media specialist will issue an outdoor authorization, confirming all of the details, or specifications, of the buy. These are then confirmed with the client and the seller, and the purchase can proceed.

With digital out-of-home, the ads can be bought programmatically, either directly with a billboard company or through a programmatic exchange. More on programmatic buying is covered in Chapter 7.

Benefits of Out-of-Home Advertising to Advertisers

The advantages of billboards and other forms of outdoor advertising have contributed to the medium's popularity over the past two centuries. Four of the most consistent and important benefits are size, mobility, diversity, and message reinforcement. Each of these advantages is discussed next.

Big Is Better

The size of the poster or bulletin means that outdoor advertising gets noticed. In fact, at a typical busy location in the center of a city, more than 10,000 people are likely to pass a poster within a given month. In addition, the message is there constantly, for 12 to 24 hours (and many are illuminated at night).

Mobility

Outdoor messages can be placed in many locations, not just on streets and highways. The out-of-home category is extremely broad, allowing advertisers to reach their target in specific locations or during specific activities. You could place ads for Samsonite luggage aimed at business executives at airports to catch them when they travel or advertise Chiquita bananas near the Kroger supermarket where your target audience shops. Additionally, mobile technology allows advertisers to send geo-targeted or contextual messages to people as they move within the vicinity of an outdoor panel.

Diversity

With out-of-home advertising, you can tailor your message to members of a particular ethnic group using their own language or cultural attributes yet still reach a mass audience within a specific market. You can buy billboards or transit ads in areas with heavy concentrations of Hispanic, Chinese, or Korean people, for example, reaching them where they live, work, and shop. Moreover, it is valuable to be able to reach non-native English speakers in their first language, whatever language that might be.

Reinforcing the Message

Out-of-home advertising is a good supplementary medium, helping to add reach and frequency to a media schedule at a reasonable cost. A fairly typical outdoor billboard buy could reach over 80 percent of adults in a given area in a month. In addition, the fact that the out-of-home message can be there all the time means that frequency builds up and the message can be a constant reminder. The ability to locate out-of-home messages in shopping areas helps to reinforce the message very close to the point of purchase.

Drawbacks of Out-of-Home Advertising

In considering what part of your advertising budget to commit to out-of-home advertising, you will need to keep in mind the two drawbacks of the medium: short exposure time and the potential for criticism from environmentalists.

Brief Message Exposure

Since the average outdoor message is only seen for between 3 and 7 seconds, the copy needs to be extremely concise and compelling. For products that need a lot of explanation, outdoor is clearly not the right medium. One way to gauge whether there is too much copy on a billboard is to estimate how quickly people are going to pass by it. You can try the exercise yourself and see how much of the message you can take in as you drive or walk by. Because most of the viewing is done at high speed, especially for bulletins situated along the highway, the advertisement must also be eye-catching and interesting enough to attract the driver's (or passenger's) attention.

Environmental Criticism

The outdoor industry, as noted earlier, has come under criticism for cluttering up the environment. This is felt in two ways. First, there is the literal problem of boards covering up the natural landscape. Second, there is the metaphorical "clutter" of forcing people to be exposed to brand messages that, some believe, simply add to human insecurities or anxieties, making them want products and services.[34] While this is a long-standing argument against advertising as a whole, the point about outdoor advertising is that there is no escape from it. Advertisers might shy away from the medium to avoid legal or ethical disputes, especially in areas with a recent history of environmental controversies.

Research on Out-of-Home Advertising

The outdoor industry has not been an extensively researched mass medium. Studies have focused mostly on proving that the medium works, as shown by Fortenberry and McGoldrick who explored how outdoor helps enhance not just awareness but also customer retention. Page et al. used Bluetooth technology to validate the reach of outdoor ads. [35] One study in the Netherlands looked at what factors enhance recognition of outdoor ads, while another examined the impact of crowds on people's attention to out-of-home ads. More information on how the medium has been researched can be found on the website of the Outdoor Advertising Association of America (www.oaaa.org).

Summary

There are numerous paid media opportunities with audio, print, and out-of-home channels. It is helpful to understand both traditional and digital options of each one, from AM/FM radio, printed magazines and newspapers, and billboards to pure-play digital audio and podcasts, to digital print and digital billboards. It is critical to know how consumers use each media channel, and how to include them in media plans and buys. Understanding the key terms and considerations used in planning and buying, such as time spent listening for audio, circulation for print, and "eyes-on" for out-of-home, will make it easier to include them in client recommendations. Knowledge of the individual benefits and drawbacks of the various options, such as radio's format-driven audience, print media's desirable audience, or outdoor's mobility and diversity, will help determine whether—and to what extent—each should be included in the final plan.

Notes

1   The Infinite Dial, 2020, Edison Research & Triton Digital.
2   Nielsen Total Audience Report, Q2 2020.
3   Nielsen Audio Today, Q2 2019.
4   The Infinite Dial, 2020, Triton Digital/Edison Research.
5   The Infinite Dial, 2020, Triton Digital/Edison Research.
6   The Infinite Dial 2020, Edison Research & Triton Digital.
7   "Radio: Live On-Air and Everywhere," NPR and Edison Research, April 2021.
8   Imagery Transfer Study conducted by Statistical Research, Inc., 1999; Radio (re) Discovered by Nielsen Audio, 2017.
9   Nielsen Audio, Radio (re)Discovered, June 2016.
10 Radio: The ROI Multiplier Report, Radiocentre 2020. https://www.radiocentre.org/why-use-radio/the-roles-for-radio/radio-for-growing-roi/.
11 Emma Rodero, "Do Your Ads Talk Too Fast To Your Audio Audience? How Speech Rates of Audio Commercials Influence Cognitive and Physiological Outcomes," *Journal of Advertising Research*, September 2020, 60 (3), 337–349. James H. Leigh, "Information Processing Differences Among Broadcast Media: Review and Suggestions for Research," *Journal of Advertising*, vol. 20, no. 2, June 1991, 71–76. Darryl W. Miller and Lawrence J. Marks, "Mental Imagery and Sound Effects in Radio Commercials," *Journal of Advertising*, vol. 21, no. 4, December 1992, 83–94.
12 2020 Doublebase, MRI-Simmons.
13 "At The Journal, A Battle Rages Over the Future," Edmund Lee, *The New York Times*, April 11, 2021, Sunday Business, pp 1, 6–7.
14 Turvill, William. October 22, 2020. https://www.pressgazette.co.uk/top-ten-us-news paper-circulations-biggest-print-titles-have-lost-30-of-sales-since-2016-election/.
15 "Who Is Going to Save Newspapers? Billionaires Dip Their Money in Ink," Nicholas Kulish, *The New York Times*, April 11, 2021, Sunday Business, pp 1, 7.
16 Izadi, Elahe. College newspaper reporters are the journalism heroes for the pandemic era," retrieved from www.washingtonpost.com, September 19, 2020.
17 "A City's Push To Restore Local News It Had Lost," Katherine Q. Seelye, *The New York Times*, June 21, 2021, B1/B5.
18 Shearer, Eliza, and Amy Mitchell. January 12, 2021. https://www.journalism.org/2021/01/12/news-use-across-social-media-platforms-in-2020/.
19 "Coronavirus-Driven Downturn Hits Newspapers Hard as TV News Thrives," Michael Barthel, Katerina Eva Mats, and Kirsten Worden, as reported on www.pewresearch.org, October 29, 2020.
20 MRI-Simmons, Doublebase 2020.

21   Newspapers Canada, 2013 Report: Newspapers Drive Purchase Decisions, as reported on Newspaper Association of America website, naa.org.

22   2020 Doublebase GfK MRI.

23   Avery M. Abernathy, "The Information Content of Newspaper Advertising," *Journal of Current Issues and Research in Advertising*, vol. 14, no. 2, Fall 1992, 63–68. Adithya Pattabhiramaiah, S. Sriram, and Shrihari Sridhar, "Rising Prices Under Declining Preferences: The Case of the U.S. Print Newspaper Industry," *Marketing Science*, https://pubsonline.informs.org/doi/10.1287/mksc.2017.1060, November 2017.

24   MPA Magazine Media Factbook 2017/2018.

25   Magazine Media Factbook, 2020.

26   Magazine Publishers of America, Magazine Factbook 2020.

27   Safaa Adil, Sophie Lacoste-Badie, and Olivia Droulers, "Face Presence and Gaze Direction in Print Advertisements: How They Influence Consumer Responses—An Eye-Tracking Study," *Journal of Advertising Research*, vol. 58, no. 4, December 2018, 443–455. Thorsten Teichert, Dirk Hardeck, Yong Liu, and Rohit Trivedi, "How to Implement Informational and Emotional Appeals in Print Advertisements: A Framework for Choosing Ad Appeals Based on Advertisers' Objectives and Targeted Demographics," *Journal of Advertising Research*, September 2018, 58 (3), 363–379. Claire E. Norris and Andrew M. Colman, "Context Effects on Recall and Recognition of Magazine Advertisements," *Journal of Advertising*, vol. 21, no. 3, September 1992, 37–46. Youjae Yi, "Contextual Priming Effects in Print Advertisements: The Moderating Role of Prior Knowledge," *Journal of Advertising*, vol. 22, no. 1, March 1993, 1–10. Yunjae Cheong, John D. Leckenby, and Tim Eakin, "Evaluating the Multivariate Beta Binomial Distribution for Estimating Magazine and Internet Exposure Frequency Distributions," *Journal of Advertising*, vol. 40, no. 1, Spring 2011, 7–24. Gergey Nyilasy, Karen Whitehill King, Leonard Reid, and Scott C. McDonald, "Checking the Pulse of Print Media: Fifty Years of Newspaper and Magazine Advertising Research," *Journal of Advertising*, vol. 51, no. 1, Supplement, March 2011, 167–181.

28   Association for Magazine Media website, www.magazine.org.

29   Geopath Standards and Best Practices Document, November 2019.

30   https://geopath.org/geekout/#research.

31   "AB InBev Erects Billbobards Tracking Nation's Vaccination Progress," E.J. Schultz, as seen on www.adage.com, June 10, 2021.

32   Buzz Awards 2008, Special Advertising section in *Mediaweek*, B10.

33   Robert Klara, "Eyeballs of the World," Adweek, September 25, 2017, 8.

34   Neal Lawson, "Assaulted in Broad Daylight," *The Guardian Weekly*, April 27, 2012.

35   John L. Fortenberry, Jr., and Peter J. McGoldrick, "Do Billboard Advertisements Drive Customer Retention? Expanding the 'AIDA' Model to 'AIDAR'," *Journal of Advertising Research*, June 2020 60 (2), 135–147. Bill Page, Zachary Anesbury, Sophia Moshakis, and Alicia Grasby, "Measuring Audience Reach of Outdoor Advertisements: Using Bluetooth Technology to Validate Measurement," *Journal of Advertising Research*, December 2018, 58 (4), 456–463. Mukesh Bhargava, Naveen Donthu, and Rosanne Caron, "Improving the Effectiveness of Outdoor Advertising: Lessons from a Study of 282 Campaigns," *Journal of Advertising Research*, vol. 34, no. 2, March/April 1994, 46–55. Lex Van Meurs and Mary Aristoff, "Split-Second Recognition: What Makes Outdoor Advertising Work?" *Journal of Advertising Research*, vol. 49, no. 1, March 2009, 82–92. Charles R. Taylor,

George R. Franke, and Hae-Kyong Bang, "Use and Effectiveness of Billboards: Perspectives from Selective-Perception Theory and Retail-Gravity Models," *Journal of Advertising*, vol. 35, no. 4, Winter 2006, 21–34. Rick T. Wilson and Taewon Suh, "Advertising to the Masses: The Effects of Crowding on the Attention to Place-based Advertising," *International Journal of Advertising*, vol. 37, no. 3, 2018, 402–420. George R. Franke and Charles R. Taylor, "Public Perceptions of Billboards: A Meta-Analysis," *Journal of Advertising*, vol. 46, no. 3, July–September 2017, 395–410.

Chapter 7

Planning and Buying for Digital

Learning Outcomes: In this chapter you will learn how to:

- Differentiate the various forms of paid digital channels
- Understand how each one is planned and bought
- Compare and contrast the benefits and disadvantages offered by paid digital

Digital Paid Media: Multiple Choices

It is increasingly hard to remember (or imagine) life without the internet. Internet penetration rose faster than any other medium (or appliance), reaching the critical mass of 50 million users in 5 short years (it took radio 36 years to get to that point). Today, more than nine in ten (91 percent) of the U.S. can access the Web from home, and more than half (52 percent) spend two or more hours a day online.[1] The vast majority (90 percent) of those going online from home do so at high speed through broadband technology, giving them easier and faster access to everything available.[2] All of this makes digital media highly valued by advertisers. There are four paid forms of digital advertising that will be covered in this chapter: digital display, digital video, search, and social media.

The internet was first devised as a means of communication for the academic community 50 years ago. It was a fairly arcane and complex system, relying on a lot of computer language and processing. The hypertext markup language (HTML) that formed the basis of the Web is now seamlessly (and invisibly) connected to everything we do online. That was not the case originally. It was not until the late 1990s that the internet came to be seen as a genuine medium (as opposed to computer tool) that offered users far greater control than with any other existing medium. More than any other media, you select exactly where you want to go and what you want to see. You choose where to click and how long to stay there. At the same time, your digital movement has been tracked at every step, capturing each site you visit or app that you use by placing special software, known as *cookies*, on users' computers or phones to

DOI: 10.4324/9781003175704-7

monitor the path that they take while browsing different sites. This information proved invaluable in the development of digital media for advertising. Ad revenues grew rapidly; by 2020, according to eMarketer, display advertising alone had reached $78 billion, while all paid digital ad dollars totaled $142 billion.[3]

One of the most important and appealing aspects of digital advertising is its targeting capabilities. In addition to placing ads where certain types of consumers are likely to go (e.g., international travel sites for affluent consumers), advertisers can target based on where you have been online, a practice known as *behavioral targeting*. Privacy advocates have objected to this practice, and rules introduced in Europe in 2018 known as the General Data Protection Regulation (GDPR) made websites gain the consent of site visitors more explicitly to have their online movements tracked. In this way, it was designed to help protect people's personal data, giving them the "right to be forgotten." It set forth rules on how personal data is collected and processed in the European Union, but given the global nature of the internet, it effectively impacted all countries. This made it harder for advertisers to send a more relevant and, therefore, likely effective message based on tracking the cookies. If you have visited kayak.com or tripadvisor.com and looked into visiting Bali, then Samsonite or Travelpro could target you either on those sites, when you return, or on other sites you visit.

Two years after GDPR was first passed, the state of California introduced its own privacy regulation, the California Consumer Protection Act (CCPA), with the similar intent of giving people more control over their data.

The next step in the process is the removal of cookies altogether. First announced by Google in 2020, this will be fully implemented by 2023. It will no longer allow any cookies on its Chrome browser. Other browser companies made similar announcements, including Apple (Safari) and Mozilla (Firefox). While this is considered good news for consumers, it leaves marketers needing to create other ways to target audiences digitally. Indeed, the prospect of a *cookieless world* will likely, in the end, create new approaches as advertisers seek to deliver the right message to the right audience at the right time. Brands may return to more contextual digital targeting (such as food brands in food content), or they could try to collect more information directly from their customers, with explicit requests for people to opt in to provide that data for marketing purposes.

With that as background, now let's look at the different kinds of paid digital media channels.

Digital Display

At first, Web ads consisted of banners—the digital equivalent of billboards—that did little more than display a brand name or teaser and a link to another site (hence the term *display*). Companies began using Web advertising for brand-building purposes rather than simply offering information. Before long, the ability to purchase via the Web became mainstream rather than exceptional. Today, about one-third of the world's population has purchased at least once during the past year, going as high as 80 percent in Denmark or the UK.[4] Advertisers started to get more creative with display ads, changing the size of the ad messages and incorporating (as technology advanced) sound, motion, and interactivity, a phenomenon known as *rich media*. Not surprisingly, the research findings showed that these kinds of ads had a greater impact (recall, awareness) than the plain-vanilla banners. But it became more and more clear that as fast as advertisers moved to surprise consumers, those consumers became increasingly disenchanted with Web ads.

Today, when most consumers are asked about digital advertising, their responses are primarily irritation. They talk about the clutter of websites, the irrelevance of most ads that appear, and their techniques for avoiding them. In particular, annoyance with ads that pop up, or pop under, a website is considerable. More and more consumers are installing ad blockers—software that prevents ads from loading. It is estimated that, globally, about 30 percent of Web users do so. According to GWI, 33 percent of people in Italy use ad blockers to stop ads from being displayed, while in Indonesia, such blockers are used by 55 percent of the population.[5] At the same time, if an ad appears on the Web that is relevant and informative, consumers will click on it to find out more. One study in 2019 examined ways to reduce ad blocking by exploring the main drivers for consumers to use them.[6] For many, the line between the editorial material and the advertising is a narrow one, which is viewed by most people as an information cornucopia.

One of the ways that advertisers have tried to improve the digital ad experience for consumers is through technology. *Programmatic advertising* involves using the power of software to determine where best to reach the desired targets digitally and direct ads to them on the sites they visit. It is estimated that in the United States, this accounts for 85 percent of all display spending in 2020.[7] How programmatic buys are made is explained further later in this chapter.

Display ads have been standardized by the Interactive Advertising Bureau into specific sizes and shapes so that advertisers can develop creative ads that works across sites. Nonetheless, advertisers continue to test out new formats in an ongoing effort to communicate with their audiences without annoying them so much that they close the ad and ignore the message.

Digital Video

As more marketers embraced digital ads, it was not surprising that they started to deploy video. At first, these were 15- or 30-second video commercials often transferred directly from television. Today, in recognition that consumers had become less and less likely to watch that long of an ad when online, there are more 6-second digital video ads. The digital video ads mostly appear before the content runs (known as *pre-roll* ads). With longer video content, such as 30-minute TV shows, there may also be *mid-roll* ads during the program or even *post-roll* ads afterward. Research has been conducted to demonstrate the immediate, short-term impact of ads seen prior to or during digital video, with some studies suggesting that online video ads are 38 percent more memorable than the comparable ad on TV. Another study examined the impact of ad customization on brand impact for digital video ads.[8]

Digital video is not simply a consumer phenomenon, however. Companies use it for other reasons. Westinghouse's website features "how-to" videos on greener portable power, while Pantene posts YouTube videos on its website about haircare. The hardware store Home Depot uses online videos to help people learn how to do home improvements, showing the full range of products available while also providing guidance to the DIYers who shop in their stores. Increasingly, however, consumers will turn to YouTube for any brand's videos, where they can see not only the official videos posted by a company, but also user-generated content talking about the same products or services.

In 2020, Comscore reported that 267 million Americans watched videos online in an average month, watching about 594 videos. The average U.S. digital viewer was watching more than 43 hours of video per month.[9] According to Nielsen, time spent watching digital video is still fairly small relative to the hours spent watching TV on a regular set. In the second quarter of 2020, in an average week, the weekly time viewing digital video (computer and mobile) was 4 hours 16 minutes, compared to 29 hours per week watching live TV or time-shifted TV.[10] But digital video viewing will keep growing rapidly, especially given the fact that among 18–34-year-olds their time spent watching digital video is more than half the time they spend watching live TV (about 6 hours per week with digital video and 10 hours with television).

As noted above, it is impossible to discuss online videos without mentioning YouTube. This global phenomenon, which started as a way for people to share videos with each other, is estimated today to have been seen by about one-fourth of the world's population. In the United States, two-thirds of the population (65 percent) have gone to the site. A staggering 500 hours of content are said to be uploaded every minute of every day. The key benefit it offers viewers is that they can search for whatever or whomever they want, whether that is Aunt Betty's New Year's Eve party, clips from last night's *Tonight Show with Jimmy Fallon*, or live streaming sports events. It has rapidly become the destination for online video content. Nielsen notes the prime time for this media form is between noon and 2:00 p.m., suggesting there are a lot of people taking their lunch breaks in front of a digital device. From a research and account-ability standpoint, YouTube provides a trend analysis tool that gives ongoing statistics on how many people are watching each video posted to the site, show-ing the number of views along with likes, shares, and comments. Researchers have also undertaken studies to look at the impact of individual ad campaigns on YouTube, as well as the impact of the popular phenomenon of *unboxing* on that platform.[11]

Digital Search

Perhaps the digital phenomenon with the biggest impact on both consumers' lives and on digital advertising is search. Inspired by sites such as Google, which allow users to type in any word and find out what is available through-out the Web, advertisers started to realize that they could buy keywords or links and deliver ad messages to consumers when they requested those words. So, for example, if you do a search on Google for "fruit drinks" to find out if your fruit-based carbonated drink, Fruitola, is available, at the top of the screen you will see sponsored shopping ads to let you buy the product online through stores such as wholefoods.com or e-commerce sites like Ama-zon.com, followed by text ads from the brand and/or its competitors such as Tropicana or Coca-Cola.

Today, search has become the most popular way for advertisers to reach online consumers. In 2020, advertisers spent an estimated $59 billion on search alone. Google generates more revenue from advertising than magazines, radio, out-of-home, and newspapers combined, estimated at $34.3 billion in 2020. It accounts for six in every ten dollars spent on search advertising in the United States. One of the reasons for the importance of the search for advertisers is that, globally, there are an estimated 3.5 billion daily searches done on Google alone.

Search is a key component for local businesses. Advertisers can ensure that the search results will be linked to the zip code in which the consumer lives. For example, if someone lives in Urbana, Illinois, and does a search for "dog collars," PetSmart can pay to ensure that the listings that result will include information on its store in the 61801 area. Search has also grown on retail sites. Walmart and Amazon, for example, both sell search opportunities as "spon-sored" ads on their websites. If someone types in "furniture cleaner" on ama-zon.com, the first item that comes up is Leather Honey furniture cleaner, with a sponsored ad on the results page.

There are two kinds of search advertising. These are pay per click, or PPC, and search engine optimization (SEO), sometimes referred to as natural or organic search. With paid search, advertisers place bids on keywords that con-sumers type into the search engine. They are paid when those people actually click on their ad. For example, Honda might bid on keywords such as *Toyota*, *SUV*, or *best family car* so that when John Smith is searching for his next vehicle to buy, even if he is thinking about getting a Toyota, he may be curious enough when the Honda ad appears on his search results page that he goes ahead and explores that brand, too.

The benefit of all forms of paid digital marketing is that it has been possible to measure their impact. That is, if someone clicks on the results of a search or the ad that appears before the video she is watching, her subsequent digital behavior can be tracked to see if that action led to a sale. The primary measures for digital ads are the number of impressions delivered, completion rate (for digital video), and *click-through rate* (CTR), or the percentage of people clicking through to the brand website. In this way, paid digital ads can be assessed in terms of their return on investment, or ROI. For every $1 spent on these forms of advertising, how many dollars are returned through increased sales? In one survey, when marketers were asked which digital channels were hardest to measure, search marketing was at the bottom of the list, reflecting the fact that when consumers are searching they are more likely to be considering to buy a product than if they happen to see an ad on social media or in a video.[12]

Beyond the click-through rate, advertisers have other ways to evaluate the impact of digital ads, and in some cases pay based on those results. For example, *cost per click* (CPC) or *cost per acquisition* (CPA) are two measures that allow the advertiser to pay only when consumers click on their message or when a customer signs up for a service or meeting. While the ad cost will be higher than the amount paid for an impression, it represents a more defined outcome from the ad. In addition, advertisers can scrutinize the digital activity further, looking at the *bounce rate*, which shows how many people come to a website but then leave before looking at any other pages or information.

Paid Social

When social media offerings such as Facebook and Twitter were first released, advertisers were not quite sure how to use them. They knew that many consumers quickly adopted them, but today paid social media advertising is a crucial part of digital advertising. In 2020, it accounted for $46 billion of digital ad spend. Facebook (including Instagram, which it owns) accounts for about four in ten digital display ad dollars. On Twitter, companies have created branded emojis in their hashtags that consumers comment on or share (retweet). Coca-Cola, for example, included its branded Coke bottles in the #ShareACoke hashtag and received over 170,000 mentions within the first day it appeared. Other social networks, such as Instagram and Snapchat, which both began without any paid advertising, looked for ways to introduce promotional messaging in ways that consumers will accept. Instagram created a "call to action" button on their video ads so that people could see an ad for a Toyota Prius and then find the nearest dealer, for example. Snapchat introduced sponsorships of animated filters that, for instance, let people turn their faces into Taco Bell tacos. The rapid adoption of TikTok, which enjoyed a nearly ten-times revenue growth in 2020, is just the latest example of a social platform that started out as a place for its users to post their own short videos, and then turned to advertisers to generate revenue.

One of the reasons advertisers flock to social media is because of the time consumers spend on these platforms. According to eMarketer, the average U.S. adult (age 18+) is spending 35 minutes each day on Facebook, followed close behind by TikTok and Twitter, at 33 minutes each.[13] GWI reported that the total time spent per day on social media varies by country, with South Korea at the low end (1:12 hours/day), and Brazil among the highest usage (3:41 hours/day).[14] While social media initially attracted users as a way to communicate with others, it has become an increasingly important destination for entertainment. According to GWI, one-third of people say that is what they are seeking; among younger adults (under 35) that increases to nearly half (45 percent).[15] Applying different strategies based on the type of content people are looking at or the platforms they are using on social media can help advertisers generate greater engagement with their paid social messages.[16]

Today, social media have quickly become more than simply a place for paid media. They are rapidly developing as e-commerce businesses, allowing people to not only look at an item but click to buy it directly from the platform, whether a sweater seen on Instagram or a kitchen utensil on Pinterest.

As we shall see in Chapter 8, the line between paid social and earned social can often be blurry. When consumers share video ads with others via Facebook or Twitter, the advertiser is certainly earning brand impact from paid media, above and beyond the investment (and impact) of the original ad. One example is the practice of Super Bowl advertisers releasing their TV ads online prior to the big game in order to generate buzz, which appears to have an overall positive impact on consumer response.[17] Indeed, advertisers continue to try to find the optimal blend of paid and earned media.[18]

Paid Social Ad Formats

While the power of digital advertising is that it can seem to offer endless creativity, each main platform has developed several standard ad formats. On Facebook, the user will typically see display or video ads appear in their news feed as they scroll through. The brand messages are identified as sponsored, and often allow the user to react (like, comment, and share) or respond (click to website or to buy) immediately. For Instagram, ads can be shown as images or videos, or in a carousel where the user can scroll through, similar to how they scroll through friends' posts. Ads (static or video) are also available while users are scrolling through Instagram Stories, the ephemeral user posts that disappear after 24 hours. When someone clicks on an Instagram ad, they may be redirected to the brand's website where they can learn more about the product, or purchase it. On Twitter, the most basic format is a text ad, which is limited to 280 characters, but users can respond the same way they do to tweets. Video ads, carousels, and polls are also available for advertisers. A more expansive offering for brands is Twitter Live, where marketers can create live announcements for their brands, taking advantage of the news appeal of the platform.

Snapchat offers ads similar to Instagram Stories. Brands can appear in-feed as people scroll through the chats, or as pre-rolls before video content. Some brands create hashtag challenges where users are encouraged to create a hashtag for a brand or topic. Sponsorships on Snapchat may include unique geo-filters or lenses that users can adopt and play with. One area of advertising that Snapchat has taken the lead in is augmented reality (AR), which lets users explore the product more closely as if they were seeing it in person. For instance, they can look at make up or clothing items in different colors or styles, and merge themselves with the product on screen. An estimated 200 million people have tried Snap's AR function.[19]

Other paid social channels, such as Pinterest, LinkedIn, and TikTok, each offer the standard display and video ads, customized for their individual platform. So, Pinterest offers brands promoted pins and featured boards. TikTok offers brand takeovers and branded hashtags. LinkedIn, as a business-oriented channel, includes Lead Generation forms and Conversation ads to enable advertisers to "speak" with the professional target of interest.

Mobile

Although mobile advertising is more about the device on which digital ads are received than a separate media channel, any discussion of paid digital needs to include an understanding of the mobile platform.

There are now more mobile devices than people in the world. In 2020, it was estimated that there are 5.2 billion mobile phone subscribers worldwide, of whom 53 percent have smartphones (with Web access). Globally, mobile phone penetration had reached 63 percent worldwide in 2019, ranging from a high of 83 percent in the United Kingdom and a low of 16 percent in Pakistan.[20]

The introduction of 5G services in 2020 offered higher speed and bandwidth, helping to expand access to and usage of mobile devices for internet access. In several countries, nearly all the time spent online is now done via a mobile phone. The highest level seen is in India, where 94 percent of internet time is on a mobile device. The United States is behind when it comes to smartphone usage during the purchase journey. In Latin America, 59 percent of digital transactions now occur on a mobile device, compared to 47 percent in North America.[21] People not only use the phone to find a store location or search for an item, but they will check prices, research the product, or read reviews before making a purchase. There is an increasing distinction between what people do on a desktop or laptop (work-focused) and their mobile (social media and entertainment), which might impact how they respond to the ads.[22] Understanding consumer motivations for using apps can also help brands be more effective.[23]

Mobile search is increasingly used by consumers, with about one-third of smartphone owners in the United States saying that they do so. The potential is much greater; in Japan, 65 percent use this application on their phone. One of the biggest growth areas in mobile advertising has been advertising on apps since these dominate consumer mobile phone use. According to Comscore, nearly 7 of every 8 minutes of phone usage is taken up with apps. While the average smartphone user downloads about two apps per month, these users spend nearly half of their time on their number one most used app. Meanwhile, tablet users spend almost two-thirds of their time on their number one app.[24] The most popular app categories are social networks (such as Facebook), games (such as Angry Birds or Words with Friends), and radio (such as Spotify or Pandora). This skew toward entertainment and communication should guide advertisers as they figure out how to best deploy their brands' messages. If you are eagerly involved in looking at a Snapchat story or playing against the clock in a game of Jelly, how receptive would you be to a banner ad for McDonald's or a video promoting fall fashions at TJ Maxx? On the other hand, a location-based ad for Olive Garden that appeared in the Snapchat post from your friends or a short video for Pepsi at the end of a tense game might be relevant and appreciated. Researchers have looked at ways to optimize location-based ads. [25]

In 2020, U.S. mobile advertising spend had reached over $100 billion. About eight in ten of those dollars are spent on in-app ads (rather than mobile Web), reflecting the fact noted above that consumers spend most of their time on a mobile device with apps. The vast majority of these ads are either display, video, or search formats.

Tablets are considered a secondary mobile device for advertisers. First introduced to the marketplace in 2010, tablets are now owned by about half (52 percent) of the U.S. population. The category was initially dominated by Apple, with its iPad, but today Android devices have become significant competitors, accounting for nearly half of all tablets sold. While tablet ownership was initially the domain of younger men, the profile has broadened, with a near-even gender split and adoption across all ages.

Perhaps the biggest strategic value of mobile for advertisers is the phone's geo-location data. That is, marketers can target potential customers when they are within the vicinity of a store. Honda can send ads to people known to be in the market for a new vehicle when those phones show up either within, say, 5 miles of the North City Honda dealership in Chicago, Illinois, or when the devices are seen visiting the Toyota Grossinger lot nearby. Burger King took advantage of mobile advertising in a campaign on the Waze mobile app, where they targeted people who passed by a billboard with a Burger King ad, as well as anyone who was looking for competitor fast-food restaurants on that app. The result was an increase in the number of store visits, as well as higher ad recall of those exposed to the ad.[26] With increased concerns over consumer privacy, Apple began requiring all apps to explicitly request consumer authorization to track their location rather than have it be buried in the terms and conditions that appear when users first download the app.

Online Gaming

One of the fastest-growing areas in the digital ecosystem is online gaming. It is estimated that two-thirds (65 percent) of all U.S. homes own one or more devices to play video games. Advertisers now spend about $1.5 billion on ads and sponsorship to reach this growing audience. The COVID-19 pandemic is thought to have expanded the number of online gamers quite significantly, since most live sports were either canceled or delayed for months during 2020. Indeed, the boundary between traditional sports and e-Sports is starting to blur, with the move of the Overwatch League of 20 international virtual teams from YouTube Gaming to Disney-owned television channels ESPN, Disney, and ABC in 2019. Companies such as State Farm Insurance, T-Mobile, and Coca-Cola are all key sponsors, whether through product placement or to offset the cost of the game/event.[27]

Driving a Digital Buy

Today's media specialists have the choice of working directly with individual websites, such as Epicurious.com, or placing buys programmatically, which is a more automated system that relies on real-time bidding. We will explain each in turn, but one key difference from traditional forms of paid media is that digital buys are based on delivering ads to selected and often narrowly defined audiences, and only those individuals, instead of programs or titles where broad groups of people defined only by age and gender (e.g., adults aged between 18 and 49) are likely to turn.

With direct sales, the media buyer negotiates the ad placement (fixed position or rotation) and cost. This type of buy can be based on *behavioral* targeting, where the target audience is defined based on his or her prior digital activity. For example, if you visit Amazon.com on a regular basis to look at the latest kitchen gadgets, then you might be sent an ad from Williams-Sonoma or crateandbarrel.com, because your behavior indicates you have an interest in those items. The benefit for advertisers is that they can find their target audience in places where they might not have expected them to be to find sites that the target considers *contextually relevant*. This may mean relevance to the campaign, such as an ad for Kellogg's Special K cereal that touts its value in a dieting plan on e-diets.com. Or it can be relevance to the target's mindset, such as ads that include JD Power award rankings appearing when a user is clicking on an automotive website searching for information.

In addition, the buyer has to determine with the seller the basis for the sale—cost per thousand impressions, cost per click, or cost per transaction, for example. Research of those who come to the site is often included as a "value-added" bonus, though the drawback here is that it could be biased in favor of the site if they are conducting or hosting the survey. An alternative is to pay for neutral third-party research through companies such as Comscore, Kantar and Nielsen. In either case, the idea is to sample every nth person who comes to the site and offer them a survey that can include questions about advertising recognition or brand attitudes and compare those exposed to the ad to the non-exposed control group.

Today, the vast majority of digital advertising transactions occur *programmatically*, where both buying and selling are done automatically to reach precisely defined target audiences. Data about those potential audiences sit in a data management platform (DMP) that gathers together both the advertiser's own information about its customers (first-party data) as well as other attitudinal, lifestyle, or behavioral information from outside companies (third-party data). The software allows for very rapid slicing and dicing of the DMP data to create audience segments. That data is then accessed by ad exchanges, which aggregate the data and allow buyers to bid on the inventory. Advertisers place bids on different online inventory through their demand-side platforms (DSPs), stating how much they are willing to pay to reach their desired target audiences on various sites. The publisher can then sell that space to the highest bidder. This is all occurring in real time, creating a programmatic marketplace that is akin to a financial stock market.

Programmatic buying has caused huge changes in how ads are bought and sold. Its goal, providing the opportunity to connect the right message to the right consumer at the right time and place, using data and technology, offers advertisers a more efficient and transparent digital ad buying process. More ads are delivered to the target audience, thereby saving money on wasted ad impressions. The costs for using the DMP or DSP or programmatic platform are clearly identified in advance. More than eight in ten display ad dollars are now traded this way, while two in three digital video dollars are. As this marketplace has grown and evolved, there are distinctions in how the trading takes place. Nearly three-quarters of programmatic dollars are spent directly with individual publishers such as Facebook and Amazon, while the remainder go through real-time bidding either in an open marketplace where anyone can bid on the inventory or in a private marketplace where a select number of buyers are invited to bid on inventory from one or a few individual publishers.[28]

Although programmatic buying was born in the digital display arena, it is now implemented across all media channels. Print publishers have created private marketplaces; digital audio such as Spotify or video such as YouTube can be bought in programmatic buys; even digital out-of-home is moving to programmatic buying. As noted in Chapter 5, connected TV is a rapidly growing means for advertisers to reach consumers through digital video. Slightly more than half of the connected TV ads are now purchased programmatically. Other media companies have been gradually automating their technology and processes to facilitate this kind of trading. As digital companies such as Google and Apple, along with regulatory changes, impose greater restrictions on digital tracking of individual consumers, there will likely be changes in the kinds of data used for programmatic buys, but few believe that its growth trajectory will be halted.

Considerations for Digital Advertising

Although the traditional terms of ratings, reach, and frequency are employed for digital campaigns, their meaning differs from other media. Unlike TV or magazines, for example, where the number or percent of the target reached is based on the content in which an ad appears, for digital, the viewers' exposure to a web page may not necessarily be the same as their exposure to the ad on that page. The ads are served when the viewer requests a page, so the more frequently he or she does so, the more opportunities there are for ad exposure. The concept of ad *viewability* is now the norm for digital ads, with the requirement that half or more of a display ad is visible for at least one second, while for video there is a two-second minimum. According to Comscore, 60 percent of digital display ads meet the viewability guideline, while 70 percent of digital video ads do so.

In addition, the ad delivery can be further refined to ensure *brand safety*. There are ongoing industry efforts to eliminate fraudulent impressions from robots

(bots) or other non-human ad views. Measurement companies also help to verify, or validate, the proportion of ads correctly delivered to the desired target group.

Although paid digital ads are delivered to devices, the reach of those ads is in some ways more precise and accurate than for other media because it is possible to measure the outcome of the ad exposure. With search ads on Google, people are directly requesting information (including ads); when they click on the ad, the publisher knows precisely how many digital devices were reached and how many times.

Benefits of Paid Digital Media to Advertisers

As the uses and forms of digital advertising change over time, the benefits of this medium for advertisers are still being explored. Four of the current advantages for paid digital ads are flexibility, targeting, reach, and measurability. Each is examined below.

Flexibility

There are many forms of digital advertising. Unlike other mass media, where choices come down to 15- or 30-second commercials or full-page versus half-page ads, there really is little limit to the imagination when it comes to digital ads. From traditional banner ads to online video to search or social media, paid digital ad messages can appear in numerous forms.

Targeted Messages

The Web is the first mass medium able to offer a targeted, personal advertising message. Although direct response has been doing so for many years, it was not possible for most of their history for TV, radio, newspapers, magazines, or billboards to talk to anything less than a sizable audience. With digital ads, however, brands can send messages to more narrowly defined groups, such as basset hound lovers (those visiting a website devoted to the topic or watching YouTube videos featuring that dog breed), people dealing with weight management issues (those who search on words related to weight control), or those who have "liked" a brand's page on Facebook. It is assumed that such messages, by being more relevant to that individual, are more likely to be accepted and absorbed. The assumption, however, that advertisers should focus more on niche sites to reach their narrowly defined targets has been questioned as it runs the risk of double jeopardy, where brands cannot increase their penetration because they only talk to their current customers. [29]

The ability to deliver messages to consumers when they are in or near specific locations has enormous appeal for advertisers, allowing them to reach the target audience closer to the point of purchase. Advertisers such as Best Buy can deliver ads to any device that is detected within a 5-mile radius of one of their stores, encouraging people to come in now (and perhaps incentivize them further with a mobile coupon). Similarly, Burger King could send digital ads to people who are within range of a Wendy's to let them know how close they are to being able to purchase a Whopper instead of a Wendy's hamburger.

Reach

Although paid digital does not offer as broad a reach as television, campaigns that appear on a range of websites can indeed reach a high proportion of everyone online. In addition, online reach can be reported against specific advertising messages, not just the sites on which those messages appear (i.e., ad exposure, not just opportunity to see).

Measurability

For advertisers, the ability to measure who is doing what on the Web would seem to be answering one of the Holy Grail questions of the industry. But because the measurement is device-based rather than person-based, the measures are not as precise and valuable as they might at first appear. Having said that, digital measurement is certainly far more detailed than for any other paid ad medium, where at best the media specialist can look at opportunities to be exposed to the ad rather than actual viewer, reader, or listener behavior. Starbucks could send Dan Smith a digital ad offering him $0.50 off a coffee if he goes to his nearest store in the next 48 hours. When he presents the offer via his phone, the company can quickly tally just how effective that advertising was. Several advertisers have undertaken cross-media studies of ad impact on the Web compared to other media (using statistical modeling) and found that digital ads are usually more effective at enhancing brand image and consideration than other media types. Initially, paid digital advertising was sold based on *click-throughs* (users clicking on web ads to link to advertisers' sites), but it soon became clear that if digital advertising was to be comparable to other ad media, the cost metric had to be the same. Today, most paid digital ads are priced based on the cost per thousand (CPM) reached. Web measurement services provide data on the demographics and lifestyles of Web users, as well as Web traffic to individual sites and/or ads.

Drawbacks of Paid Digital Advertising

As powerful as digital advertising is, it still cannot provide advertisers with everything they would want to reach their desired targets at an acceptable cost.

Following is a summary of the downside to paid digital advertising, in terms of consumer irritation, brand safety, and non-standard metrics.

Consumer Irritation

The plethora of paid digital advertising is not always appreciated by consumers. Although users have the option to click on an ad to find out more information, there are more and more messages that appear on a site that the user has to actively remove if he or she does not want to look at them. Moreover, since people tend to use digital media to look for specific information or to catch up with friends (rather than passively consuming a TV program or browsing a magazine's pages), the irritation level with the high number of paid ad messages in digital media (display banners, video pre-roll, search ads) can become overwhelming, detracting from the impact of any one particular message.

Brand Safety

During the 2020 U.S. Presidential election, there was a heightened awareness by advertisers of where their ads appeared online. Examples of major brands showing up on websites promoting racial hatred or terrorism lead to companies moving significant media dollars out of sites and apps such as YouTube and Facebook until the publishers could better verify that brands would only show up in "brand safe" environments.

Beyond the concern over the suitable environment, another challenge with digital advertising is fraud. It is estimated that advertisers lost nearly $6 billion globally due to ad response that was generated by robots (bots) rather than real people. Part of the problem is that there are different methods used to detect invalid digital traffic, and no single standard for how to prevent, or even report it. Researchers have offered ways to overcome these issues.[30]

Privacy Concerns

As marketers have taken advantage of being able to target and reach people anywhere and anytime, their ability to do so is premised on capabilities that, for many people, are deeply concerning. That is, the geo-location function of a phone, identifying where a person is at any moment, makes some consumers deeply uncomfortable that their privacy has been compromised. When that is combined with the behavioral targeting prevalent on the Web (knowing you like dogs because you visited a dog website, for example), it can make digital advertising seem downright creepy. The new restrictions on marketers by companies such as Apple and Google are a response to that.

Measurement Confusion

Despite its use as an advertising medium for well over a decade, the industry is still developing fully standardized measurement metrics. Each digital platform (Facebook, Google, etc.) tries to operate within its own ecosystem, leading to the term of a *walled garden*. Even the measurement services use slightly different methods to measure the ads. Some platforms will sell advertising based on audience impressions, others on site visits (clicks), and yet others on actual sales. The Interactive Advertising Bureau has worked hard, however, to standardize the ad unit sizes so that there is consistency for the consumer and for the creative developers on rectangular billboards, pop-ups, or skyscraper ads. The guidelines include not only the size (in pixels) but also recommendations on the size of the file that has to download onto the page it appears on, along with the duration of the ad. Even standards such as the viewable impression have been changing, with some buyers insisting on 100 percent viewability. There is also a growing push toward cross-platform measurement, where digital video and traditional TV could be compared using the same metric, such as a duration-weighted viewable impression.

Research on Digital Media

This area of research has blossomed in the past five years. Initial work tried to model the uses and gratifications of Web use, finding that those looking for information tend to interact more with messages on websites, whereas those looking for social interaction turn to the Web for human-to-human communication.[31] Additional studies have looked at the ability of various paid digital forms to enhance both upper funnel (awareness, preference) and lower funnel (sales) measures, examined consumer avoidance to digital ads, and considered how the location of paid social media ads can impact effectiveness.[32]

Research on mobile marketing has also been growing, with more emphasis on the value and meaning of location-targeted messages.[33]

Which Paid Media Should You Use?

Now that you have some basic information on each paid media category, we can start to consider why you might or might not wish to include them in your media plans. To make this process less cumbersome, we'll recap some of the most important advantages and disadvantages that each one offers. These are summarized in Exhibit 7.1.

Exhibit 7.1 Pros and Cons of Paid Media

Medium	Pros	Cons
Television	True to life	High cost
	Pervasive	Brief exposure
	Reaches masses	Clutter
	Digital targets	Poor placement
Audio	Local appeal	Background medium
	Targeted audience	Sound only
	Imagery transfer	Short message life
	Lower cost	Fragmentation
	Close to purchase	
	High frequency	
	Flexible message	
Newspaper	Wide reach	Short message life
	Timeliness	Active readers
	Desirable audience	Black and white
	Editorial context	
	Local/regional	
Magazines	Upscale and niche audiences	Long planning cycle
	Reader involvement	Shift to digital
	Long issue life	
Outdoor Billboards/ Out-of-home	Large size	Brief exposure
	Mobility	Environmental criticism
	Diversity	
	Reach	
	Supplementary exposure	
Digital Display/ Video /Search/Social	Flexibility	Consumer irritation
	Targeted message	Brand safety
	Reach	Measurement confusion
	Measurability	

Summary

While digital media are newer than other types of paid media such as TV and radio, they now capture a huge (and still growing) proportion of advertiser spend. A myriad of paid digital options are available for the planner, from display and video to search, and paid social, with numerous ad formats to consider. Each digital channel offers the benefits of highly targeted and flexible messages that can generate high reach of the audience. They are also all very measurable, with each click captured. That wealth of data has been collected, analyzed, and automated to enable programmatic buys that can reach narrowly defined audiences at the right moment for the desired cost. As changes in government or company regulations alter the way the data can be collected and used, paid digital media will continue to evolve.

Notes

1 MRI-Simmons, Doublebase 2020.
2 Ibid.
3 eMarketer, "Digital Ad Spend by Format," 2020.
4 eMarketer, "Digital Buyer Penetration by Country," December 2020.
5 Global Web Index, Q2 2020–Q1 2021.
6 Johanna Söllner and Florian Dost, "Exploring the Selective Use of Ad Blockers and Testing Banner Appeals to Reduce Ad Blocking," *Journal of Advertising*, vol. 48, no. 3, 2019, 302–312.
7 eMarketer, "Programmatic Digital Display Ad Spending," 2020.
8 Mark Loughney, Martin Eichholz, and Michelle Haggar, "Exploring the Effectiveness of Advertising in the ABC.com Full Episode Player," *Journal of Advertising Research*, vol. 48, no. 3, September 2008, 320–328. Yan Huang and Thomas Franklin Waddell, "The Impact of Ad Customization and Content Transportation on the Effectiveness of Online Video Advertising," *Journal of Current Issues & Research in Advertising*, vol. 41, no. 3, 2020, 284–300.
9 Comscore Vido Media Metrix, January–December, 2020.
10 Nielsen Total Audience Report, Q2 2020.
11 Yang Feng, Huan Chen, and Li He, "Consumer Responses to Femvertising: A Data-Mining Case of Dove's 'Campaign for Real Beauty' on YouTube," *Journal of Advertising*, vol. 48, no. 3, 2019, 292–301. Hyosun Kim, "Unpacking Unboxing Video-Viewing Motivations: The Uses and Gratifications Perspective and the Mediating Role of Parasocial Interaction on Purchase Intent," *Journal of Interactive Advertising*, vol. 20, no. 3, 2020, 196–208.
12 "The Leadership Outlook on Revenue Attribution," DemandLab, December, 2020.
13 "Average Time Spent per Day by US Users on Social Media Platforms," eMarketer March 2021.
14 Global Web Index Social Media Report, 2021.
15 Global Web Index, Q3 2020.
16 José Manuel Gavilanes, Tessa Christina Flatten, and Malte Brettel, "Content Strategies for Digital Consumer Engagement in Social Networks: Why Advertising Is an Antecedent of Engagement," *Journal of Advertising*, vol. 47, no. 1, 2018, 4–23. Hilde A. M. Voorveld, Guda van Noort, Daniël G. Muntinga, and Fred Bronner, "Engagement with Social Media and Social Media Advertising: The Differentiating Role of Platform Type," *Journal of Advertising*, vol. 47, no. 1, 2018, 38–54.
17 Jennifer Lee Burton, Kristen M. Mueller, Jan Gollins, and Danielle M. Walls, "The Impact of Airing Super Bowl Television Ads Early on Social Media: Benefits and Drivers of Watching, Liking, and Sharing Advertisements on Social Media," *Journal of Advertising Research*, vol. 59, no. 4, December 2019, 391–401.
18 Rob Jayson, Martin P. Block, and Yingying Chen, "How Synergy Effects of Paid and Digital Owned Media Influence Brand Sales: Considerations for Marketers

When Balancing Media Spend," *Journal of Advertising Research*, vol. 58, no. 1, March 2018, 77–89.

19 Harvey, Bill. July 8, 2021. https://www.mediavillage.com/article/digital-context-and-augmented-reality/.

20 Newzoo's Global Mobile Market Report 2019.

21 Comscore Global State of Mobile, 2020.

22 Comscore Global State of Mobile, 2020. Caroline Lancelot Miltgen, Anne-Sophie Cases, and Cristel Antonia Russell, "Consumers' Responses to Facebook Advertising across PCs and Mobile Phones: A Model for Assessing the Drivers of Approach and Avoidance of Facebook Ads," *Journal of Advertising Research*, vol. 59, no. 4, December 2019, 414–432.

23 Marina Nascimento Lemos Barboza and Emílio José Montero Arruda Filho, "Green Consumption Values in Mobile Apps," *Journal of International Consumer Marketing*, vol. 31, no. 1, 2019, 66–83.

24 Comscore U.S. 2017 U.S. Mobile App Report.

25 Ginger Rosenkrans and Keli Myers, "Optimizing Location-Based Mobile Advertising Using Predictive Analytics," *Journal of Interactive Advertising*, vol. 18, no. 1, 2018, 43–54.

26 "Burger King used targeted ads on Waze to launch 'Master Burger,'" as reported on https://www.waze.com.

27 Comscore State of Gaming, 2021.

28 eMarketer, U.S. Programmatic Ad Spending Forecast 2020, October 2020.

29 Harsh Taneja, "The Myth of Targeting Small, but Loyal Niche Audiences: Double-Jeopardy Effects in Digital-Media Consumption," *Journal of Advertising Research*, vol. 60, no. 3, September 2020, 239–250.

30 Patricia Callejo, Ángel Cuevas, Rubén Cuevas, Mercedes Esteban-Bravo, and Jose M. Vidal-Sanz, "Tracking Fraudulent and Low-Quality Display Impressions," *Journal of Advertising*, vol. 49, no. 3, 2020, 309–319.

31 Hanjun Ko, Chang-Hoan Cho, and Marilyn S. Roberts, "Internet Uses and Gratifications," *Journal of Advertising*, vol. 34, no. 2, Summer 2005, 57–70.

32 Amy Errmann, Yuri Seo, Yung Kyun Choi, and Sukki Yoon, "Divergent Effects of Friend Recommendations on Disclosed Social Media Advertising in the United States and Korea," *Journal of Advertising*, vol. 48, no. 5, 2019, 495–511. Gunwoo Yoon, Cong Li, Yi (Grace) Ji, Michael North, Cheng Hong, and Jiangmeng Liu, "Attracting Comments: Digital Engagement Metrics on Facebook and Financial Performance," *Journal of Advertising*, vol. 47, no. 1, 2018, 24–37. Apollo Demirel, "An Examination of a Campaign Hashtag (#OptOutside) with Google Trends and Twitter," *Journal of Interactive Advertising*, vol. 20, no. 3, 2020, 165–180. Steven Holiday, Travis Loof, R. Glenn Cummins, and Amber McCord, "Consumer Response to Selfies in Advertisements: Visual Rhetoric for the Me Me Me Generation," *Journal of Current Issues & Research in Advertising*, vol. 40, no. 2, 2019, 123–146. Sangruo Huang and Jisu Huh, "Redundancy Gain Effects in Incidental Exposure to Multiple Ads on the Internet," *Journal of Current Issues & Research in Advertising*, vol. 39, no. 1, 2018, 67–82. Mehedi Hasan and M. Sadiq Sohail, "The Influence of Social Media Marketing on Consumers' Purchase Decision: Investigating the Effects of Local and Nonlocal Brands," *Journal of International Consumer Marketing*, vol. 33, no. 3, 2021, 350–367. Nancy Berenice Ortiz Alvarado, Marisol Rodríguez Ontiveros, and Claudia Quintanilla Domínguez, "Exploring Emotional Well-Being in Facebook as a Driver of Impulsive Buying: A Cross-Cultural Approach," *Journal of International Consumer Marketing*, vol. 32, no. 5, 2020, 400–415. Judy Ma and Brian Du, "Digital Advertising and Company Value: Implications of Reallocating Advertising Expenditures," *Journal*

of Advertising Research, vol. 58, no. 3, September 2018, 326–337. Gian M. Fulgoni and Marie Pauline Morn, "Whither the Click? How Online Advertising Works," *Journal of Advertising Research*, vol. 49, no. 2, June 2009, 134–142. Stephanie Flosi, Gian Fulgoni, and Andrea Vollman, "If an Advertisement Runs Online and No One Sees It, Is It Still an Ad? Empirical Generalizations in Digital Advertising," *Journal of Advertising Research*, vol. 53, no. 2, June 2013, 192–199. Steve Millman and Zhiwei Tan, "What Is the Cost of an Unseen Ad?" *Proceedings of Print and Digital Research Forum*, 2015. Gayle Kerr, Don E. Schultz, Philip J. Kitchen, Frank J. Mulhern, and Park Beede, "Does Traditional Advertising Theory Apply to the Digital World? A Replication Analysis Questions the Relevance of the Elaboration Likelihood Model," *Journal of Advertising Research*, vol. 55, no. 4, December 2015, 390–400.

33 Shintaro Okazaki, Akihiro Katsukura, and Mamoru Nishiyama, "How Mobile Advertising Works: The Role of Trust in Improving Attitudes and Recall," *Journal of Advertising Research*, vol. 47, no. 2, June 2007, 165–178. Gian M. Fulgoni and Andrew Lipsman, "The Future of Retail Is Mobile: How Mobile Marketing Dynamics Are Shaping the Future of Retail," *Journal of Advertising Research*, vol. 5, no. 4, December 2016, 346–351. Paul E. Ketelaar, Stefan F. Bernritter, Jonathan van't Riet, Arief Ernst Hühn, Thabo J. van Woudenberg, Barbara C. N. Müller, and Loes Janssen, "Disentangling Location-Based Advertising: The Effects of Location Congruency and Medium Type on Consumers' Ad Attention and Brand Choice," *International Journal of Advertising*, vol. 36, no. 2, 2017, 356–367. Mirja Bues, Michael Steiner, Marcel Stafflage, and Manfred Krafft, "How Mobile In-Store Advertising Influences Purchase Intention: Value Drivers and Mediating Effects from a Consumer Perspective," *Psychology and Marketing*, vol. 34, no. 2, February 2017, 157–174. Hilde A. M. Voorveld, Guda van Noort, Daniël G. Muntinga, and Fred Bronner, "Engagement with Social Media and Social Media Advertising: The Differentiating Role of Platform Type," *Journal of Advertising*, vol. 47, no. 1, 2018, 38–54.

Chapter 8

Planning and Buying Beyond

Learning Outcomes: In this chapter you will learn how to:

- Differentiate the various forms of owned and earned channels
- Understand how each one is planned and bought (or paid for)
- Compare and contrast the benefits and disadvantages offered by earned and owned media   .

As the cost of paid media has continued to go up, and as consumers have gained ever greater control over their media usage, starting with the TV remote control and then with digital platforms and devices, marketers have turned more to media opportunities that they can own or that they can earn from customers or prospects. That is, there are ways in which a company or brand can use its name, its values, and/or its position in consumers' minds to convey advertising messages to its target audience in ways that will enhance sales or other metrics and enhance the performance of paid media. And whether the brand is using paid or owned media, marketers have increasingly looked for ways to interact with and talk about their brands (ideally, in a positive way) so as to earn consumer trust and confidence in their offerings. In these naturally occurring moments advertisers can see how much their brands have "earned" consumer awareness, liking, preference, or other effects outlined in Chapter 2.

In this chapter, we will focus on both the areas that a brand can own, and the ways they use earned media. While there are still costs to be paid to initiate and run some of these opportunities, they all provide the company with a way to put their brands in consumers' hearts and minds, with the goal of driving sales and growth.

Owned Media: Expanding the Impact of Brands

The placement of brand names somewhere besides paid commercials has a long history. Indeed, the first movie to win an Oscar as "best picture" in 1927 included a Hershey chocolate bar. As noted in Chapter 5 and explored below,

DOI: 10.4324/9781003175704-8

early television programs featured brand names in their titles in acknowledgment of the marketers' sponsorship. Kraft Television Theater, Philco Television Playhouse, and Hallmark Hall of Fame filled American viewers' screens in the 1940s and 1950s. Here we look at the current array of owned media: product placement, brand integration, brand website, sponsorship, influencer marketing, and custom events.

Product Placement

While $74 billion is spent each year in the United States on paid television advertising (commercials), another way for advertisers to reach consumers with their brands is through product placement. Here, advertisers pay the program producer to put their brands into the storylines or content of TV shows. This began back in 2001, when contestants on the reality show *Survivor* were shown happily consuming cans of Pepsi's Mountain Dew. Sometimes the product is overtly written into the script, such as having the characters in the FX series *Sons of Anarchy* ride Harley-Davidson motorbikes. The success of a brand placement is not guaranteed. Three brands were originally placed in the hugely popular show *American Idol*: Coca-Cola, Ford, and Cingular (then AT&T). While consumers readily accepted and remembered the soft drink (consumed by the judges) and the phone company (linked to the text messages they sent in), there was no clear connection with a vehicle. As a result, Ford's brand equity actually declined during its time on the program.[1]

Many advertisers today are pulling dollars out of regular national television and switching it into product placement deals that have a lower out-of-pocket cost. It was estimated that in 2019, a total of $20.6 billion was spent on product placement globally, according to PQ Media. There are benefits both to the brand and to the content creators. Advertisers can get additional attention on their products and services that are (or should be) naturally integrated into the story. Production companies gain additional revenue that can offset the cost to make the content, allowing them to fund additional cast members or special locations, for example.

Of course, placement is nothing new. It was how commercial TV got started, with the product sponsorship of the Texaco Star Theater or daytime dramas brought to you by Tide and Dreft (i.e., soap operas). It grew to greater prominence thanks to James Bond movies, where the hero drove specific brands of cars and drank certain kinds of alcohol. In the 2018 hit movie *Black Panther*, Lexus paid to have a special version of its LC 500 vehicle in the film; following the huge success of the film, Lexus used the superhero in one of its Super Bowl commercials a month later. Unlike content integration (discussed later), with product placement the product appears more or less as a prop, such as a character opening a box of General Mills' Lucky Charms cereal rather than Brand X.

While there is no legislation aimed specifically at this type of owned advertising, questions are raised from time to time about whether the public should be explicitly informed when a company has paid to place their product directly in a program.

Research on product placement looks at it from all angles, including theories that help explain it, understanding how to contextualize it, and exploring how it impacts consumers who are multi-tasking. A selection of articles is suggested.[2]

Brand Integration

This type of owned media is an extension of product placement. The major difference is that with brand integration (sometimes called *content integration*) a more holistic experience is created with the brand that involves developing unique content specifically for that brand. This can be done across media, from customized magazines (Kraft Foods' *Food & Family* magazine) to original TV programs or movies (Mattel's movie division is creating content around its licensed toys, such as Barbie or Hot Wheels) to digital content (Healthy Choice online videos on tasty.co on Buzzfeed or the Red Bull YouTube channel).

To successfully integrate a brand into existing content, the key consideration is fit. That is, does it make sense to put your brand in that context? This can be done figuratively, in terms of shared values, or literally. When upscale automaker Lexus was used as the inspiration for the aspiring fashion designers on Bravo's reality TV program *Project Runway*, the challenge was to create evening wear suitable for the Emmys award show. The fit here was conceptual and symbolic rather than concrete. That is, it was about the high style of both the fashion challenge and the vehicles Lexus makes. For Dyson, the vacuum maker, an integration into the Netflix sitcom *Grace and Frankie* went one step closer. Here, one of the regular characters is seen with one of the company's vacuum models as she cleans her house while on the phone talking with her sister.

Indeed, as viewers pay decreasing attention to commercials, brands are looking for deeper integration into program content, where people are less likely to avoid the brand. In *Top Chef*, which has had brands sponsoring individual cooking challenges since it first aired in 2006, the goal now is to be seen (and mentioned) on a more regular basis. BMW not only provides the cars that contestants drive to pick up their groceries, but it was also featured in one of the cooking challenges at a drive-in movie theater. When the Season 18 chefs reached for any cheese or butter for their recipes, viewers saw the prominent display of Tillamook.[3]

For some brands, no existing content seems an appropriate fit for them. In such a case, some advertisers create content. This is not the same as making an *infomercial*, a long-form commercial that lasts several minutes or more. Rather, a full-length (30 minutes or longer) program is developed in which the brand is integrated. With the continuing decline of traditional TV program ratings, more brands are turning to developing programs themselves. In March 2021, a documentary on HBO called "The Day Sports Stood Still" did not have any ads or overt sponsor mentions, but Nike was seen throughout. The documentary was created by Imagine Brands, a division of a regular entertainment production company, Imagine Entertainment. Other large advertisers, such as Procter & Gamble and Ford Motor Company, are getting actively involved in creating content involving their brands.[4] Pepsi worked with ViacomCBS to develop a reality dating show where its Pepsi Mango flavor could be prominently displayed.[5]

One of the challenges for brand integration is how to measure it. Since it is, by definition, unique, it is unlikely to get captured in traditional syndicated measures of viewership or readership, for example. Today, however, there are a variety of ways to do so. Both Nielsen and Comscore, the TV audience measurement services in the U.S., have created services specifically to measure brand integrations in streamed content to provide the number of impressions delivered when the brand appears. The social impact of the integration is readily assessed by looking at the trending of brand mentions on platforms such as Twitter, Instagram, or Facebook. For any integrated digital content, consumer visits to a unique site or branded page can be quantified through digital audience measurement companies. To focus specifically on consumer reactions to a particular integration, in terms of shifts in their attitudes or feelings about the brand, advertisers can undertake custom research such as an online survey among those who have visited integrated digital content.

A variation of brand integration is direct response TV (DRTV). Here, advertisers purchase time on local TV stations or, more often, on cable networks. This time could be anywhere from a 2-minute infomercial to a 30-minute program. What the consumer sees is an informational message with an immediate opportunity to purchase (online or by telephone). On a Saturday morning, for example, viewers can watch programs featuring purse-maker Dooney & Bourke, Total Gym, or Shark Vacuum Cleaners. This kind of direct-to-consumer approach works well for certain types of marketers and has typically been used by smaller or independent companies offering unusual products, such as the Snuggie blanket or NordicTrack fitness equipment. The media rates can be up to 75 percent lower than the cost of buying regular commercial time. Bigger companies occasionally use DRTV to good effect. Marketers such as LifeLock, Audible, Hyatt, and New York Life have launched products or run campaigns this way. In the past several years, marketing solely direct to consumers without traditional media has become a huge trend, greatly disrupting the product categories these brands are in. Dollar Shave Club, Warby Parker, Casper, and Barkbox were each launched by selling online without paid media.

Native advertising is another type of brand integration. This originated in print media, but is now most commonly seen online. As with the above examples, brands help create content that appears in a newspaper or magazine or website, such as Nike providing support to an article in *Bleacher Report* celebrating female athletes on International Women's Day, or HBO Max providing an interactive feature on "which bingeable series should you watch next?" on the Apartment Therapy website. In all cases, the content provider should include a disclaimer that the content is brought to you by the brand, but questions have arisen as to how transparently that is shown as well as the effectiveness of this type of owned media.[6]

Brand Website

The strongest and perhaps most obvious owned media available is the brand's website. In our fictional example of Fruitola, the creation of a website with original content related to the brand's values and positioning can be important ways to communicate with the desired customers. It can link to all areas of marketing. Site visitors could explore the *package* and get nutritional information. They could find which stores in their area stock the brand (*place*) as well as see where Fruitola is sponsoring events in their local community. Online coupons or other discounts could be placed on the site (*promotion*). Product users could be encouraged to submit their own experiences with the brand or suggest drink recipes.

Today, just about every brand has its own website. Type a brand or company name into a web browser, and you will arrive at the website. Increasingly, the site is used to develop a relationship with the customer that goes beyond the function of the brand. When people visit pampers.com, not only will they get information about diapers but broader material related to pregnancy and childrearing, including e-commerce links to purchase other companies' baby products such as strollers or travel cribs. At dove.com, for example, the consumer can find out more about the various skincare and beauty products the company sells. But she can also learn more about Dove's mission to bolster girls' self-esteem, explore the #RealVoices community where consumers can share their own experiences, or purchase any of the company's products directly. Taking that one step further, Dove, like many brands, encourages visitors to its website to register their information to receive a digital newsletter or special offers. The Container Store website has the more obvious elements to it of promoting what is going on in the store, but it lets the user get expert tips and watch how-to videos about home improvement or read about the company's Employee-First Fund, which gives grants to its employees in need, providing a sense of an employee-first community for its workers.

Advertisers are looking at their owned media channels more holistically today, producing content that not only appears on their website, but is also shared on their social media channels, and then converted into 15- or 30-second TV spots that can run in paid media. One brand that took this approach is

Miracle-Gro, the lawn and garden company. It created a six-episode series called "How I Grow," designed in part to move the brand's image from simply a one-season offering to an always-on panoply of products that can be used year-round.[7]

The research on how to make brand websites most impactful has focused on how to encourage consumer interaction with them and how they work with other media forms.[8]

Sponsorship

As advertisers have had to work harder to reach their target consumers, one of the owned forms of communication they have turned to is sponsorship. This involves paying an organization a fee to put a company or brand name at the head of an event or as the key sponsor of that event. Examples include State Farm Insurance's sponsorship of an ice skating competition, Citibank's sponsorship of the U.S. Olympic team, and the renaming of sports stadiums after companies (e.g., Chase Center in San Francisco, Little Caesar's Arena in Detroit, and Guaranteed Rate Field in Chicago). The practice of sponsorship in North America is now estimated to be worth about $24 billion, while globally it is close to $66 billion.

The majority of sponsorship spending (70 percent) goes toward sports-related events, followed by entertainment tours (10 percent), causes (9 percent), arts (4 percent), festivals (4 percent), and associations (3 percent). The growth of cause-related marketing, where companies link up with non-profit groups and become sponsors of their causes, continues to expand. Examples include Avon's long-standing support of an annual three-day walk to raise funds for breast cancer research and Coca-Cola's connection with the World Wildlife Fund to protect polar bears (the brand's symbol). Even though sponsorship is generally considered to be undertaken to reach a national audience, there are often significant local opportunities, too. Sponsorship of local sports teams can enhance a business' reputation in those particular markets, while companies that choose to sponsor a local annual festival often receive positive coverage in the local media. There are also benefits to be gained by sponsoring grassroots or community festivals and fairs, especially among multicultural audiences.

The reasons companies choose sponsorship in addition to paid advertising are many. They include the opportunity for heightened visibility for their brand name, thereby increasing the chances of shaping positive consumer attitudes ("I like ice skating, therefore since State Farm sponsors a skating competition, I like State Farm more, too"). Sometimes, sponsorship works well for smaller companies. While they may have smaller ad budgets compared to bigger competitors, their sponsorship of a key event or attraction can make them seem an equal in consumers' eyes. Asics spends much less than competitors like Nike or Reebok, but through its sponsorship of the New York City Marathon, the runners or viewers of the race do not see one company as a "better" or necessarily bigger sponsor than another.

Consumer research suggests that people are indeed more likely to have positive feelings toward a sponsoring brand and are more likely to consider buying it in the future. One study, conducted by the GroupM Next agency, found that one-third or more of consumers indicated these positive feelings toward brands that sponsor award shows, TV shows, sports events, or musical acts.[9] The Olympics are often considered the apotheosis of the sponsorship world. The International Olympic Committee places restrictions on any form of advertising that does not come from one of the official sponsors of the games, companies that have paid up to $100 million for that privilege.

Nonetheless, one of the risks of sponsorship is *ambush marketing*. This occurs when another marketer (frequently a competitor) uses other media (paid and earned) around the sponsored event so that consumers end up believing that the ambusher is in fact the sponsor. For example, during the African Cup of Nations, for which Pepsi was the official sponsor, Coca-Cola reinvigorated Egyptians' love of the game (and their team) by creating an online video reminding people to support their country's team. The campaign, which never mentioned the tournament itself, brought fans back to the team, as well as to the brand, by strengthening the association between Coke and soccer.[10] A research study into ambush marketing created a typology of this strategy to help further explain how it is used.[11]

Even less mature brands can benefit from the Olympics. Although Peloton is not an official Olympics sponsor, it began a campaign in April 2021 that featured nine athletes who have been or are currently competing in the Olympic or Paralympic Games. While the Olympics organizers had previously prohibited most athletes from being in ads for non-sponsors, those rules were relaxed somewhat. Still, companies such as Peloton are forbidden from mentioning the word Olympics in any of their messaging.[12]

Sponsorships can be harmed by any controversy. When cyclist Lance Armstrong was found guilty of using performance-enhancing drugs, it not only damaged his career; it had a negative effect on the image of his team's sponsor, the U.S. Postal Service. The cost to the brand can sometimes be significant. The golfer Tiger Woods, who was accused of cheating on his wife and driving under the influence, is estimated to have cost the companies he endorsed and helped promote up to $12 billion.[13]

The media are getting more actively involved in creating sponsorships for advertisers. *Teen Vogue* magazine created an event in 2019 called the Teen Vogue Summit in New York City, where inspirational and inspiring speakers were brought in to discuss issues and encourage activism. Sponsors included Motorola, TOMS, and PB Teen, all brands that target this demographic group. Sponsorships are, like other owned media, useful connectors between paid and earned opportunities. That is, most marketers who sponsor something (or someone) will benefit from their brand being mentioned or visible during their TV or digital or print ads and can use social media and influencers to amplify the impact of the sponsorship. For example, as part of Budweiser's World Cup sponsorship, the company sponsors the Man of the Match, which means that the key player of each game is pictured in front of their brands. That photo is then posted to the competition's Instagram and Facebook pages.

The number of research papers published on sponsorship has steadily increased over time. Studies have focused either on the practical elements of how to maximize the impact for a sponsor or on understanding the theoretical underpinnings of how it works.[14]

Influencer Marketing

The power of celebrities to help brands succeed goes back many decades, with some of the most famous actors appearing in commercials for everything from cigarettes and chocolates, to cars and credit cards. There has been extensive research examining how and why consumers have a heightened trust in celebrities they like or admire, and that these people bring greater credibility to the brand message.[15] The growth of social media channels gave lesser-known individuals the opportunity to promote products themselves, resulting in a newer type of owned and earned media opportunity. Influencer marketing is a combination of sponsorship (or endorsement) and social media. While much of it grew natively, without brands doing too much, today's savvy marketers take full advantage of and engineer the overt endorsement of their brands by willing spokespeople. Influencer marketing involves creating (paid-for) relationships with people who are considered influential and persuasive in a particular category or field so that they can influence others to change attitudes toward or behavior about a particular brand. Most of this activity occurs on social media—with influencers posting on Instagram or Twitter, for instance—to let their followers know that they love Prada or Oreos. Between 2019 and 2020, the volume of promoted posts on Instagram (labeled with #Ads) grew by nearly 25 percent, reaching 6.12 billion posts globally; the estimated total spend in this channel has grown from about $1 billion in 2016 to about $10 billion today. According to influencer marketing company Izea, the top three categories for influencer marketing are beauty, fashion, and travel.

Influencer marketing is not just an American phenomenon. Global marketers are seeing influencers as an opportunity to localize their appeal and broaden their message beyond traditional media channels. In India, for example, Colgate employed 200 influencers to build up interest in a new brand they were launching by sending mystery items to expand consumer curiosity for their new toothpaste. The campaign reached nearly 24 million people.[16]

Influencer marketing can be broken down into subcategories, based largely on the number of followers. The basic three categories are the macro-influencer, who is the social media equivalent of a celebrity marketer. These people are often well-known entertainers or athletes whose fans happily follow their every move, recommendation, or opinion. According to Hopper HQ, a company that offers an Instagram scheduling tool to help people manage their social activity, the highest-paid celebrity (Kylie Jenner) earns $1 million per paid-for social media post.[17] The standard classification for such people is that they have more than 10,000 followers. Next, the micro-influencer is the "regular" person whose expertise in or knowledge of a topic (combined with savvy use of social media) attracts people to follow him or her in more of a grassroots way. These individuals have fewer than 10,000 followers.[18] And lastly, the increasingly popular nano influencer tends to be a niche specialist with 5,000 or fewer followers. Marketers are turning more to these lesser-known influencers, realizing that having their brands promoted to smaller, but more engaged audiences may in fact be a more effective strategy.

One key to this type of marketing is that it represents a significant shift in how a brand communicates with and impacts its audiences. With most forms of paid media, the brand invests in placing ads that provide one-way messages to consumers (along with some opportunity to respond on digital platforms). Earned media let audiences indicate their sentiment or enthusiasm for the brand in terms of likes, shares, or tweets. Influencer marketing helps move the control from the brand to the individual. That is, consumers hear about and react to the brand via another person who has decided to speak out about that product or company. While marketers may go in believing that this is simply a type of sponsorship, all indications are that there are important differences in how consumers respond to influencer messages that will require additional research to understand more fully.

Research on influencers has grown rapidly, comparing their impact to other forms of marketing, as well as exploring the theory behind what makes this approach successful.[19]

Custom Events

Sometimes there are ideas for a brand that don't fit in to any marketing category. They are completely owned by the brand and designed solely for it. These are called *custom events*, and they are defined as activities or programs specifically built to promote a brand, and have consumers talk about it to friends and family.

One version of this type of communication is to recreate a scene or an experience so that consumers can touch or feel the product. When IKEA opened a new store in Japan, the company took over a train and outfitted the cars with items that could be purchased in the new store, including price tags. In addition to the benefit of having consumers look at the products, IKEA was sticking to one of its strategic objectives of demonstrating how it can help people furnish small spaces.

A very different way to use a subway was seen in Toronto, where the tourism bureau of the province of Alberta, to encourage visitors to travel there, recreated scenes from its rocky mountain scenery, changing rail seats into ski lifts and surrounding commuters with photos of the idyllic landscape. Visits to the bureau's website more than doubled during the two months of the campaign.

Sometimes these custom event campaigns are not even real. To launch a new car model in the United States, BMW created a pseudo-festival called Rampenfest that featured a video of a BMW car driving on an enormous ramp in a tiny town in Austria. The catch was that the ramp and the town itself were not real, and neither was the festival. But the buzz that surrounded the campaign certainly was, with an estimated 10 million visitors to the vehicle's website.[20] Custom events can grow from one-offs to become established. American Express first created Small Business Saturday in 2010 to encourage people to shop at local businesses on the Saturday after Thanksgiving. It quickly became an annual shopping tradition, bringing in nearly $20 billion on that single day in 2019. While American Express is not used for all payments, it generates considerable goodwill for supporting small and local businesses.

Custom events may also be used for charitable purposes. At any major marathon or triathlon, people who participate are often raising funds for the charity they support, such as research institutes or hospitals. Many charities themselves organize national or local custom events, such as the Walk to End Alzheimer's or the annual Hunger Walk organized by the Greater Chicago Food Depository. The shoe company, TOMS, started its "buy one, give one" program from its inception and has so far donated more than 86 million pairs of shoes to children in need.

Investing in Owned Media

Although it might seem like an oxymoron to pay for media that a brand or company owns, the opportunities noted here do often require investment and, sometimes, negotiation. Sponsorships, for example, are typically sold by the venue (sports stadium, concert promoters). Product placement or brand integration into TV shows and movies is typically offered by the producers of the entertainment, though TV networks have started to move into this highly profitable arena. Influencers receive some kind of payment for promoting specific brands. For custom events, the cost discussions would occur with whatever company (media or otherwise) is hired to create and manage that event.

Owned Media Measurement

For several forms of owned media, the key measure to consider is how many people will be in attendance or the *traffic* that will be generated. Attendance to sports stadiums is easy to capture, as are the number of people at a rock concert or movie theater (e.g., if your product is the concert sponsor or is being given away as samples in the theater lobby). While not a substitute for actual impact, traffic measures at least give an indication of how many people will have the opportunity for exposure. For word-of-mouth efforts, the number to determine is how many people could potentially be influenced by the viral efforts.

Some owned media are as measurable as paid digital. Brand websites, for example, can be evaluated based on the number of people that clicked on them (impressions), along with information on where those users came from beforehand and where they clicked to afterward. For product placement and brand integration, the metric can be based on television audience ratings. That is, it is assumed that viewers of *The Voice* will be exposed to Starbucks drinks consumed by the judges. Additional measurement is also undertaken to confirm the percentage of people that actively remember seeing the brand in its program context, using survey research, along with any attitudinal change that can be attributed to the placement or integration.

Given that it is not enough for marketers to have their name placed in front of hundreds or thousands of happy but disinterested bodies, it is also important to assess the value of those expected impressions relative to the cost of obtaining them. Here, it is probably good to consider the contextual relevance of the impact. It might make sense to have Adidas be a featured sponsor at tennis tournaments but less so for a prescription drug such as Viagra to be present at those same events. For digitally based owned media forms, such as brand websites or Facebook pages, the costs may be relatively low, but the impact may also be small depending on the brand. While the Airbnb website is at the heart of its travel-booking business, that is less true for Charmin's website or Facebook page. The cost of developing a television program based on or incorporating a brand can be high, but the value may be worthwhile if the brand is able to reach its desired—and potentially hard-to-reach—target audience.

The success of influencer marketing can be measured in several ways. The digital impressions generated, along with engagement metrics such as likes, shares, or comments, help brands understand how much consumers are responding to influencer activity. More concretely, influencers often provide direct links for people to purchase the product, which provides marketers with actual sales that can be traced back to the influencer.[21]

Benefits of Owned Media to Advertisers

There are five main benefits of owned media to advertisers: broader awareness, endless creativity, lower cost, indirect impact, and implied trust.

Broader Awareness

While advertisers continue to invest in paid media such as television to generate brand awareness, owned media expands the ways in which consumers are exposed to the brand, whether that is seeing Coors beer consumed by the lead actor in Netflix' *Cobra Kai*, or noting the sponsor name of the White Sox home ballpark, Guaranteed Rate Field in Chicago. Those who follow style and beauty influencer Rachel Talbott on YouTube may well learn about brands such as YSL or Anastasia when they watch her videos, generating relatively low-cost awareness for those companies.

Endless Creativity

One of the advantages to brands owning the media properties is that they have more, if not total control over what they create. That could be a website that showcases how Home Depot works in the community or events that magazines develop that become synonymous with the brand, such as the *Food & Wine* Festival in Aspen, Colorado. As noted earlier, brands are becoming more actively involved in creating TV shows or producing films where they have more creative freedom than is available in a full-page print ad or 30-second TV commercial.

Lower Cost

Advertisers look at several types of owned media as a potentially cheaper way to promote their brand, compared to traditional advertising. There may be no cost to place a Hershey chocolate bar in a TV episode, or an influencer could receive free samples of a new face cleanser in lieu of payment. At the same time, it is important to remember that owned media alone, without other types of paid media promotion, may produce an initial favorable reaction, but in isolation, that impact is likely to be short term and brief.

Indirect Impact

For brands that are placed in a high-performing media vehicle and endorsed by or referred to by the vehicle or celebrity, the effect on consumers can be very positive. Dunkin's placement of its bright orange cups on the judges' table in *America's Got Talent* is a subtle reminder to viewers that if these celebrities are enjoying the Dunkin treats, then maybe they should buy them, too. The good feeling you have toward Nike in its sponsorship of many high school sports teams may not directly lead you to buy their apparel or footwear, but it could well enhance your consideration and preference of their brands.

Implied Trust

The reason that brands are rushing to establish relationships with influencers is that in a world where consumers feel over-saturated with ad messages, they are much more willing to trust the opinions of people they admire and follow; if those individuals recommend a brand that they like and/or use, then the belief is that their followers will buy and use it, too. A similar inherent benefit can come from product placements and brand integrations. Sales of Eggo Waffles soared after they were featured in an episode of *Stranger Things*.

Drawbacks of Owned Media

The most common concerns mentioned for owned media are irritation, strategic weakness, lack of control, and measurement challenges.

Consumer Irritation

The notion of creating a media property that has a brand in its title may seem ideal to a marketer, but from the consumers' perspective, it could lead to intense annoyance. If they already feel bombarded by ads during a program or throughout a magazine or all over a website, then the exposure to the brand in the name of the content could just irritate them further, harming the brand's equity rather than helping it. If an influencer fails to mention she has been paid to promote the Athleta shirt she is promoting, that can also annoy the consumer and backfire on the brand.

Strategic Weakness

When marketers set their goals of trying to sell a certain number of widgets or increasing awareness or recall by X percent, owned media are rarely included as a means to accomplish this. Unless a product sells a lot directly from its own, or a third-party website (such as Amazon), then determining how the site will be used to directly impact the goals becomes a challenge. How placement of the Chevy Malibu in the film *Coming 2 America* helped sell more vehicles is not clear.

From a marketer's perspective, it may make all the sense in the world to pay for placement of an airline in a sitcom when the character talks about taking a trip, but if the viewer is sitting there scratching her head wondering why that particular airline was mentioned several times (or worse, ignoring it), then the impact on the brand could be completely negative. When the product is misplaced, or fits badly, consumers are less likely to remember it or associate it correctly.

Lack of Control

The strategy behind using Alec Baldwin as a spokesman for various brands may have been strong, but then when the actor was accused of making homophobic comments in 2013, or was arrested over a parking space dispute in 2018, those same brands have to face the consequences of negative publicity and not having full control over the celebrities they select. This is even more marked in influencer marketing, which cedes much of the control a company has over its brand messaging and marketing to individuals who may end up publicizing comments or opinions that are not aligned with the corporate approach. This is a trade-off with having "real people" be additional spokespersons for your brand. Brands are increasingly including a "morality clause" in their contracts so that if the influencer says or posts something considered inappropriate or offensive, the brand can easily cut off the relationship. Such was the case with Olivia Jade Giannulli, who lost her endorsement deals with Sephora and Amazon after her parents were arrested and found guilty in the 2019 U.S. university admissions scandal.

Measurement Challenges

Owned media can sometimes be difficult to measure in terms of their impact. A specially created TV program, digital program, or print title may have such a small audience that standard methods cannot detect it and more customized approaches may be required.

You can tell sponsorship works—when it works! Event attendance may increase, perceptions may improve, sales may even go up. But proving that it was caused by the sponsorship is a tricky proposition. Some research has been done to assess the financial fundamentals of a company employing sponsorship, but it can be challenging to determine cause and effect. Did the company's fortunes change due to the sponsorship, or was the sponsorship the result of the company's situation?

Earned Media: Getting Brand Conversations Going

Beyond using a brand's owned (or acquired) assets, today's marketers look for ways to earn further trust, loyalty, and engagement from consumers by finding ways to encourage people to talk about the brands they like and use. Of course, in ceding that control to consumers, brands accept the risk that what people say about them may not be uniformly positive. The expanded consumer conversation generated through earned media is considered a welcome extension of impact beyond paid and owned media. We examine each of these opportunities below, from word of mouth to social media, and organic search to public relations.

Word of Mouth: Who Says What?

While considered by many to not be a true "medium," word of mouth is a popular way for brands to be promoted. When companies pay for that experience, it may be referred to as *viral* marketing, using the metaphor of spreading good words about a brand the way that a virus can spread among people. There is also a strong connection with influencer marketing, where brands are paying selected individuals to actively promote them online. For earned media, however, word of mouth occurs naturally, earning the brand some kind of (hopefully positive) consumer response, but is monitored carefully by marketers. It is estimated that word of mouth helps drive 19 percent of sales (one-half of which are online).[22]

Word of mouth is not always positive, however. Consumers may be more likely to share their negative experiences with a brand or company, telling others to avoid using Brand X or relaying a poor service experience with Company Y. Larger companies try to remain alert for these occurrences, often publicly responding immediately to allay concerns. On TripAdvisor, for example, hotel managers often write directly to people who post negative comments.

Indeed, word of mouth is often thought of as solely occurring in digital media, particularly through social conversation, but most of the talk about brands (72 percent) actually occurs face to face, with digital accounting for about 12 percent.[23] One analysis of online versus offline conversations about brands showed that there was little overlap between people talking in those ways and little correlation between the topics covered.[24] During the COVID-19 pandemic, word of mouth held steady, even though there was an unsurprising shift in the categories that consumers talked about (more on healthcare and financial services, less on sports and travel).[25]

Nonetheless, from an advertising perspective, it is digital media that offer the most earned brand opportunities. That could happen on personal blogs, where people who are passionate about a topic will share content that others can read and respond to. Another venue for sharing opinions about brands is online reviews. If you like a movie, you are encouraged to share your opinion on sites or apps such as Fandango, IMDB, or Rotten Tomatoes. Each time you make a purchase on Amazon, you are invited to share your feelings there, and, as noted above, you can spread the word about your experiences on TripAdvisor or Airbnb when you travel. In fact, the number of places that let you do so in today's digital landscape is almost infinite. Many of today's brands "listen" carefully to what consumers say about them, often dedicating staff to responding directly to positive or negative comments in the reviews.

Research on word of mouth focuses more now on differentiating the impact of offline versus online forms.[26]

Earned Social Media

The notion of community is paramount to the explosive growth of social media platforms. Companies such as Facebook or Wei-bo (in China) give users the ability to connect with friends and family locally and globally to exchange messages, videos, music, or photos. According to Insider Intelligence, four out of five web users (81 percent) go on social media sites. While advertisers invest significant portions of their media dollars in paid social media, here we will focus on the ways that brands can earn additional consumer attention through these channels.

The biggest social platform today is Facebook. Created by Harvard undergraduate Mark Zuckerberg in 2004, Facebook began as a way for college students to communicate with each other. It blossomed and grew exponentially, with 2.1 billion users worldwide, and today has an estimated stock value of $750 billion, despite considerable scrutiny in 2018 over how it shared its user data with other companies. Other key social network offerings are Instagram (now owned by Facebook), with more than 500 million users each day who view and share visual messages and stories. Snapchat, used by 265 million people per day globally, is particularly popular with younger age groups, who share brief content that automatically disappears after a few seconds. Twitter, focused on brief (140- or 280-character) messages, has 187 million active users per day. Growing very rapidly as the next global platform is TikTok, with 680 million daily active users, who share their own video content with others. Last but not least, LinkedIn, a Microsoft-owned social platform, is used by 740 million users worldwide to network for business reasons. The biggest shift in social network usage in recent years has been from desktop to mobile. About one-quarter of the time that people in the U.S. spend with apps on their mobile devices is on social networks, second only to digital audio,[27] and 90 percent of social network users today are accessing these platforms via mobile.

In the United States, Facebook users spend, on average, 33 minutes per day on the site (second only to TikTok).[28] For big events, the platform is becoming an increasingly important way to reach many at one time. Over 10 million people rang in the start of 2018 on Facebook Live, which was more than three times its typical December daily average.[29] That makes Facebook and other social networks extremely appealing from an earned media perspective. Research has looked at how Facebook brand posts engage consumers.[30]

Early research conducted by digital measurement company Comscore in 2011 found that the addition of friends of the fans of a brand can expand its online reach by anywhere from one-third to twice as much as the fans alone.[31] And both fans and friends of fans were more likely to have visited the brands' websites than the "regular" Web user. The sharing on social media is staggering. Social media measurement company Shareablee reported that in 2020, people shared posts on Facebook and Twitter more than 5 billion times.[32]

Indeed, from an earned media perspective, the sharing phenomenon is what brands hope for. Shareablee notes that in 2020 brands received 290 million comments across social media, with a brand seeing about 900,000 posts each on Facebook, Instagram, and Twitter. In food and beverages, for example, there were nearly 70 million actions or reactions of some kind (comments, shares, retweets, likes) for Red Bull in 2020.[33] For media-related brands, such as TV shows or networks, earned media has become a crucial metric of success. In 2020, *Grey's Anatomy*, a long-running series on ABC, saw almost 97 million sharing activities, while the Netflix show *The Umbrella Academy*, generated 512 million.[34] For brands considering where to place ad dollars, these kinds of numbers provide an indicator of viewer engagement that, potentially, would spill over to the ads in commercial breaks (in *Grey's*) or products integrated into the content (*Umbrella*).

Twitter is a social network focused on sharing comments. The most popular activity on Twitter is to read a news or sports story, and its power and influence was felt strongly during the 2020 U.S. presidential election. Brands can connect to their customers through Twitter. Harley-Davidson, which spends only 15 percent of its marketing on traditional media, uses social media not only to encourage customers to share their own stories but also casts real riders from among its Twitter followers in ads.

While social networking began among college students, today's social network users span the age spectrum. In January 2021, Facebook reached nearly nine in ten (88 percent) of U.S. adults aged between 35 and 54, and 82 percent of those 55 and older. Most other social networks see their highest reach among those aged between 18 and 34, making their ability to earn brand interest, liking, and consideration from that younger segment even more desirable.[35]

Today, it is the norm for a company and each of its brands to have a strong and pervasive social media presence to earn the trust of, share information with, and strengthen the relationship with customers. When done properly, the personality of the brand (or company) is readily apparent. Netflix, for example, uses its Twitter feed to post tongue-in-cheek comments, often about its own content.[36] Starbucks creates Instagram stories that feature its latest drink or promote the company's education initiatives for its employees.

The power of social networks to spread impactful messages is quite profound. In 2014, the Ice Bucket Challenge to raise money for ALS research generated enormous "earned" impact. By asking people to pour a bucket of ice-cold water on their heads or donate to the ALS charity, the charity generated more than $100 million in donations. That was four times the amount the organization raised the year before.[37] The success was attributed to the fact that it was easy for people to participate, they felt part of a community, and they could tell their own stories.

Research on earned social media has grown exponentially, in line with the expansive growth of its popularity.[38] Its dual role as a paid channel and one that earns consumer value has drawn attention to the need for a more holistic theory of how social media work.[39]

Organic Search

Today, when consumers are looking for information about a topic, they usually go to Google (or another search engine). If you type in "Android phone," for example, the search will come up with various articles about different phones in the category, as well as images for them. This is known as an *organic search* because it has been sought out naturally by an individual. As noted in Chapter 7, however, companies respond at the top and to the right of the page with paid search ads, based on the keywords that consumers choose.

Marketers use search engine optimization (SEO) to increase the chances that consumers will see their brand appear in the search results. There is a built-in credibility to organic search results that can make people more willing to click on them rather than words or links identified as "paid for." Like the paid version, organic search is measurable since, if it works, there will be a digital trail of clicks and/or conversions or sales. It may take longer than paid search to generate those results. When someone types into the Google search bar, they may be curious and want to learn more, but are probably not yet ready to buy. So organic search is thought to have more impact on upper-funnel measures such as consideration or favorability. In contrast, if a person clicks on a paid search result that is labeled as an ad, it is believed they are closer to making the purchase. Most advertisers use a combination of SEO and paid search (buying keywords) so they can then compare organic to non-organic click-throughs, to better understand the relative impact of each. When doughnut brand Krispy Kreme created a campaign in the U.S. offering the Graduate Dozen to graduating high school seniors who could not attend their graduation ceremony because of the COVID-19 pandemic, they noted not only a 36 percent increase in same-store sales, but a 43 percent lift in organic search for the brand.

Public Relations

Although this area of media and marketing is really worthy of a whole book on its own (and several are listed at the end of the chapter), it is important to mention how marketers can consider their public relations (PR) efforts as part of their earned media. That is, how consumers think about brands and companies may well be influenced (or improved upon) by the efforts of PR companies to help earn their trust or support or consensus. The use of PR as a form of earned media is not, most of the time, without any cost on the part of the brand. That is, when a marketer wants or needs to change or enhance its image, it does need to invest in deliberate campaigns (that utilize paid or owned media) to make that happen. In 2019, according to the U.S. Census, an estimated $11.3 billion was spent on PR in the United States.

Marketers do recognize its importance. In one survey of marketers, more than eight in ten (83 percent) cited public relations as one of their most effective marketing tactics to influence buyer decisions, right behind advertising and content marketing. For example, when IKEA in France wanted to enhance awareness of the company's commitment to sustainable practices, it launched a PR campaign that invited influential food bloggers to participate in a cooking contest in each IKEA store that was called "Zero Waste." By promoting these events, the company not only increased the number of its followers on social media but also won an award for sustainable development.

Often, public relations efforts focus on the latter word—*relations*—with employees or potential employees. The oil company BP wanted to hire experienced people to work at one of its key processing terminals in an offshore Scottish island where it was ramping up production. Through promotions of the benefits of working in that area and by engaging with the local council and key islanders, the company saw a 40 percent increase in job applications for that location.

Public relations efforts are often used to enhance other marketing strategies. The "Like a Girl" campaign, which personal-care brand Always created to promote the idea that young teen girls should not lose their self-confidence as they hit puberty (a time when they start to need Always' products), used public relations successfully to promote the campaign itself, generating almost 50 million online video views and winning many industry awards. PR can be used in the opposite case, where brands make a misstep and need to use this type of earned media to rescue their reputation. Starbucks, for example, faced a large public outcry when two African-American men were arrested at a store in Philadelphia. The company immediately responded not only through paid full-page newspaper ads apologizing for the incident but by launching a large-scale public relations campaign to promote a mandatory half-day racial bias training for all store employees in an effort to restore its image as a company whose core values include creating a culture of diversity and inclusion.

Earned Media Value

It is ironic that although a brand's earned social media, such as its Facebook likes and Twitter posts, are captured immediately and passively the second they occur, advertisers are still determining what the *value* is of these often-impressive numbers. It may not cost much to generate millions of followers or fans to a brand, but how that translates into increases in awareness or product sales continues to be tested.

For traditional (non-digital) word of mouth, the media specialist needs to consider value, too, although it is harder to quantify. What happens to a brand's value when it receives either negative or positive comments from consumers? Sometimes this is expressed in terms of its stock price. In January 2021, after an apparently orchestrated discussion on social media platform Reddit, the electronic game retailer, Game Stop, saw its stock price unexpectedly soar, only to drop back down a few days later. At that time, however, some investors were able to make large sums of money. If a local radio or TV buy includes the on-air talent talking about your brand (*added value* negotiated as part of the deal), how much can you measure the impact at the cash register or to your website?

In addition, the media specialist needs to ensure that what a brand earns through earned media is part of a holistic communications plan, rather than just used for the sake of it, and that there are clear objectives for what the earned media should achieve for the brand.

Benefits of Earned Media to Advertisers

There are three primary advantages to using earned media for brands: consumer-driven communications, minimal cost, and enhanced brand value.

Consumer-Driven Communications

When people are asked if they are affected at all by advertising, the majority always responds no. But when questioned on what made them choose a particular product or brand, the answer is often the recommendation of a friend or relative. This benefit, the fact that the "advertisement" was, in effect, from someone they know or trust, clearly works to the advantage of earned media.

With millions of Americans turning to social media each month, advertisers have a huge opportunity to reach large numbers of people in a less overt way than paid digital ads. By creating content about the brand that consumers enjoy and will share, advertisers are able to engage with both current and prospective buyers. The ability to then track the activity (how many likes, shares, or comments) makes that type of earned media highly measurable, including basic information on those engaged in the practice, since social media sites require user registration (such as age and gender).

Enhanced Brand Value

As noted in Chapters 5, 6, and 7, there are various ways for brands to use paid media. By combining that with earned activity as well as owned media (such as brand-related content), advertisers can create a media plan that connects with the target audience in multiple ways. For example, Sargento Cheese could create short videos showing ways to use the product in easy-to-make recipes. This owned content could not only be posted to the brand's website but also be included in paid ads on Facebook or Instagram, which busy moms will then share with friends and family through those or other social networks to amplify the impact.

Minimal Cost

Due to the viral nature of most kinds of earned media, it is an extremely cost-efficient means of communication. If done correctly, it acts like a pebble dropped in a pond, with ripple effects that go far beyond where the brand mention started. And the marketer may pay nothing or just for the paid media advertising!

Although much of the focus of this book is on using paid media to help advertise and promote brands, the ability of earned media to impact perceptions that people have of those brands (and the companies that make them) should not be underestimated. It is one of the key benefits that earned media can provide—to make consumers feel good (or better) about the items that they purchase. It ideally works seamlessly with other elements of marketing and media to amplify the impact of a campaign through carefully planned promotional and publicity efforts that encourage consumers to talk about the brand and share their (hopefully positive) feelings or actions with others.

Drawbacks of Earned Media

When brands are considering earned media, they should note the potential disadvantages of lack of control, challenges on measuring impact, and questionable value.

Lack of Control

It is always serendipitous for a brand to generate positive word of mouth without even trying (as noted above for Eggo Waffles when they appeared in the hit Netflix series *Stranger Things*), but there is no guarantee that the reverse will not occur, with celebrities or even regular consumers creating a negative buzz about the product. Either is hard, if not impossible, to control, and this should be taken into consideration when implementing a WOM campaign.

Despite the enormous power of social media and other forms of earned media to change opinions and influence people, sometimes it can lead to unintended consequences due to the fact that what gets shared and amplified within one's group of friends or acquaintances may not tell the full story. When the CEO of Chick-fil-A spoke out against gay marriage in 2012, there was an immediate outcry on social media and an exhortation to boycott the chain; however, the company saw a healthy increase in sales for that same quarter, as people continued to patronize the quick service restaurant regardless.[40] A more serious outcome of misinformation took place in India, where fake rumors of child kidnappers posted and shared on WhatsApp and Facebook incited mob violence that resulted in more than 20 people being killed.

Weak Measurability on Impact

While there are many ways used to measure the impact of traditional paid media forms (TV, radio, etc.), the growth and development of earned media has in some ways outpaced the industry's understanding of how best to measure it. Certainly, for the digital forms such as organic search and earned social, it is possible to gather clickstream data on clicks or likes, comments, and shares, but fully connecting that to consumer impact measures, such as brand awareness or purchase intent, has been harder to do. Since consumers primarily go to Google or Facebook or Twitter to get information and communicate with others about topics besides brands, the proportion of earned media users who choose to take action with brands, compared to those who are going to these sites for information, entertainment and communication, is still relatively small.

Measurement for word of mouth tends to rely either on panels of consumers who report on what they are talking about (and with whom) or passive data capture, which automatically monitors the digital "conversation." While the latter can track vastly more data, it cannot necessarily get to the nuances of human conversations. The former can do so—but typically with smaller samples and the unreliability of self-reported data.

Similarly, it is difficult to quantify or demonstrate definitively the impact of many public relations campaigns. Consumer surveys can be used (before and after a PR campaign) to see how people say they feel about a brand, and response can also be measured through digital media (clicks, views, etc.)—but attributing the latter response solely to public relations may be difficult.

Questionable Value

As much as brands believe, or want to believe, that the original content they develop is appealing and interesting for consumers (and, therefore, worth liking or sharing), most of the time consumers are not going to be interested in hearing about the benefits of Brand A drain cleaner or do not have time to spend with a 10-minute video of Brand B's latest SUV showing off all its features. Even if someone has a blocked drain or is in the market for a new car, the chances that they will choose to like or share that branded content are still pretty slim. For earned media to be effective, brands do have to give serious consideration to whether they are doing or creating things that not only gain the attention of the recipient but are worth more than a few seconds of their time.

Additionally, while much of the conversation in earned media is generated at no cost to the brand, this is not always the case. With public relations, for example, a company is usually paying something to communicate information about the brand through media. While the results are often significant in terms of corporate reputations and consumer perceptions, it should be recognized that, even as it "earns" value for the brand, it does come at a cost.

Which Owned and Earned Media Should You Use?

Now that you have some basic information on each major owned and earned media category, we can start to consider why you might or might not wish to include each option in your media plans. Exhibit 8.1 summarizes the most important advantages and disadvantages that owned and earned channels offer.

Exhibit 8.1 Pros and Cons of Owned and Earned Media

Channel	Pros	Cons
Owned Media	Broader awareness Endless creativity Lower cost Indirect impact Implied trust	Consumer irritation Strategic weakness Lack of control Measurement challenges
Earned Media	Consumer-driven communications Enhanced brand value Minimal cost	Lack of control Questionable value Measurement challenges

Summary

In considering owned and earned media, the specialist must still focus on how each media type will enhance and achieve the plan's strategic objectives. Whether looking at the various forms of owned media, from product placement to custom events, and earned media, including word of mouth, earned social, and public relations, media experts need to assess the benefits and drawbacks of each and how to incorporate them seamlessly into the overall media plan.

Notes

1 "Why 'Idol' Works for Coke—But Not for Ford," Martin Lindstrom, *Advertising Age*, November 17, 2008, 18.
2 Cristel Antonia Russell, "Expanding the Agenda of Research on Product Placement: A Commercial Intertext," *Journal of Advertising*, vol. 48, no. 1, 2019, 38–48. Talé A. Mitchell and Michelle R. Nelson, "Brand Placement in Emotional Scenes: Excitation Transfer or Direct Affect Transfer?," *Journal of Current Issues & Research in Advertising*, vol. 39, no. 2, 2018, 206–219. Sukki Yoon, Yung Kyun Choi, and Sujin Song, "When Intrusive Can Be Likable: Product Placement Effects on Multitasking Consumers," *Journal of Advertising*, vol. 40, no. 2, Summer 2011, 63–76. Reo Song, Jeffrey Meyer, and Kyoungnam Ha, "The Relationship Between Product Placement and the Performance of Movies: Can Brand Promotion in Films Help or Hurt Moviegoers' Experience?" *Journal of Advertising Research*, vol. 55, no. 3, 3 September 2015, 22–338. Brigitte Naderer, Jörg Matthes, Franziska Marquart, and Mira Mayrhofer, "Children's Attitudinal and Behavioral Reactions to Product Placements:

Investigating the Role of Placement Frequency, Placement Integration, and Parental Mediation," *International Journal of Advertising*, vol. 37, no. 2, 2018, 236–255.

3 "'Top Chef' Bakes In Deeper Brand Integrations To Reduce Reliance On Skippable Ads," Jessica Wohl, *Advertising Age*, April 5, 2021, 10.

4 "As Ads Drop, Brands Make Own Content," Nicole Sperling and Tiffany Hsu, *New York Times*, March 24, 2021, B1/B5.

5 "'Top Chef' Bakes in Deeper Brand Integrations to Reduce Reliance on Skippable Ads," Jessica Wohl, *Advertising Age*, April 5, 2021, 10.

6 Yoori Hwang and Se-Hoon Jeong, "Editorial Content in Native Advertising: How Do Brand Placement and Content Quality Affect Native-Advertising Effectiveness?" *Journal of Advertising Research*, vol. 59, no. 2, June 2019, 208–218. Kasey Windels and Lance Porter, "Examining Consumers' Recognition of Native and Banner Advertising on News Website Home Pages," *Journal of Interactive Advertising*, vol. 20, no. 1, 2020, 1–16. Martin Eisend, Eva A. van Reijmersdal, Sophie C. Boerman, and Farid Tarrahi, "A Meta-Analysis of the Effects of Disclosing Sponsored Content," *Journal of Advertising*, vol. 49, no. 3, 2020, 344–366.

7 "Miracle-Gro Pivots from Seasonal Flights To 'Always On' Ad Strategy," Larissa Faw, *MediaPost Agency Daily*, April 20, 2021.

8 Hilde A. M. Voorveld, Peter C. Neijens, and Edith G. Smit, "The Relation Between Actual and Perceived Interactivity: What Makes the Web Sites of Top Global Brands Truly Interactive?" *Journal of Advertising*, vol. 40, no. 2, Summer 2011, 77–92. Brigitte Miller, Laurent Flores, Meriem Agrebi, and Jean-Louis Chandon, "The Branding Impact of Brand Websites: Do Newsletters and Consumer Magazines Have a Moderating Role?" *Journal of Advertising Research*, vol. 48, no. 3, September 2008, 465–472. Frank Harrison, "Digging Deeper Down into the Empirical Generalization of Brand Recall: Adding Owned and Earned Media to Paid-Media Touchpoints," *Journal of Advertising Research*, vol. 53, no. 2, June 2013, 181–185.

9 GroupM Next, "The New Music Model for Brands: How Live Events and Digital Are Changing the Sound of Things," February 2015.

10 "Coca-Cola: Hijacking the African Cup," WARC Awards, Grand Prix, Effective Content Strategy, and Multiplatform Special Award, 2018, from WARC.com.

11 Nicholas Burton and Simon Chadwick, "Ambush Marketing Is Dead, Long Live Ambush Marketing: A Redefinition and Typology of an Increasingly Prevalent Phenomenon," *Journal of Advertising Research*, vol. 58, no. 3, September 2018, 282–296.

12 "How Peloton is Tapping into Olympics Fever without a Sponsorship," as seen on www.adage.com, April 14, 2021.

13 "How to Choose the Right Celebrity Endorser for Your Brand," Janet Comenos, *Adweek.com*, March 21, 2018.

14 T. Bettina Cornwell, "Less 'Sponsorship As Advertising' and More Sponsorship-Linked Marketing As Authentic Engagement," *Journal of Advertising*, vol. 48, no. 1, 2019, 49–60. Lane Wakefield, Kirk Wakefield, and Kevin Lane Keller, "Understanding Sponsorship: A Consumer-Centric Model of Sponsorship Effects," *Journal of Advertising*, vol. 49, no. 3, 2020, 320–343. Francois A. Carrillat, Eric G. Harris, and Barbara A. Lafferty, "Fortuitous Brand Image Transfer: Investigating the Side Effect of Concurrent Sponsorships," *Journal of Advertising*, vol. 39, no. 2, Summer 2009, 109–123. Nigel Pope, Kevin E. Voges, and Mark Brown, "Winning Ways: Immediate and Long-Term Effects of Sponsorship on Perceptions of Brand Quality and Corporate Image," *Journal of Advertising*, vol. 38, no. 2, Summer 2009, 5–20. Erik L. Olson and Hans Mathias Thjomoe, "Explaining and Articulating the Fit Construct in Sponsorship," *Journal of Advertising*, vol. 40, no. 1, Spring 2011, 57–70.

Francois A. Carrillat, Alain d'Astous, and Marie-Pier Charette Couture, "How Corporate Sponsors Can Optimize the Impact of Their Message Content. Mastering the Message: Improving the Processability and Effectiveness of Sponsorship Activation," *Journal of Advertising Research*, vol. 55, no. 3, September 2015, 255–269. Francois A. Carrillat, Paul J. Solomon, and Alain d'Astous, "Brand Stereotyping and Image Transfer in Concurrent Sponsorships," *Journal of Advertising*, vol. 44, no. 4, 2015, 300–314. Jonathan A. Jensen and Joe B. Cobbs, "Predicting Return on Investment in Sport Sponsorship: Modeling Brand Exposure, Price, and ROI in Formula One Automotive Competition," *Journal of Advertising Research*, vol. 54, no. 4, December 2014, 435–447. T. Bettina Cornwell, *Sponsorship in Marketing: Effective Communications Through Sports, Arts, and Events*, USA: Routledge, 2014. Gerard Prendergast, Aishwarya Paliwal, and Marc Mazodier, "The Hidden Factors Behind Sponsorship and Image Transfer: Considerations for Bilateral Image Transfer among Sponsors and Events," *Journal of Advertising Research*, vol. 56, no. 2, June 2016, 132–135.

15 Marcela Moraes, John Gountas, Sandra Gountas, and Piyush Sharma, "Celebrity Influences on Consumer Decision Making: New Insights and Research Directions," *Journal of Marketing Management*, vol. 35, no. 13–14, 2019, 1159–1192. Lars Bergkvist, Hanna Hjalmarson, and Anne W. Mägi, "A New Model of How Celebrity Endorsements Work: Attitude Toward the Endorsement as a Mediator of Celebrity Source and Endorsement Effects," *International Journal of Advertising*, vol. 35, no. 2, 2016, 171–184. Christian Schimmelpfennig, "Who is the Celebrity Endorser? A Content Analysis of Celebrity Endorsements," *Journal of International Consumer Marketing*, vol. 30, no. 4, 2018, 220–234. Yadvinder Parmar, Bikram Jit Singh Mann, and Mandeep Kaur Ghuman, "Impact of Celebrity Endorser as In-Store Stimuli on Impulse Buying," *The International Review of Retail, Distribution and Consumer Research*, vol. 30, no. 5, 2020, 576–595. Kofi Osei-Frimpong, Georgina Donkor, and Nana Owusu-Frimpong, "The Impact of Celebrity Endorsement on Consumer Purchase Intention: An Emerging Market Perspective," *Journal of Marketing Theory and Practice*, vol. 27, no. 1, 2019, 103–121.

16 Kunal Sinha, "How Colgate, Philips and Durex Do Influencer Marketing in India," downloaded from WARC.com, September 2016.

17 "The Instagram Rich List Shows How Insane the World Is," Melissa Locker, *Fastcompany.com*, July 26, 2018.

18 "Micro-Influencers vs Macro-Influencers," Georgia Hatton, *Social Media Today*, February 2018.

19 T, Bettina Cornwell and Helen Katz, *Influencers: The Science Behind Swaying Others*, London: Routledge 2021. Courtney Carpenter Childers, Laura L. Lemon, and Mariea G. Hoy, "#Sponsored #Ad: Agency Perspective on Influencer Marketing Campaigns," *Journal of Current Issues & Research in Advertising*, vol. 40, no. 3, 2019, 258–274. Eunjin (Anna) Kim, Margaret Duffy, and Esther Thorson, "Under the Influence: Social Media Influencers' Impact on Response to Corporate Reputation Advertising," *Journal of Advertising*, vol. 50, no. 2, 2021, 119–138. Rebecca K. Britt, Jameson L. Hayes, Brian C. Britt, and Haseon Park, "Too Big to Sell? A Computational Analysis of Network and Content Characteristics among Mega and Micro Beauty and Fashion Social Media Influencers," *Journal of Interactive Advertising*, vol. 20, no. 2, 2020, 111–118. Shupei Yuan and Chen Lou, "How Social Media Influencers Foster Relationships with Followers: The Roles of Source Credibility and Fairness in Parasocial Relationship and Product Interest," *Journal of Interactive Advertising*, vol. 20, no. 2, 2020, 133–147. Chen Lou, Sang-Sang Tan, and Xiaoyu Chen, "Investigating Consumer Engagement with Influencer- vs.

Brand-Promoted Ads: The Roles of Source and Disclosure," *Journal of Interactive Advertising*, vol. 19, no. 3, 2019, 169–186. Chen Lou and Shupei Yuan, "Influencer Marketing: How Message Value and Credibility Affect Consumer Trust of Branded Content on Social Media," *Journal of Interactive Advertising*, vol. 19, no. 1, 2019, 58–73. Priska Linda Breves, Nicole Liebers, Marina Abt, and Annika Kunze, "The Perceived Fit between Instagram Influencers and the Endorsed Brand: How Influencer-Brand Fit Affects Source Credibility and Persuasive Effectiveness," *Journal of Advertising Research*, vol. 59, no. 4, December 2019, 440–454. Cristel Antonia Russell and Dina Rasolofoarison, "Uncovering the Power of Natural Endorsements: A Comparison with Celebrity-Endorsed Advertising and Product Placements," *International Journal of Advertising*, vol. 36, no. 5, 2017, 761–778.

20 "Herd on the Street," Robert Klein, *Mediaweek*, December 8, 2008, 12–13.

21 T. Bettina Cornwell and Helen Katz, *Influencer: The Science Behind Swaying Others*, London: Routledge, 2020.

22 Study by Engagement Labs, as reported on their website, December 2017.

23 Keller Fay research study, 2015, as seen on website www.kellerfay.com.

24 Engagement Labs, "5 Myths About Social Influence, 2017."

25 Engagement Labs, "America's Changing Brand Buzz Since COVID-19," April 29, 2021.

26 Brad Fay, Ed Keller, and Rick Larkin, "How Measuring Consumer Conversations Can Reveal Advertising Performance," *Journal of Advertising Research*, vol. 59, no. 4, December 2019, 433–439.

Ed Keller, "Unleashing the Power of Word of Mouth: Creating Brand Advocacy to Drive Growth," *Journal of Advertising*, vol. 47, no. 4, December 2007, 448–452. Ed Keller and Brad Fay, "The Role of Advertising in Word of Mouth," *Journal of Advertising Research*, vol. 49, no. 2, June 2009, 154–158. Lars Groeger and Francis Buttle, "Deciphering Word-of-mouth Marketing Campaign Reach: Everyday Conversation versus Institutionalized Word of Mouth," *Journal of Advertising Research*, vol. 5, no. 4, December 2016, 368–384. Yu-Hui Fang, Kwei Tang, Chia-Ying Li, and Chia-Chi Wu, "On Electronic Word-of-mouth Diffusion in Social Networks: Curiosity and Influence," *International Journal of Advertising*, vol. 37, no. 3, 2018, 360–384. Shu-Chuan Chu and Juran Kim, "The Current State of Knowledge on Electronic Word-of-mouth in Advertising Research," *International Journal of Advertising, International Journal of Advertising*, vol. 37, no. 1, 2018, 1–13.

27 eMarketer Report: Mobile Time Spent, 2020, January 2021.

28 eMarketer, Time Spent with Social Networks, January 2021.

29 Facebook.com, 2018.

30 Keith A. Quesenberry and Michael K. Coolsen, "What Makes Facebook Brand Posts Engaging? A Content Analysis of Facebook Brand Post Text That Increases Shares, Likes, and Comments to Influence Organic Viral Reach," *Journal of Current Issues & Research in Advertising*, vol. 40, no. 3, 2019, 229–244. Taemin Kim, Hyejin Kim, and Yunhwan Kim, "How Do Brands' Facebook Posts Induce Consumers e-Word-of-Mouth Behavior? Informational versus Emotional Message Strategy: A Computational Analysis," *Journal of Advertising Research*, vol. 59, no. 4, December 2019, 402–413.

31 Comscore, "The Power of Like," 2011.

32 Shareablee, "State of Social Media 2020," March 2021.

33 Ibid.

34 Ibid.

35 Comscore Media Metrix, January 2021.

36 "15 Tweets That Show Netflix Is Great at Twitter All over the World," www.best social.media.

37 "Remember the Ice Bucket Challenge? Here's What Happened to the Money," Ethan Wolff-Mann, *Time.com*, August 21, 2015.

38 Louis Leung, "Generational Differences in Content Generation in Social Media: The Roles of the Gratifications Sought and of Narcissism," *Computers in Human Behavior*, vol. 29, no. 3, May 2013, 997–1006. Anita Whiting and David Williams, "Why People Use Social Media: A Uses and Gratifications Approach," *Qualitative Market Research*, vol. 16, no. 4, 2013, 362–369. Frank Harrison, "Digging Deeper Down into the Empirical Generalization of Brand Recall: Adding Owned and Earned Media to Paid-Media Touchpoints," *Journal of Advertising Research*, vol. 53, no. 2, June 2013, 181–185. Judit Nagy and Anjali Midha, "The Value of Earned Audiences—How Social Interactions Amplify TV Impact: What Programmers and Advertisers Can Gain from Earned Social Impressions," *Journal of Advertising Research*, vol. 54, no. 4, December 2014, 448–453. Malte Brettel, Jens-Christian Reich, Jose M. Galivanas, and Tessa C. Flatten, "What Drives Advertising Success on Facebook? An Advertising-Effectiveness Model Measuring the Effects on Sales of 'Likes' and Other Social-Network Stimuli," *Journal of Advertising Research*, vol. 55, no. 2, June 2015, 162–175. Theo Araujo, Peter Neijens, and Rens Vliegenthart, "What Motivates Consumers to Re-tweet Brand Content? The Impact of Information, Emotion, and Traceability on Pass-Along Behavior," *Journal of Advertising Research*, vol. 55, no. 3, September 2015, 284–295. Xia Liu, Alvin C. Burns, and Yingjian Hou, "An Investigation of Brand-Related User-Generated Content on Twitter," *Journal of Advertising*, vol. 46, no. 2, April–June 2017, 236–247. Atanu Roy, Jisu Huh, Alexander Pfeuffer, and Jaideep Srivastava, "Development of Trust Scores in Social Media (TSM) Algorithm and Application to Advertising Practice and Research," *Journal of Advertising*, vol. 46, no. 2, April–June 2017, 269–282. Tania Yuki, "What Makes Brands' Social Content Shareable on Facebook? An Analysis that Demonstrates the Power of Trust and Attention," *Journal of Advertising Research*, vol. 55, no. 4, December 2015, 458–470. George D. Deitz, Marla B. Royne, Michael C. Peasley, Jianping "Coco" Huang, and Joshua T. Coleman, "EEG-Based Measures versus Panel Ratings: Predicting Social-Media Based Behavioral Responses to Super Bowl Ads," *Journal of Advertising Research*, vol. 56, no. 2, June 2016, 217–227. Yongjun Sung, Eunice Kim, and Sejung Marina Choi, "#Me and Brands: Understanding Brand-Selfie Posters on Social Media," *International Journal of Advertising*, vol. 37, no. 1, 2018, 14–28. José Manuel Gavilanes, Tessa Christina Flatten, and Malte Brettel, "Content Strategies for Digital Consumer Engagement in Social Networks: Why Advertising Is an Antecedent of Engagement," *Journal of Advertising*, vol. 47, no. 1, 2018, 4–23. Gunwoo Yoon, Cong Li, Yi (Grace) Ji, Michael North, Cheng Hong, and Jiangmeng Liu, "Attracting Comments: Engagement Metrics on Facebook and Financial Performance," *Journal of Advertising*, vol. 47, no. 1, 2018, 24–37. Ilyoung Ju, Yi He, Qimei Chen, Wei He, Bin Shen, and Sela Sar, "The Mind-Set to Share: An Exploration of Antecedents of Narrowcasting Versus Broadcasting in Digital Advertising," *Journal of Advertising*, vol. 46, no. 4, 2017, 473–486.

39 Rodoula H. Tsiotsou, "Introducing Relational Dialectics on Actor Engagement in the Social Media Ecosystem," *Journal of Services Marketing*, December 2020.

40 "Brands Heed Social Media. They're Advised Not to Forget Word of Mouth," Janet Morrissey, *New York Times*, November 26, 2017.

Chapter 9

Putting the Plan Together

Learning Outcomes: In this chapter you will learn how to:

- Understand the key elements that go into a media plan
- Consider alternatives to a proposed plan
- Examine a sample media plan

Putting together a media plan represents the culmination of all the thinking, planning, and organizing that we have discussed in earlier chapters. That is, with sound advertising and media objectives, a knowledge of who it is we wish to reach with our messages, and a clear idea of what different paid, owned, and earned media can offer us, we are now in a position to start assembling the plan. The key idea to keep in mind when doing this is your *media strategy*. What is it you are hoping to achieve by using media vehicle X as opposed to Y? How will your combination of media categories and vehicles help fulfill your advertising and media objectives? As with any process, there are several steps to the creation of the plan. These are outlined in this chapter.

Connecting the Target Audience to Media

The first step in building the media plan is finding out which media your target audience uses and what their relationships are with those media. There is not much point in putting your message about Allstate insurance on hundreds of radio stations across the country if the 25–54-year-olds you are trying to reach tend to be heavy television viewers. As noted in Chapter 3, you can discover the media habits of your potential customers through syndicated services such as MRI-Simmons, GWI, or through custom studies that you conduct or commission on your own. Another alternative, which is the cheapest but may be less accurate, is to do some mini research on your own. You can use your own website or Facebook page to gather feedback, keeping in mind that if someone is on that site or page, they may well be biased in your favor. You

DOI: 10.4324/9781003175704-9

could directly ask your clients or customers where they have seen your ads; if you have been sponsoring the local Little League club for years but nobody mentions it, then that might indicate the need for a different approach.

By this point, given what you now know about what each media type can offer (and what it can't), you are probably starting to see how the various media will fit in to your particular strategy. If your goal is to increase awareness of your beauty salon's new manicure and massage treatments, you might turn to the media best suited to that awareness goal—television and out-of-home. On the other hand, if you want to increase the frequency of visits to Pizza Hut restaurants, then local radio or digital might be a better bet because you can place a large number of ads at a reasonable cost and keep repeating the message to remind people of that establishment.

Once you think you have a handle on which media should be used, you should then consider more closely the *relationship* of your target audience with their media. This notion, as explained in the earlier chapters, explores the relationship of consumers to media in order to understand how and why they use the media they select.

For example, the 25–54-year-old insurance prospects might watch more television than average, according to the syndicated audience measurement data. But do they do so as an escape from their routines, because they are constantly looking for new information, or because they cannot afford other forms of entertainment? By understanding the target's motivations for media use, the planner will be better able to select the right media types and vehicles to communicate the advertiser's message.

As you start to assemble your media categories and vehicles, you also need to think about several other considerations: the timing of the plan, its scheduling, and its geographic variations. We consider each of these in turn.

Timing of the Plan

For many products, the timing of the plan is self-evident. That is, you want to advertise snow blowers in winter and sunscreen in summer. Other items are tied to specific days or weeks of the year, such as Valentine's Day candies or Thanksgiving turkeys. But for the majority of goods and services, you would ideally want to promote them continually, getting your message out on a very regular and frequent basis to reach as many people as you can as often as possible. Indeed, one of the popular theories on *how brands grow* is that most brands' buyers only purchase that brand occasionally, so that in order to keep the brand top of mind, marketers need to maintain a certain level of reach to all category buyers so that when they are ready to buy, they will remember your brand.[1]

There are a couple of challenges here. First, most advertisers, particularly small businesses, simply cannot afford to do continuous advertising. And second, there are good reasons *not* to bombard the media constantly with your message. People are going to tire more quickly of your ads, making them tune out or ignore them sooner. They may even grow so irritated by seeing or hearing them all the time that they actually develop less favorable opinions of your brand or company. Most of all, there is no point advertising something unless you have something worth saying. Remember, an advertising message has to tell the consumer about something that they will be interested in. If all you did was place a message in the paper or online 365 days of the year saying "I'm here", you would be unlikely to see much effect, if any, on your sales.

You need to focus your efforts on particular months, weeks, or days. Deciding when to do so is not all that difficult. Most businesses have some seasonality to them, even those that are used or frequented all the time. You probably know, for example, that people stock up on office supplies at the end of the financial period (quarterly or semi-annually); they flock to health clubs at the start of the new year and when the weather begins turning warmer. The peak season for home renovations runs from April to September each year.

You might want to use one of two tactics here. You could focus your efforts on promoting your product right before the peak period, reminding people of your existence and trying to take additional share points away from your competitors, or you could try to build up sales at other times of the year. Or you could try a combination of the two, maintaining a strong presence during the height of your "season", but also keeping a high profile at a couple of other times during the year, too. If you do choose to advertise when people may not be thinking about your product, then it is even more important that you tell them something new and interesting. Perhaps you lower your membership rates to the health club in March or October and announce that on digital displays and on billboards. You need not be confined to "typical" seasonal patterns either. You can create an event for your business at any time of the year. *Vogue* magazine sponsors an annual two-day global fashion event called *Forces of Fashion* that includes presentations and discussions from designers, editors, and celebrities, supported by sponsoring brands such as Porsche. Or you can find a charitable cause to support that can enhance your image among your target audience. Conagra Foods, for example, which makes well-known brands such as Reddi Whip, Hunts tomato sauce, and Banquet frozen meals, supports many initiatives that help fight hunger, including making food donations, encouraging employees to volunteer at food banks, and conducting financial education classes to help families struggling to make ends meet. Since the key target for many of Conagra's brands is women with children, this is an approach that likely makes those moms think more highly of them when they are in the store. These kinds of special activities not only provide excellent opportunities for self-promotion in the media, but they can also generate additional coverage through public relations efforts and social media.

It is also worthwhile to consider the seasonality of the media you are planning to use. Most media categories have seasonal variations—the fourth quarter (October–December) is often very tight, for example, because of pre-holiday advertising. For media sold on a supply-and-demand basis, such as radio and television ads, this can affect prices considerably. There are only a fixed number of minutes of commercial time available. Even for those media that can add space, such as magazines or newspapers, heavy media demand during those months may mean it is especially important to place orders well in advance. Other events happen less frequently but have a predictable impact on media buys. Congressional elections every other year and presidential elections every four years mean that the spring primaries and fall elections can have a significant impact on media availability and pricing in those time periods. In the sporting world, the winter and summer Olympics, alternating with each other every two years, affect national media buys around the time of those special events.

Balancing Reach and Frequency

As you develop your media plan, it is important to keep track of how well it will perform. That is, you need to keep calculating your reach and frequency measures to compare one potential plan against another. The goal is to find the right medium, or combination of media, that will realize your media objectives, given the amount of money you have to spend. You can do so using the calculations shown in earlier chapters, based on the size of your target audience and the ratings of the individual media vehicles.

It may turn out that you will not be able to achieve the specific number you set as your goal for reach and/or frequency. In that event, you need to consider several possibilities. It may be that a 55 percent reach of the target is acceptable, even though you had originally planned to reach 65 percent, or that a frequency of three is all right when four was the ideal. And keep in mind, again, that we are dealing here with plan *estimates* rather than actual reach figures. You may be restricted in the actions you can take. If your client demands that his message is seen on television, then that medium must remain in the plan. But perhaps you can opt for lower-rated networks instead of the largest, most expensive TV programs, and, by reducing the cost, be able to place the message more frequently and across more channels, thereby increasing the reach.

Alternately, you might want to rethink your timing and scheduling strategies. Maybe instead of advertising every two weeks for six months, you could place your message every week for three or four months, concentrating your efforts on the most important period and increasing your reach and frequency within that time span. And the addition of owned and earned media efforts will likely enhance your brand presence even when there are no paid media being used.

ROI and Attribution

While media planners should have a good understanding of all the media concepts outlined in Chapter 4, today's advertisers and agencies rely heavily on media models to perform the calculations. A media model is a statistical routine performed by software that goes through the data and manipulates it to project the effectiveness and efficiency of a plan. Various kinds of models are used, all with the overall goal of providing numbers to support the plan. The models are usually based on original numbers of actual audiences to a media type (magazine readership, TV viewership, digital tracking, etc.). They then rely on statistical techniques, such as regression, to project out from that data to other demographics, time periods, or markets (depending on the scope of the model).

The main goal of these models is to try to figure out what marketing (and media) elements are driving actual sales. In so doing, they attempt to measure the media's return on investment, or ROI. As noted in Chapter 4, the key question to be answered is: for every dollar spent on television or radio or digital, how much is returned in sales? The goal is to receive at least $1 of net profit for each dollar that they invest. If they obtain much less than that, then some argue the money is being wasted. Conversely, if the ROI is much higher than $1, it can suggest they are not spending enough because if the advertising and media are having such an impact, then they should be spending more to make the most of that effect. The techniques used are fairly complex; they try to account for external factors beyond just media spend such as consumer confidence, weather patterns, or economic indicators, for example. The idea of holding advertising media more accountable for their performance is one that has found favor among high-ranking executives at many corporations. Some find it difficult to believe that any kind of model can truly determine the proportion of sales delivered by any form of indirect and/or brand image advertising (as opposed to truly measurable direct response, promotional, or digital advertising). But as marketing budgets have faced increasing scrutiny, these types of models have gained in popularity and use.

Much of the interest in ROI has been propelled by the enormous growth in digital spending. With that type of advertising, it became possible to look at the behavioral response to an ad. How many viewed it? How many clicked on it? And of those who clicked, how many went through to purchase the product (or take some other action)? The precision of tying exposure to sales (or some other action) has been a strong driver of digital's growth. Today, most paid media have created ways to demonstrate a similar level of accountability. Some, such as radio or magazines, have relied primarily on custom research using marketing mix models to show sales driven by ads on their platforms. In television, the tuning data collected at the household level pulled back from cable boxes or smart TV sets has provided new ways to measure the precise impact of TV spots. The subscriber or registered user information can be linked to a myriad of other data, from frequent shopper loyalty cards, to auto registrations, to credit card spending, to an advertiser's own customer database, allowing them to measure directly the link between TV ad exposure and product sales.

An extension of a marketing mix model that has become popular is the multitouch attribution (MTA) model. This approach considers the collective and fractional impact of various media exposures not just in predicting sales but also in the way they work together over time. It helps marketers understand, for example, whether the TV ad works best if delivered before the digital ad or if an event sponsorship is most effective when promoted with TV and digital simultaneously.

Most accountability studies focus on the short-term impact of the advertising. Did it generate immediate sales of the brand? It is much harder to precisely measure the long-term impact. Let's say your ad for Fruitola fruit drink appears in a monthly magazine. Your target sees the ad but is unlikely to rush out and buy the product immediately, but when she is next at the grocery store, she sees the product, remembers the ad, and decides she will try it. Many accountability models would not be able to capture that kind of longer-term effect.

Another hard-to-measure effect is what is called the *halo effect* of advertising. You might see an ad campaign for Fantastik cleaning spray that talks about how SC Johnson, its manufacturer, cares about keeping families healthy by removing germs from their homes. Your favorable impression of the brand may be transferred to other products made by the same company, such as RAID or Pledge, even if they are in other cleaning categories. That halo is very hard to capture in statistical models, simply because it is difficult to measure through direct data. How much of the sales results for RAID, for example, can be attributed to consumers' reaction to the Fantastik advertising?

Indeed, advertising's impact is not always reflected solely in terms of sales. Many brands use media to convey a message that is designed to improve awareness or enhance brand loyalty or increase brand consideration. If every ad was supposed to generate an immediate sale, companies that make cars or laptops or other high-ticket items would be wasting the vast majority of their ad dollars! Despite these reservations, more and more advertisers expect answers on the ROI of their media spending. While you as a media specialist may not have simple answers, you should at least be aware of the discussions going on around the topic.

Scheduling Ads

You may have a good idea about when to start running your ads. The next question to think about is how to schedule them. Do you want them running each week for six weeks (*continuity*), or twice a month all year (*bursts*), or for alternating six-week periods (*flighting*)? The answer to this question will depend primarily on two interrelated factors: your media objective and your sales pattern. There should always be a timing component stated in your objective, which will give you some guidance for the scheduling of the plan. If you hope to reach 60 percent of your target during the next six months with the message that your hospital was rated the number-one pediatric hospital in the city by a *U.S. News* analysis, then you may want to disperse your ads throughout the period to reach as many different people in your audience as possible. For H&R Block, which wants to expose people to its message about how fast it can generate tax refunds, there would be good reason to schedule most of the ads in the three months prior to the April 15 tax deadline date, building up the frequency of the message at the time of year when it is most appropriate.

You should also think about the scheduling of different media and their combination. Perhaps you could advertise your Panera store on local radio every week of the year and supplement it with outdoor billboards, digital display ads, or mobile ads around the time of each special promotion. A brand's owned or earned media presence may be continual and supplement or complement the paid media schedule.

Much of what we know about scheduling tactics comes from our general knowledge of reach and frequency. That is, if you wish to reach as many *different* people as possible in your target audience, then you want to disperse your messages across media, vehicles, or days and dayparts, for example. On the other hand, if you want to ensure that your audience hears or sees your ads several times in a given period, you should concentrate them on fewer media, vehicles, days, or dayparts.

The pattern of scheduling does not seem to make a difference, however, in terms of total reach. Whether your ads appear in two sequential weeks or alternate weeks (one week on, one week off) or are placed one week a month over four months; the final reach will be approximately the same. One thing to keep in mind, however, is that if you schedule too many ads within a short time frame, your audience is likely to ignore or tune out those messages because they are tired of seeing them, a phenomenon known as *wearout*.[2] The timing element could be critical, depending on your product. It would not make much sense to spread ads for a highly seasonal item, such as suntan lotion or Christmas decorations, across many months; but, if you are promoting your Charles Schwab office through newspaper ads and in digital media, there is something to be said for having a fairly constant presence during the year (perhaps changing the message to tie in to the financial cycle).

Two television scheduling tactics that are occasionally used among major advertisers are double-spotting and bookending. *Double-spotting* refers to placing two spots within the same program. The effect of this technique is to increase the likelihood of multiple exposures to your ad message (i.e., increased frequency). When these ads appear at the beginning and end of the commercial break, this is a tactic known as *bookending*. Part of the expectation is that, even if you have tuned away at the start of the break, you will see the ad at the end of the break when you are returning to watch the program content.

In the 1990s, considerable research was conducted on how best to schedule ad messages to impact sales. A study done by John Philip Jones examined the purchase records of households who also had their TV viewing captured via TV set meters (to record what channels were viewed). The results clearly showed that to achieve the greatest short-term advertising strength, or STAS, the best scheduling tactic was to place at least one message per week across as many weeks as possible. In this way, the plan could impact more people closer to the time of purchase. While the study had some significant limitations (it only looked at packaged goods, only dealt with television advertising, and only examined households rather than people), its impact was noteworthy. Advertisers began switching their scheduling, moving away from trying to achieve a 3+ reach (reaching the target audience three or more times) in a month. Instead, they began looking at a 1+ reach per week, a strategy known as *frequency planning*. Here, the schedule calls for fewer GRPs per week, spread across more weeks of the year. While this doesn't make sense in many categories, especially those that require lengthy or high-involvement decisions by consumers (cars, houses, financial services), for many packaged goods manufacturers, frequency planning became the norm.

Cost Efficiencies

Costs are obviously very important for the media plan. So, in addition to keeping track of reach and frequency figures as you create the plan, you must also consider the costs involved. Of course, these are closely related. If you need to increase the frequency of your message, it is going to require more media time or space, which means more money. But as we noted previously, it might be possible to find a cheaper medium or vehicle to help your funds go further. Cost efficiencies can be calculated in terms of cost per thousand of the audience reached (CPM) and through cost per rating points (CPP), both of which were explained in Chapter 4. The more "mass" the medium, the cheaper it will be on a CPM basis, but the less targeted it will be for your situation. That is, there will be a lot of waste exposures of people who are probably not interested in what you have for sale. For a widely used product or service, such as car tires or a muffler shop, that might not be a bad thing. But if you are trying to reach a narrower group of people, such as Tesla car owners, to offer them a specially designed luggage rack that sits on the roof of the car, then you would be better off paying a higher CPM in a more targeted environment, such as car enthusiast websites or streaming audio focused on the classic rock music you know that target enjoys. The growth of more advanced forms of

TV advertising, noted in Chapter 5, helps to reduce, or eliminate completely, this waste by sending ads to—and charging the advertiser for—the people you really want to talk to.

Tactical Considerations

As you develop your plan, there are probably going to be numerous additional considerations that are specific to your product or service. These might include trade merchandising, consumer merchandising, national–local integration, and testing.

Trade Merchandising

For many goods and services, the trade plays a critical role in the brand's development and sales. Many media plans that are geared primarily to the consumer market also have some side benefits for the trade. When Frito-Lay promotes its Doritos corn chips, it is telling its distributors and retailers that it is pushing the brand and helping to increase their revenues, too. National ads for Burger King, or the Cadillac XT6 SUV, are also designed to help the local franchisee or dealer.

In putting the plan together, therefore, it is important to look at what trade-merchandising elements may be attached to it. Perhaps for a chain of Jiffy Lube oil-change shops, you can bring all the operators together for a kick-off party when the media campaign begins. Even something as simple as buttons with your new campaign slogan can help give the trade a sense of being part of the program. Sending them copies of the new ads and/or materials lets them know what message is being promoted to customers. The media can help here as well, particularly if you are one of their valued customers. They may be willing to co-sponsor an event for your distributors or retailers, for example.

One particular type of trade merchandising is *cooperative* (coop) advertising. With this, two groups agree to divide the cost of the advertising space or time. This may be as simple as a tag placed at the end of a retailer's commercial that mentions the address of the local store, or it can be a joint promotion of a theme park and a soft drinks company, where the latter is helping fund the ads of the former since it makes money on the drinks sold in the park. For local businesses, there are significant benefits to this type of merchandising. If you are a small health food store in Madison, Wisconsin, your ability to advertise on cable TV or in the Wisconsin tourism guide is going to be greatly enhanced if you can get supporting (coop) funds from Clif Bar & Company, whose products you sell in your store. Not only would it allow you to promote your business in more types of or more expensive media, but you will also most likely be able to afford better-looking ads! There are potential disadvantages, however. Sometimes the manufacturer will impose restrictions on the ads in terms of both their content/appearance and their distribution and scheduling. But even with those limitations, the coop approach works well in many cases.

Consumer Merchandising

Although we focus here almost exclusively on advertising media, it is important to keep in mind many of the other ways in which you can gain additional exposure for and mileage out of your media plan through owned and earned media. There are a multitude of consumer merchandising possibilities available, from sampling to community festivals to exhibitions and displays. If you are promoting a line of gourmet preserves, then perhaps in addition to the digital display and paid search ads that you run, you can talk to the local grocery stores to set up sampling booths in their stores and feature the dates and locations in the online ads. For a wireless phone company promoting the latest cell phones, you could go to local community festivals and let consumers see them, buying local search keywords or radio ads to inform consumers about which events you will be attending. Whatever you do, however, should remain within the overall communications objectives of your plan—increasing awareness, obtaining customer preference, encouraging brand selection, and so on.

To gain as much advantage as possible from consumer promotions, you should consider increasing other paid media weight when you are featured at a community event or placing more digital or other media ads the week that you are holding the promotion, as well as incorporating them into your earned media efforts (promoting on Instagram stories, setting up a Twitter hashtag, or adding information to your Facebook page).

National–Local Integration

While some products, such as new movies or product launches, are advertised primarily on a national level, and others, such as the neighborhood coffeehouse, appear only in local ads, the majority of name brands include both national and local advertising in their media plans. If that is the case, you need to ensure not only that the message is consistent (something handled by the creative team), but also that the media placements are aligned. There are different ways of doing this. For some, particularly the higher spending advertisers, the local media weight is added to make an even greater impact on the national spending, such as buying spot TV on top of network TV, or placing digital ads in locally focused websites in addition to your national digital presence. For others, typically with smaller budgets, the addition of local media helps to stretch the paid media dollars further, helping to create the illusion (in selected markets) that the advertiser has a constant presence. Digital media are critical here, since it is possible to target ads to specific geographical locations such as the zip codes in which your franchises are located. In all these situations, you should ensure that there is no unwanted duplication and that the messages do not drown out each other to the point of irritating the consumer or that they are so inconsistent that the consumer is faced with competing messages.

Testing

For smaller advertisers, the notion of testing a plan may seem unnecessary. If you only have a few thousand dollars to spend, then it doesn't seem worthwhile. However, if you are about to change your entire marketing and media strategy, it is a good idea to see first—on a small scale—whether your new approach is likely to increase sales or harm them. For example, in 2014, Procter & Gamble had been advertising its Swiffer cleaning products primarily through coupons and national magazines. The following year, it pulled dollars out of the print medium, and started investing in digital ads. That test seemed to work for the next few years, where it continued to increase its proportion of spend in digital.

Testing is also a good idea for making changes in media weight (GRPs). If you are trying to persuade your client to increase annual spending from a few hundred dollars to several thousand, and you face resistance to the idea, then you might suggest a test of the proposed strategy in one or more markets to see what impact those added dollars would have to the bottom line.

Presenting the Plan

Whenever you present your completed plan, whether it is to senior management at your own company or to your client, you need to keep three points in mind. The first is to *be visual*. Most people either hate or fear media because they believe it is a morass of numbers, most of which they don't understand. The more you can do to present the information in ways that they can *see* what is going on, the better off you will be. That means using charts, graphs, pictures, photos, or videos to liven things up and bring the numbers to life. For instance, if you are presenting the demographic statistics on your target, then you can do so via a short video that depicts these people in real life or present charts or photos that demonstrate who they are.

The second point to remember is to *be brief.* Although you want to have all of the backup materials and numbers to support what you are doing, when you make a presentation you should focus on the key points. Assuming you have an interested audience, they will look at the details afterward or ask you questions as you go along. Again, this helps to overcome the common perception of media that it is a mind-numbing experience, filled with mathematical formulas and statistics that are, quite simply, boring.

Third, and perhaps most importantly, *remember the consumer*. Ultimately, your plan is designed to help your client sell more widgets to actual people. If your plan simply recites a hundred different statistics and presents all of the numbers in charts, tables, and flowcharts, it may be totally accurate but will seem completely removed from the marketing reality that your client lives in.

Fortunately, there are ways around these problems. The first, keeping it visual, can be accomplished through the use of a flowchart. This shows, at a glance, when the ads will run, in which media and vehicles, at what cost, and to what effect (reach and frequency). These can be made for each target in a given plan and be broken out by medium, if desired. An example is shown later in this chapter. There are numerous ways of creating flowcharts. You can simply draw one yourself, use a spreadsheet program, or use a custom media flowchart package.

Being brief is harder to do. It usually comes down to practice. Running through your presentation with a friend or colleague and asking for their advice can be useful. It is particularly helpful to present your work to someone outside of your area; if they can understand your concise explanations of media terms, then you are doing fine! Remember, however, to include all the pertinent information (including calculations for how you arrived at your conclusions) in the deck of materials you leave behind. In addition, remember to show how your media plan fits in with and enhances the brand's marketing and advertising objectives and strategies.

Learn as much as possible about the end-user of your product, and include some of those findings in your presentation. You might want to survey some of the customers or do a couple of focus groups to find out how they currently use media and advertising in your category. Include a few of the verbatims (what consumers actually said, in their own words), or even some video of your conversations with customers, to remind your client that you know you are, in the end, dealing with people.

Last, but not least, it is crucial to remind your audience that you are presenting estimates. Some of those may be informed by years of experience, but many are based on your best judgment, syndicated data sources, or mathematical reasoning. People tend to believe that because you, as the media specialist, have placed a number on something, then that turns it into reality. If that were so, media planning would be completely automated and done by rote, a pure science, rather than the combination of art and science that it remains today.

A Media Plan Example

Let's go through an example for a fictitious brand of granola bar, Bene-Bar. This is a nationally distributed health-oriented brand that was first introduced in 2015. The company now wishes to introduce a new line that only has natural ingredients in it, called Bene-Bar Natural. It will compete primarily with the natural granola bars of KIND and Nature Valley along with cereal-focused Kellogg's.

Situation Analysis

Through the end of calendar year 2021, Bene-Bar sales are flat versus a year ago.

Marketing objectives/strategies: Introduce new Bene-Bar Natural among granola bar eaters in two ways:

1 Year-round focus on natural benefits of new Bene-Bar Natural granola bar.
2 Heavy-up during primary granola bar months (spring/summer).

Advertising time period: January through December 2023
   Media budget: $20.0 million

Marketing Background

Competitive Analysis

- Nature Valley: Total spending, $30 million; 50 percent cable television, 25 percent network TV, 15 percent local radio, 8 percent magazines, 2 percent online video
- Kellogg's: Total spending, $25 million; 80 percent cable television, 10 percent magazines, 5 percent paid social, 5 percent online video
- KIND: Total spending, $15 million; 70 percent cable television, 20 percent network TV, 5 percent paid social, 5 percent online video
- Category total: Total spending, $90 million; 50 percent cable television, 15 percent magazines, 10 percent network TV, 10 percent paid social, 10 percent online video, 5 percent local radio

Seasonality

Granola bar usage tends to peak in the spring/summer months, but the product is used throughout the year.

The following chart shows usage for each two-month period compared to usage throughout the year. Where a number is 100, that means the usage in that period is the same as the annual average. If the number is above 100, usage is greater than average; if the number is below 100, usage is less than average in that time period.

Exhibit 9.1 Bene-Bar Seasonality

Bene-Bar

J/F	M/A	M/J	J/A	S/O	N/D
80	110	126	130	105	70

Granola Bar Category

J/F	M/A	M/J	J/A	S/O	N/D
95	98	105	121	102	80

Advertising Objectives

Generate awareness among the target of the natural ingredients of the new line of Bene-Bar Natural granola bars, with a goal of 40 percent by the end of calendar year 2023 (from 0 percent at the start of the year).

Media Objectives

1   Advertise to granola bar eaters. The demographics and psychographics of this target are:

- Women aged between 25 and 54, household income $100,000+, with children
- Well-educated, professional or managerial, health and wellness-oriented

The target consists of 32 million women who can be defined as granola bar users. They represent 25 percent of all women.

2   Achieve the following communication goals: Average four-week delivery.

Exhibit 9.2 Bene-Bar Media Objectives

Peak period	Rest of year
Reach 35% of target reached 3+ times	Reach 10% of target reached 3+ times

3   Provide year-round media support to encourage trial and repeat usage throughout year, with additional weight during the peak summer months.

4   Provide national advertising support.
5   Include paid, owned, and earned media support.

Media Strategies

Following the success of the primary brand during the past six years, the 2023 media plan recommends an awareness-building media strategy using television as the primary paid medium and online video and selected magazines as the additional paid media types. Bene-Bar Natural will work with influencers such as Kayla Itsines or Krys Campbell, as well as create integrations into Bravo's *Top Chef* and HGTV's *Christina on the Coast*, both of which will be promoted on the brand's website and social media channels such as Facebook, Instagram, and Pinterest. It will use paid social media to share tips for helping on-the-go women.

Television

As the primary medium, national TV provides:

- High reach/awareness builder
- Sight, sound, and motion
- Immediacy of message
- Targetability (niche networks)
- Continuity (lower cost networks)
- Contextual relevance
- Emotional connection to viewer/consumer.

The plan will include cable TV shows that appeal to the target audience. These fall into genres such as sitcoms, movies, and reality/news.
   The following cable networks are more likely to be viewed by the target:

- HGTV
- Food Network
- Bravo
- TLC
- Lifetime

One-half of the weight will be in prime time, with the remainder split between weekend and late night. Prime time programming offers a broad reach. Late night helps expand that reach, and weekend will reach the target when they are relaxing at home or planning for the week ahead.
   Bene-Bar will also include some non-linear television (over the top and connected TV).

Digital Video

As the second medium, digital video provides:

- Additional reach
- Response-based measurement
- Contextual relevance
- Audience based targeting.

The digital impressions will be purchased programmatically against the desired strategic target audience of women aged between 25 and 54 who buy granola bars and are interested in health and fitness. Links to the brand's website and social media pages will be included, along with digital promotions during peak seasons.

In addition, Google will be used to drive search on natural health-related keywords.

Magazines

As the third medium, magazines provide:

- Long message life
- Repeat exposure
- Targetability—ability to provide a contextually relevant and engaging message
- Editorial compatibility.

Magazine ads will include both hard copy print (one-page, four-color) and the digital version of those ads wherever possible. The latter will have links to the brand's website and social media pages and allow the reader to interact with related nutritional information.

The preferred position will be:

- Health and fitness—fitness section
- Food—front of the book
- General interest—news section.

The recommended magazines, which are more likely to be read by the target, are shown in Exhibit 9.3.

Owned Media: Brand Website

The Bene-Bar Natural website will provide diet and health information, including video clips from the TV shows it sponsors, *Top Chef* and *Christina*

Exhibit 9.3 Magazine Delivery for Bene-Bar

Magazine	Coverage	Index
Parents	8.4%	268
Cosmopolitan	10.6%	216
US Weekly	7.8%	209
Women's Health	8.0%	208
Food Network Magazine	6.8%	148

on the Coast. It will also offer helpful tips on how to maintain health and fitness while on the go.

Branded Integration

For its connection to *Top Chef* and *Christina on the Coast*, Bene-Bar Natural will get mentions during the episodes in which it is featured, in addition to commercial time, and a significant presence on the TV show's websites and social media pages. It will include sponsored program-related quizzes and games in those venues where consumers can sign up to receive weekly on-the-go tips.

Earned Media: Influencers and Social

Bene-Bar Natural will create relationships with at least two influencers to help drive awareness of and engagement with the brand. These people could include one of the hosts on Food Network or HGTV, along with one or more healthy lifestyle bloggers. As the relationship grows, these people would be featured in paid media messages, included in the brand's owned media efforts, and featured at local events in which the brand appears.

On its social media pages (Facebook, Instagram, Pinterest), Bene-Bar Natural will position itself as the healthy "helping hand" for busy women trying to fit 25 hours into every day.

The Final Plan

The total cost of this plan will be $20 million (including a 5 percent amount as a contingency). The flowchart in Exhibit 9.4 depicts how the plan would be laid out during the year.

Exhibit 9.4 Sample Flowchart: Bene-Bar Natural 2023 Media Plan

		January					February				March				Totals
		3	10	17	24	31	7	14	21	28	7	14	21	28	TRPs/$000
Bene-Bar Natural															
PAID															
Television	Cable: Prime time	10	10	10	10	10					10	10	10	10	
	Cable: Weekend/Late night	5	5	5	5	5					10	10	10	10	
	OTT/CTV	2	2	2	2	2					2	2	2	2	
	Total TRPs	**17**	**17**	**17**	**17**	**17**	**0**	**0**	**0**	**0**	**22**	**22**	**22**	**22**	
	Total Cost ($000)						*$1,500*								
Digital	Video														
	Search														
	Total Impressions						*10,000,000 Imps/month*								
	Total Cost ($000)						*$650*								
Magazines	All Titles														
	Total TRPs						*25 TRPs/month*								
	Total Cost ($000)						*$1,200*								
OWNED															
Brand Integration	*Top Chef*										5	5	5	5	
	Christina on the Coast						5	5	5	5					
	Total Cost ($000)						*$300*								
EARNED															
Social	**Total Cost ($000)**						*$300*								
															308/$3,350

Bene-Bar Natural

PAID

		April 4	11	18	25	May 2	9	16	23	30	June 6	13	20	27	Totals TRPs/$000
Television	Cable: Prime time	15	15	15	15	10	10	10	10	10	15	15	15	15	
	Cable: Weekend/Late night	5	5	5	5	5	5	10	10	10	10	10	10	10	
	OTT/CTV	2	2	2	2	2	2	2	2	2	2	2	2	2	
	Total TRPs	**22**	**22**	**22**	**22**	**17**	**17**	**22**	**22**	**22**	**27**	**27**	**27**	**27**	
	Total Cost ($000)							$3,200							
Digital	Video														
	Search														
	Total Impressions							*10,000,000 Imps/month*							
	Total Cost ($000)							$800							
Magazines	All Titles														
	Total TRPs							*25 TRPs/month*							
	Total Cost ($000)							$1,200							
OWNED															
Brand Integration	*Top Chef*	5	5	5	5	5	5	5	5	5					
	Christina on the Coast										5	5	5	5	
	Total Cost ($000)							$300							
EARNED															
Social	**Total Cost ($000)**							$500							431/$5,800

(Continued)

Exhibit 9.4 (Continued)

		July				August					September				Totals
		4	11	18	25	1	8	15	22	29	5	12	19	26	TRPs/$000
Bene-Bar Natural															
PAID															
Television	Cable: Prime time	15	15	15	15	10	15	15	15	15	15	15	15	15	
	Cable: Weekend/Late night	5	5	5	5	10	10	10	10	10	10	10	10	10	
	OTT/CTV	2	2	2	2	2	2	2	2	2	2	2	2	2	
	Total TRPs	22	22	22	22	22	27	27	27	27	27	27	27	27	
	Total Cost ($000)							$2,200							
Digital	Video														
	Search														
	Total Impressions					15,000,000 Imps/month									
	Total Cost ($000)							$750							
Magazines	All Titles														
	Total TRPs					25 TRPs/month									
	Total Cost ($000)							$1,400							
OWNED															
Brand Integration	*Top Chef*														
	Christina on the Coast	5	5	5	5	5	5	5	5	5					
	Total Cost ($000)							$200							
EARNED															
Social	**Total Cost ($000)**							$500							
															446/$5,050

Bene-Bar Natural

PAID

	October 3	October 10	October 17	October 24	October 31	November 7	November 14	November 21	November 28	December 4	December 11	December 18	December 25	Totals (TRPs/$000)
Television														
Cable: Prime time	15	15	15	10	10					10	10	10	10	
Cable: Weekend/Late night	10	10	10	10	10					10	10	10	10	
OTT/CTV	2	2	2	2	2	2	2	2	2	2	2	2	2	
Total TRPs	**27**	**27**	**27**	**22**	**22**	**2**	**2**	**2**	**2**	**22**	**22**	**22**	**22**	**366/$4,800**
Total Cost ($000)							$1,800							
Digital														
Video														
Search														
Total Impressions							20,000,000 Imps/month							
Total Cost ($000)							$1,000							
Magazines														
All Titles														
Total TRPs							30 TRPs/month							
Total Cost ($000)							$1,500							
OWNED														
Brand Integration														
Top Chef	5	5	5	5	5	5	5	5	5	5	5			
Christina on the Coast														
Total Cost ($000)							$300							
EARNED														
Social														
Total Cost ($000)							$500							

Total TRPs	1,551
Total Budget ($000)	$19,000
5% safety	$1,000
Total Budget ($000)	$20,000

Although this is a very generalized and simple version of what to include in a plan, it provides the basic information that has been covered earlier in this book. You should note that all of the recommendations need to be backed up by research data, wherever possible, beyond simple tables showing indices or coverage for individual media vehicles or gross expenditures for the year. Here is a brief list of the kinds of analyses that could be included in the backup for this plan:

- Demographic/lifestyle analysis of granola bar users
- Category geographic analysis (BDI versus CDI by region)
- Purchase volume for brand and category
- Seasonality analysis
- Purchase behavior of target (online and in-store)
- Media usage of the target
- Cable TV network comparisons
- Daypart/program rankings by target
- Magazine comparisons
- Brand website traffic patterns
- Social media usage (e.g., likes, shares, tweets for brand and competitors)
- Social media page traffic patterns and analysis
- CPM comparisons (e.g., TV versus print versus digital)
- Detailed reach and frequencies by medium

Once you have completed your media plan, you might think your task is over. Even as you are creating the plan, you should be starting to think about possible alternatives. These are covered next.

Spending More Money

The opportunity to gain a larger budget than you were originally expecting does not happen very often, and certainly not as often as a media specialist might like! However, there are several good reasons for being prepared to spend more on paid advertising media than was originally proposed. It is your job as the media specialist to prove to the client how much more effective the media plan *could* be if there were more dollars available.

To some people this might sound wasteful. But for the most part, research supports the notion that placing more dollars in advertising media to reach more people on more occasions (assuming, of course, that they are the right people for your product) will increase sales.

So, how do you best prepare to offer the alternative of spending more? In many situations, the best way is to simultaneously create a second media plan that has a larger budget. If your primary plan has an annual media budget of $2 million, then you might consider creating an additional one at the $3 million level to see how that would perform. In doing so, you should not simply throw extra media weight around randomly. Instead, you should revisit your advertising and media objectives and consider what you might set as your goals if you had that extra money to spend. If, for instance, your original goal was to boost awareness of the latest Target store to open in Atlanta to 35 percent of the surrounding communities, then, perhaps if your budget was to be 20 percent larger, you might think about setting your objectives higher, proposing that with the additional funds you could increase awareness to 40 percent in that same time period.

An additional option with increased funding is to increase the efforts in owned and earned media. If your paid media plan for Tropicana Orange Juice for kids consists of network television and magazine ads, then the extra dollars you are recommending could permit you to feature the brand at local community festivals. Or keyword searches could be purchased related to juice or children's nutrition, and paid TikTok and Instagram ads could promote the brand socially.

Of course, in suggesting where and how this extra money could be spent, you must always show what will be achieved in return. That is, you need to quantify, wherever possible, the positive impact those dollars will have. This can be done through reach and frequency calculations that show how many additional people in the target will be reached and how many more times they will have the opportunity to be exposed to the message. Supplementary funds may also end up *lowering* the cost of individual ads, either through volume or frequency discounts, or by reducing the cost per thousand (CPM). So, although the bottom-line cost of the plan may go up, the cost efficiency may actually improve.

Another advantage to spending more media dollars is that they may allow you to reach a secondary target more readily. If you are putting a plan together for the Beef Council, where the primary target audience is women who like to cook, then perhaps expanding the plan will allow you to address more clearly a secondary target audience of restaurant chefs. You might also think about using additional dollars to reach people who can influence your primary target. For a media plan offering a college fund that is aimed at parents, you might spend the extra monies to promote your company to financial planners to whom the parents will turn for advice.

Whatever you recommend for your increased-spending scenario, you must justify it in terms of the objectives and strategies that you have stated upfront (even if you propose modifying those objectives if you get additional funds).

Spending Less Money

Unfortunately, for most media specialists, the more common case is that you will end up having to spend less than originally proposed.

Whatever the reason for the cost reductions, as you prepare an alternative plan, think carefully about how you can put together a media schedule that will come as close as possible to meeting your original objectives. There may be several ways to cut corners without decimating the plan. Perhaps you can shorten the flight times, running TV ads for two weeks at a time instead of four, or reduce the digital programmatic video buy, or rely more on owned or earned media that may cost no additional money.

Creating a reduced-spending scenario should not be a case of simply cutting spots or digital placements arbitrarily. It must be done with strategic reasoning in mind. For instance, let's say you have a media plan to get more parents in your area to consider sending their children to your client's preschool program, but instead of having $300,000 to spend, you end up having only $240,000. You had originally intended to send direct mailings to all parents of young children in the vicinity, inviting them to visit the school, as well as placing digital ads on community-based websites. Now, with less money to spend, you could enhance the school's website or build a Facebook page, both at minimal cost, and promote your owned media through social media. Note that a reduction in frequency of paid media may result in the loss of some volume discounts and potentially lower your reach.

Sometimes there is no alternative but cutting one or more media forms from the plan. Before doing so, it is important to think about how important that medium is in consumers' lives. If you take out all TV from a plan, then remember that you are losing a key medium that offers sight, sound, and motion and the opportunity to deliver the message to a large audience. That might be less important for a Ford dealership, but critical for a Red Lobster restaurant where you want to showcase the food. And it also depends on how consumers interact with the media. For example, if you know that your coffee shop has generated a strong response to mobile coupons, then removing that from your plan is likely to be detrimental to the plan's impact on your audience.

One way to reduce media spending is to use briefer or less expensive ads. Instead of 30-second commercials, maybe you could switch to 15-second ones; instead of a digital video ad placed in premium content, perhaps standard display banners distributed programmatically will suffice. Once again, however, this must be considered not simply in numerical terms (such as reach or CPM), but also in terms of the impact on consumers seeing or hearing that commercial message.

It might seem appropriate, given a reduced media budget, to cut the size of your target audience, but that can turn out to be *more* costly; the more narrowly you try to target your media, the more expensive it becomes to try to reach them. If your original plan for Method cleaning products is aimed at all women 18 to 49 years old and uses a mix of TV and digital video, then by trying to narrow it further to reach only those women 18 to 49 who have household incomes of more than $75,000 and have three or more children, you will probably end up looking at more expensive media vehicles. Instead of picking a broadly popular woman's service magazine, such as *Good Housekeeping* or *Better Homes and Gardens*, you might end up with magazines that have a smaller circulation and cost more per ad page, such as *Food and Wine* or *Martha Stewart Living*. While they *will* reach more of your more narrowly defined target, the cost may be correspondingly higher, too.

Sometimes costs are cut by removing any secondary targets you had planned to reach through separate media. A plan that was intended to increase awareness of a new dog daycare business might be aimed at both neighborhood pet owners and veterinarians. Faced with a cutback in media dollars, you might consider targeting only one of those groups initially, rather than both of them at once.

Changing Targets

Sometimes after a complete media plan has been presented to the client they might ask, "Did you consider targeting X instead?" That simple question might at first induce panic, but instead should be considered on its own merits. For example, is the media target really in line with the brand's marketing target, in order to achieve the overall marketing objectives?

It could also be important to include different targets in a plan, or create a separate plan for those targets, when you think that there are critical secondary audiences who need to be addressed. This is highly dependent on the product category. For medicines or healthcare items, for example, it is often essential to communicate with the medical profession as well as consumers, because they are the ones who influence which brands are selected. With the removal in the late 1990s of restrictions on television advertising for prescription drugs, there was an enormous increase in the amount pharmaceutical companies are spending on that medium. Even though consumers must still ask their doctors to prescribe these specialized drugs (such as Humira, Lyrica, or Prolia), the advertising is aimed at influencing the consumers to ask their physicians for a specific brand-name medication, rather than simply "something to help with my depression" (or arthritis or allergies).

One area where critical secondary audiences exist is with children's products. When children are targeted, it is frequently advisable to have a separate target of moms or parents, because they are the ones who typically make the purchases. It is estimated that children influence tens of billions of dollars of spending each year. In many countries around the world, there are strict limits on which products can be advertised directly to children and how, out of concerns that they are more easily misled by advertising.

Whomever the target is, the media specialist must determine which media are needed to reach those people. That, in turn, will depend upon the marketing and advertising objectives for that distinct audience. Are they identical to the main target's goals, or do they differ in some way? How much do the two targets overlap, both in terms of those objectives and in their media usage patterns? It could be, for example, that if you are trying to encourage both consumers and contractors to select your Grohe faucets, then using digital display ads on home decorating sites would reach both groups, but more specialized trade sites will do a better job at convincing contractors of the merits of your brand, and ads on a broader array of sites could help expand brand awareness among consumers.

Changing Media

As the media specialist, your job entails considering different media from the beginning to the end of media plan development. That means taking time to investigate alternative media options as you put the plan together.

This could include assessing different media vehicles within the same media form. If you are recommending magazines, then perhaps you might look at more specialized publications or just their digital versions to reach your target. For TV, reconsider whether you should use broadcast, spot, or cable TV to convey your messages, or perhaps switch to digital video instead. With a radio plan that uses spot markets, a network buy might be more efficient and appropriate. With paid digital, you can compare buying display ads programmatically or paying for premium online video. The use of different media vehicles will depend primarily on two factors: cost efficiency and targetability. Switching from smaller local papers to bigger, more regional ones may bring you a larger audience, but those people may not be close enough to your chain of Outback Steakhouse restaurants to be worth reaching with your message.

The bigger change when thinking about different media is a switch in media forms altogether. Instead of recommending newspapers, what happens if you use digital display instead? How about using streaming audio instead of local TV? Or what would be the result of switching dollars out of product placement and into sponsorship? And how much would that change be affected by the relationship of your target with the media you are considering? The media specialist must think through these scenarios from the point of view of both strategy and cost. How would a move from newspapers to display affect your overall objective of boosting awareness of your health food store? Would the same number of people be reached? Would they be the same people? What is the cost difference? And how would message frequency be impacted? What are the creative implications of such a change? All of these questions need to be answered as you develop a plan using different media channels.

One of the tools used in helping determine alternatives for a plan is the optimizer. Developed in the U.K. in the 1980s, this software was first designed to select the optimal mix of national TV dayparts or types against a specific target. It uses algorithms that balance the reach of a plan against its cost to arrive at a solution that maximizes one or the other (cost or reach). Although optimizers are models based on historical data (ratings), they are now routinely used predictively to help media planners and buyers determine what TV dayparts or specific programs to include. Following their introduction, multimedia optimizers were created that include television, digital, radio, and print.

All these considerations about alternative plans reinforce the notion that media planning is both art and science. There are potentially hundreds of different ways that you could plan your media to obtain the designated goals. Your job as the media specialist is to come up with the one that you believe will do the most effective and efficient job, while fully understanding that there are alternatives available that might achieve the same ends.

Tests and Translations

There are two common ways to conduct tests of a media plan on a local or regional basis. They are known as *as it falls* and *little America*. Here we will consider the basic concepts for each one, rather than going through all the mathematical calculations needed to prepare such plans. Although this procedure is really a test, it is also sometimes referred to as a "test translation", to reflect the fact that a national or bigger plan is being recreated in some fashion on a smaller scale. And even though, as media specialists, we are most concerned with testing the media plan itself (increasing GRPs, trying different scheduling strategies, and so forth), tests are also often conducted to determine the impact of new creative, or to see how a new product fares in the marketplace.

As It Falls

This type of test is most often used for brands in existing product categories, where the competitors are well known. The main premise of this method is that the rating points are allowed to occur as they normally would in each market, or as it falls. So rather than have the same GRPs across all test markets, the plan's goals would vary somewhat from location to location, depending on how well the individual vehicles perform in each place. That also means that the budgets will vary by market, too. It may cost $5,000 to buy 100 radio GRPs in Boise, Idaho, but $10,000 to get the same GRP level in Milwaukee, Wisconsin. The main advantage of this testing system is that it provides a realistic scenario for assessing the impact of the test plan. If the plan were expanded to a national level, there would still be market-by-market differences similar to those seen in the as it falls test situation.

Little America

This test market procedure is used more often with new brands or products where there is no existing competition. What it sets out to do is recreate a national plan in one (or a few) markets, or get as close to that as is feasible. It usually involves more complex planning, first to determine how individual media categories perform in the markets you choose, and then to figure out how to adjust the test plan so that it matches the national delivery. Certain cities have become popular representations of the total U.S. because they match the demography of the country at a national level. Places such as Columbus, Ohio, and Nashville, Tennessee, claim this.

However products are tested, there is no guarantee of success when they are launched nationally. The marketing literature has several notable failures of items that were heavily researched but flopped miserably. The 1990s launch of New Coke is one such classic. The company extensively tested the product with consumers before it introduced the product, which was intended to taste more like its key competitor, Pepsi. Its failure was attributed to the fact that while consumers may have preferred New Coke to Pepsi, they really preferred Coke to New Coke! Barnes & Noble introduced an e-reader, the Nook, to compete against Amazon's Kindle device. While the company had seen a clear connection between its heritage as a bookstore and selling devices on which to read books, for consumers that link was never strong enough, especially when the key competitor offered a better product and a simple relationship between ordering the book on its site, then downloading to its device. All this reinforces that, for all the hard work of tests and translations, consumers can be fickle and hard to predict.

Summary

When creating a media plan, it is crucial to consider first the target audience's use of media in terms of which categories and vehicles they use. You then must determine the plan's timing, if there are seasonal sales or other elements of the marketing mix (pricing, promotion, distribution or product changes) that will affect the plan's timing. For scheduling of your chosen vehicles, financial considerations and reach and frequency goals will help determine when and how often your ads appear. Tactical elements are important, too, particularly trade and consumer merchandising, to receive maximum support from dealers, distributors, and retailers and maximize the impact of the advertising. Then plan alternatives have to be evaluated, including having larger budgets to spend, as well as fewer dollars. Areas of focus with these alternatives are the media types used and the targets to be reached. Any potential changes can be tested by translating the plan into a local or regional test market situation and seeing what happens there first.

Notes

1 Byron Sharp, *How Brands Grow: What Marketers Don't Know*, Oxford: Oxford University Press, 2010.
2 Margaret Henderson Blair, "An Empirical Investigation of Advertising Wearin and Wearout," *Journal of Advertising Research*, vol. 27, no. 6, December 1987/January 1988, 45–50.

Chapter 10

Evaluating and Measuring Plans and Buys

Learning Outcomes: In this chapter you will learn how to:

- Understand ways to evaluate a media plan
- Consider consumer research approaches for evaluation
- Compare analytical approaches for evaluation

Evaluation and measurement are not really effective if they are only thought about at the end of the media planning and buying cycle. They have to be considered before, during, and after, otherwise you end up having no idea whether all the time, effort, and money made any difference. This chapter looks at how media plans are evaluated and analyzed.

Evaluating the Plan

As noted earlier, one of the most often-repeated quotations about advertising was attributed to John Wanamaker, Philadelphia department store magnate, who said that he knew half of the money he spent on advertising was wasted; he just didn't know which half. Your job, as a media specialist, is to try to ensure that your client's dollars are not wasted. One way to achieve that is by evaluating the media plan both before it is executed, and then again after the ads have run.

The starting point for evaluation is to establish a measurement plan while the media plan is being formulated. The media specialist and advertiser client need to agree on how success will be quantified. This often involves agreeing on what the *key performance indicators* (KPIs) should be. As noted in Chapter 2, these should connect to the marketing and advertising objectives, either directly or indirectly. Similar to those initial goals, the KPIs need to be precise so that the measurement will be able to ascertain if the plan delivered. For example, if the KPI is defined as vaguely as an "increase in brand awareness", there will probably be disagreement if a 0.5 percent increase in ad recall was satisfactory, or not.

DOI: 10.4324/9781003175704-10

It is no longer true that an annual plan is left unchanged for a whole year; more and more, advertisers will make changes to at least some part of the marketing plan while the campaign is running. This may be in response to changes in any part of the marketing mix. Consumer response could end up greater or less than anticipated; product improvements could necessitate additional promotional efforts; new channels of distribution could become important; or competitive pricing strategies may require alterations to the original, approved plan. And beyond that, economic trends can affect most marketing efforts. For example, in recessionary times, most experts tend to predict that the economic hard times will be over soon, suggesting that consumer spending will improve. What often happens is that consumer confidence in the economy remains low for longer than such optimistic forecasts, leading people to continue their restrained purchasing habits. This has a marked effect on the manufacturers of high-ticket items such as cars and electronics. It also impacts overall eating habits, causing people to eat out less and stay home more.

There are four key ways that a media plan can be evaluated, before and after it runs. We have explained the concepts of reach and frequency. With today's sophisticated software, syndicated data on past purchases and media consumption can be analyzed to give a "best guess" estimate of how well a medium, or total plan, will reach the chosen target audience. This can later be compared with actual results on reach and frequency, to see how well the plan actually performed, which is crucial information for preparing next year's plan. The second type of evaluation is to check that the ads actually ran as scheduled, a practice known as post-buy analysis. It is up to the media specialist to make sure that if, for any reason, the ad did not run as planned or was not positioned in the agreed-upon place, that some form of compensation is given, either monetary or in time or space. Third, it may well be worthwhile spending additional dollars to research the consumer impact of the media (and/or marketing) plan. After you doubled the spending levels in television, are your brand's awareness levels considerably higher? How well is your commercial message being recalled now that you have switched dollars out of magazines and into digital? These kinds of questions can best be answered by talking to some of the consumers you were trying to reach. Last but not least, in the weeks and months after your plan is executed, you can use statistical models to assess the return on investment, or payout, of your plan.

Pre-Plan Analysis

The first time to evaluate the impact of the media plan is before it is presented to the client. That is, in selecting the media vehicles you think will best meet the advertising and marketing objectives, the media specialist needs to figure out which combination of vehicles will do the best job of reaching the target an acceptable number of times. Data systems and tools are readily available to help make these kinds of analyses simple and fast.

For example, let's say you were considering two alternative combinations for your media plan for Pillsbury cake mix. The first combination would use monthly insertions in *Every Day with Rachael Ray* magazine, along with periodic commercials in prime time on the Lifetime cable television network. Another possibility would be to place continuous messages on cable, with occasional ads in the magazine. In Exhibit 10.1, we can see how the two schedules might look for the year.

Exhibit 10.1 Two Alternative Schedules

Schedule One	Schedule Two
Ten insertions in *Rachael Ray* (50 GRPs) 400 GRPs in Lifetime	Four insertions in *Rachael Ray* (20 GRPs) 1,000 GRPs in Lifetime

And in Exhibit 10.2, we can see how the two schedules would perform against your target of women 25 to 54.

Exhibit 10.2 Performance of Alternative Schedules

	Schedule One	Schedule Two
Total GRPs	450	1,020
Reach 1+	34.1%	32.6%
Reach 3+	25.2%	22.7%
Frequency	13.2	31.3

So, even though you are using far more cable in Schedule Two, the impact on the overall reach is actually less than if you used more magazine advertising, as in Schedule One.

Post-Buy Analysis

What the media specialist must find out once the plan is running is whether the ads ran as scheduled, and how well the plan actually delivered. For the first part, as noted earlier, you can turn to various sources to determine that the ads did in fact run as scheduled. For newspapers, there are *tear sheets*, which are provided by commercial services, to show you examples of the actual ad in the newspaper. Magazines will usually provide copies of the issues in which your ad appears. For television and radio, you receive affidavits confirming precisely when your spot aired. With digital ads, you also receive affidavits for the ads, as well as using a third-party service to verify that the ad was viewable and the percentage of impressions that were in-target. In each case, the media specialist must check that the terms of the contract were adhered to. If you requested being in the food section of a newspaper website, or the first third of a printed magazine, or on posters opposite your competitor's retail outlets, is that where your ad appeared?

For traditional broadcast media, the task can be more complicated because program schedules are far more prone to change. You might have arranged for your radio spot to air between 6:00 p.m. and 8:00 p.m., only to find that it came on at 5:30 p.m. or 8:20 p.m. Or, you could have bought a rotation of spots (ROS, or Run of Schedule), which in theory means that your spots will run equitably in all dayparts. In analyzing the affidavits, you might discover that more than half of the messages were aired between midnight and 6:00 a.m., or some other inappropriate time. It is then incumbent upon the station to explain what happened and, in all likelihood, offer a make-good, running the ad later in the correct daypart, or providing financial compensation for the cost differences between ROS and the overnight period.

In larger agencies or organizations, this post-analysis checking is typically done by the media buyers or business service department. It is more of an accounting than a media function but, ultimately, the media specialist should know what happened, and why.

Later on, additional information from audience measurement companies shows how your ad schedule delivered. Sources such as Nielsen for television, Nielsen Audio for radio, MRI-Simmons for print media, and Comscore or Nielsen for digital media provide the ratings, impressions, and audience delivery of media vehicles to help you determine whether, in fact, you met the goals of your plan. Other companies can access this data also, acting as third-party vendors of the information.

The kinds of questions the data can help you answer include what percentage of the target was reached by the media (and vehicles) that you used (reach), and how often, on average, was the target exposed to them (frequency)? It is worth emphasizing again that these terms refer to media exposure, and not to actual exposure to the ads themselves, so are therefore *opportunities to see* your message. Many advertisers will discount, or weight the exposure levels to account for this distinction, assuming, for example, that only half of the people reached by the media vehicle will actually see the ad. Or they may only look at the proportion of the target that is exposed a certain number of times (*effective reach*), knowing that people will require several opportunities to see your message before they in fact will do so.

Consumer Research

The importance of evaluating the plan's impact on consumers once it has gone into effect cannot be underestimated. By finding out, first, whether you got what you (or your client) paid for and, second, whether the plan worked as you intended, you can be better prepared for next year's plan too. This may be by undertaking surveys of consumers, either before and after their exposure to your ads or comparing the exposed group to a non-exposed (control) group, to assess differences in brand recall and any brand attitude shifts. Or it could be through qualitative research such as focus groups or in-depth interviews, where consumers are asked to explain their feelings about their media exposure in greater detail. Why did they pay attention to the connected TV ads but ignore the digital display ads, for example? Were the mobile ads effective in influencing their purchase decision? Although, ultimately, the impact of the media plan, and the other elements of the marketing mix, is determined at the cash register, it is helpful to be able to analyze the individual parts to find out what is, or is not, working. Having said that, and acknowledging the truth to the earlier comment by John Wanamaker, you should keep in mind that it is sometimes difficult to determine the precise effect of advertising media messages on consumers. We know *when* it is working, though we may not always know *how*.

Without evaluating how a media plan performs, we may be left even more in the dark than when we began. In effect, it means that each time we create a plan, we end up recreating the wheel. This can lead you down two paths. Either the same plan is reproduced because it "seemed to work" (or at least, didn't cause any disasters). Or the plan is completely changed to see if that makes a difference in sales, or awareness, or attitudes. Both of these options are flawed. To continue doing exactly the same thing as before without knowing whether it is working, or if it could possibly be improved upon, is detrimental to your product (and client), keeping them from performing at their best. Similarly, to overturn the plan without analyzing how it worked (or didn't work) means that you run the risk of losing the momentum your ads might have started to build, and jeopardizes your chances for success.

So, although there is a strong temptation, once the media plan is completed and the ads are running, to file it away and move on to the next task, the real media specialist will carry on through to the end. He or she is responsible for ensuring not only that the ads run as intended, but also that they delivered what was planned. If these evaluation tasks are carried out successfully, you will not only have a more satisfied client, but will also have already taken an important step forward in preparing for next year's media plan.

Analytics

The challenge of fully understanding how well a plan and buy performed and delivered is, today, undertaken by highly sophisticated statistical analysis. While the people that undertake this type of work may have varied names (data scientists, analytical insights, data intelligence), the focus of their efforts is similar. That is, they apply statistical rigor to try to determine the value of every dollar the advertiser invests in media. They do so by analyzing large sets of raw or unstructured data to either understand a change or predict an outcome.

While there are specialized books that provide the detailed formulas and mathematical explanations behind these approaches, here we will look at a few key types of analysis that help advertisers to determine whether the plan "worked" or not.

Structured Testing

This type of analysis tries to determine which media tactics work best. Should ads be scheduled every week or every other week? What is the optimal way to use 15-second and 30-second TV ads? These, and many other questions, can be answered by setting up test scenarios that are rigorously run, and then analyzed to help determine the best approach to execute.

Market Mix Modeling

The use of market mix modeling, or MMM, is one of the most popular kinds of analytics for marketers. As noted earlier, the fundamental question to be answered is how to maximize the advertiser's return on investment. Secondarily, but sometimes as importantly, this analysis helps determine how much the advertiser needs to spend in media overall, and by media channel. An MMM analysis involves the development of an econometric model to quantify the impact of both marketing and non-marketing activities to drive business outcomes. Going back to the "4Ps" mentioned in Chapter 1, these models look not only at media spend, but also distribution ("place"), product factors such as unit size, pricing, and other promotional activity such as discounts or co-branding efforts. External factors might include economic indicators or weather patterns. All the data are analyzed through regression techniques to see how each of these independent variables impact sales of the brand over time.

Multi-Touch Attribution

As noted earlier, multi-touch attribution, or MTA, is a more sophisticated type of analysis, looking not only at the overall return on investment by channel, but also the interactions between them. This helps the marketer to see which tactics may be less effective in the overall process, as well as how consumers may be influenced by one or several media touchpoints, and in what order those should occur. For example, a hotel chain might learn through MTA that search activity is most effective after the audience has seen TV ads, or that digital display ads work best alongside digital video. The granularity of the MTA approach can also provide insights into the optimal frequency of ad exposure to deliver a sale.

Audience Segmentation

In Chapter 3, we looked at the various ways to define and evaluate target audiences when creating a media plan. Once the plan has been executed, there are additional opportunities to determine if you are targeting the right audience. One of these is segmentation. Here, the analytics expert looks at several data *signals*, such as purchase data when available, or search activity, or location data gathered from mobile devices. With these types of *big data*, it is possible to create different segments of the audience based on their behavior. That enables different messages to be delivered to each group that are more relevant to them. For example, a casual dining restaurant such as Applebee's might discover there is one audience segment that visits these restaurants after spending time at nearby malls (from location data); a second group orders online for either pickup or delivery (based on the restaurant's online orders); a third group may be seniors (adults aged 65+) who tend to show up for early dinners (based on time of visits). Not only can different creative messages be developed, but the subsequent media plans would include quite different paid, owned, or earned channels to deliver those ads to each audience segment.

Demand Forecasting

One of the challenges with media planning is that you are creating and executing a plan to drive future sales (or other KPIs). But what if the marketer could forecast future demand for their products and services? Sometimes, the demand is predictable. Insect repellent sells better in warm-weather months, while Canada Goose coats sell more in cold-weather months. Many brands, however, expect their media to help drive demand. Statistical techniques can be applied to understand the key indicators that predict purchase consideration and sales. Then, the media can be allocated (or reallocated) to help reinforce those consumer actions.

Summary

A completed media plan is really not final until it has been evaluated to see how it has performed. This should be done both before the plan is executed, by calculating estimates of reach and frequency that the plan should achieve, and afterwards, through post-buy analyses to ensure that the ads ran as scheduled.

If the messages did not air as intended and specified in the buys, it is up to the media specialist to obtain some type of compensation. Without these checks, there is no way of knowing whether this year's plan should be continued into the following year with or without modifications. Statistical analysis can provide a deeper level of information on how well the plan delivered, in terms of the impact of advertising on sales. The process of evaluating the success or failure of the media plan in achieving the media, advertising, and marketing objectives will help the brand and the client know how to do better next year.

Key Research Resources

Advertising Age
www.adage.com
Industry trade journal, published digitally and in print 24 times a year. Student subscriptions available.

Advertising Research Foundation
www.thearf.org
Primary U.S. industry research organization that oversees *Journal of Advertising Research* and runs research-focused events.

Adweek
www.adweek.com
Industry trade journal, published in print and online regularly. Student subscriptions available.

Alliance for Audited Media (formerly Audit Bureau of Circulations)
www.auditedmedia.com
Measures print media circulation.

Comscore
www.comscore.com
Measures what people do as they use digital media (laptop/desktop, mobile, tablets, and television), in U.S., and 25+ other countries.

Contagious
www.contagious.com
Provides creative and strategic insights for campaigns, featuring best-in-class creative examples.

eMarketer (now part of Insider Intelligence)
www.emarketer.com
Provides statistics and information on trends in digital marketing, media, and commerce.

Foresight Factory
www.foresightfactory.co
Provides global consumer and cultural trends, both qualitative and quantitative, in U.S. and global markets.

Forrester Research
www.forrester.com
Research and advisory firm in the technology space.

Ipsos Affluent Study
www.ipsos.com
Provides media, demographic, and lifestyle information for upper-income adults.

IRI
www.iriworldwide.com
Collects and reports marketer and shopper information using supermarket checkout data.

JD Power & Associates
www.jdpower.com
Provides annual demographic, lifestyle, and media information linked to automotive industry.

Kantar
www.kantar.com
Parent company to several audience research companies (Kantar Health, TGI), as well as measuring advertisers' media spending across 20 media types, in multiple countries around the world.

Media Rating Council
www.mediaratingcouncil.org
Organization tasked with administering audits of audience measurement companies to ensure those services are valid, reliable, and effective.

Media Ocean
www.mediaocean.com
Third-party software platform and systems to process audience data for buying and selling media; also major bill payment system for advertising agencies.

Mintel
www.mintel.com
Global market and consumer intelligence on product categories and consumer trends.

MRI-Simmons
www.mri-simmons.com
Measures demographic, media, and lifestyle information among 50,000 adults per year; used for target and audience analysis.

Netbase Quid
www.netbase.com
Global social listening and analytics company.

Nielsen
www.nielsen.com
Key provider of national and local television viewing information on which buys are transacted.

Nielsen Audio
www.nielsen.com
Key provider of national and local radio audience measurement.

Nielsen IMS
www.nielsen.com
Third-party media software that provides media planning tools to assess multimedia audiences.

Nielsen Scarborough Research
www.nielsen.com
Measures demographic, media, and lifestyle information in 75 local markets.

SRDS
www.srds.com
Provides databases to compare media rates and information on all major media categories.

Statista
www.statista.com
Statistics portal for advertising and media.

Telmar
www.telmar.com
Third-party media software company that provides media planning tools to assess multimedia audiences for media planning.

WARC
www.warc.com
Global database of campaign case studies and best practices.

Key Media Organizations

Advertising Club of New York
www.theadvertisingclub.org
Forum for ad professionals.

Advertising Council
www.adcouncil.org
Organization sponsoring and promoting public service advertising.

Advertising Research Foundation
www.thearf.org
Industry organization that tries to further, through research, the scientific practice of advertising and marketing.

American Advertising Federation (AAF)
www.aaf.org
Considers itself the 'unifying voice of advertising'; sponsors annual National Student Ad Competition (NSAC) and has more than 140 college chapters with 4,000+ student members; offers many internship opportunities.

American Association of Advertising Agencies (AAAA)
www.aaaa.org
Main trade organization of advertising agencies.

American Marketing Association
www.ama.org
Professional association for marketers with strong educational component.

ANA Educational Foundation
www.aef.com
Connects advertising, marketing, and academic communities to enhance understanding of marketing and advertising in society. Operates the Visiting Professors Program, MADE (Marketing and Advertising Education) internships, and campus speakers.

The Association of Magazine Media
www.magazine.org
Primary national trade association promoting the consumer magazine industry.

Association of National Advertisers (ANA)
www.ana.net
Main trade organization for national advertisers. Now includes the DMA (Data & Marketing Association).

Geopath
www.geopath.org
Industry organization that oversees measurement of the out of home industry.

Hispanic Marketing Council
www.hispanicmarketingcouncil.org
National trade organization representing the Hispanic communications industry.

Interactive Advertising Bureau (IAB)
www.iab.net
Trade group that empowers the marketing industry to thrive in the digital economy. Includes initiatives on data privacy, as well as monitoring digital ad spending.

International Advertising Association (IAA)
www.iaaglobal.org
Professional group focused on advertising as a global industry; has chapters in 30 countries, and at many U.S. universities.

Localogy
www.localogy.com
Trade association focused on growing the local marketplace.

Mobile Marketing Association
www.mmaglobal.com
Trade association representing all sides of mobile industry.

National Association of Broadcasters (NAB)
www.nab.org
Trade group promoting radio and television broadcasters.

News Media Alliance
www.newsmediaalliance.org
Trade group serving as the voice of the news media industry.

The One Club for Creativity
www.oneclub.org
Group that celebrates and supports the global creative community. Offers Portfolio Night for students, as well as workshops and Young Ones Student Awards.

Outdoor Advertising Association of America (OAAA)
www.oaaa.org
Trade group promoting the out of home advertising industry.

Radio Advertising Bureau (RAB)
www.rab.com
Trade group promoting radio advertising.

She Runs It
www.sherunsit.org
Forum to advance women in the field of communications (formerly known as Advertising Women of New York). Includes largescale mentoring program.

Television Bureau of Advertising (TVB)
www.tvb.org
Trade group promoting the local broadcast television industry.

Video Advertising Bureau (VAB)
www.thevab.com
Trade organization promoting premium video content across screens.

World Federation of Advertisers
166 Avenue Louise, 1050 Brussels, Belgium
www.wfanet.org
Trade group representing the global interests of marketers.

Index

References to illustrations are in *italics*
References to tables are in **bold**